POLITICS, DIALOGUE AND THE EVOLUTION OF DEMOCRACY

HOW TO DISCUSS RACE, ABORTION, IMMIGRATION, GUN CONTROL, CLIMATE CHANGE, SAME SEX MARRIAGE AND OTHER HOT TOPICS

POLITICS, DIALOGUE AND THE EVOLUTION OF DEMOCRACY

How to Discuss Race, Abortion, Immigration, Gun Control, Climate Change, Same Sex Marriage and Other Hot Topics

---

KENNETH CLOKE

BOOKS BY KENNETH CLOKE

Mediation: Revenge and the Magic of Forgiveness, Center for Dispute Resolution, Santa Monica, California, 1996

Mediating Dangerously: The Frontiers of Conflict Resolution, Jossey Bass / Wiley Publishers Inc., 2001

The Crossroads of Conflict: A Journey into the Heart of Dispute Resolution, Janis Publishers Inc., 2006

Conflict Revolution: Mediating Evil, War, Injustice and Terrorism, Janis Publishers Inc., 2008

The Dance of Opposites: Explorations in Mediation, Dialogue and Conflict Resolution Systems Design, Good Media Press, 2014

Conflict Revolution: Designing Preventative Systems for Chronic Social, Economic and Political Conflicts, (Second Edition) Good Media Press, 2015

Ordinary Ecstasy: A Meditation Home Companion, Center for Dispute Resolution, Santa Monica, California, 2018

Words of Wisdom: Profound, Poignant and Provocative Quotes, illustrations by Brad Heckman, to be published by GoodMedia Press, 2018.

BOOKS BY KENNETH CLOKE AND JOAN GOLDSMITH

Thank God It's Monday: 14 Values We Need to Humanize the Way We Work, Irwin/McGraw Hill, 1997

Resolving Conflicts at Work: A Complete Guide for Everyone on the Job, Jossey Bass/Wiley Publishers Inc., 2000

Resolving Personal and Organizational Conflicts: Stories of Transformation and Forgiveness, Jossey Bass/Wiley Publishers Inc., 2000

The End of Management and the Rise of Organizational Democracy, Jossey Bass/Wiley Publishers Inc., 2002

The Art of Waking People Up: Cultivating Awareness and Authenticity at Work, Jossey Bass/Wiley Publishers Inc., 2003

Resolving Conflicts at Work: Eight Strategies for Everyone on the Job (Second Edition) Jossey Bass/Wiley Publishers Inc., 2005

Resolving Conflicts at Work: Ten Strategies for Everyone on the Job (Third Edition) Jossey Bass/Wiley Publishers Inc., 2011

CONTENTS

Part Four
INTEREST-BASED DEMOCRACIES AND ALTERNATIVES TO CONFLICT

GoodMedia Press
An imprint of goodmedia communications, llc
25 Highland Park Village, 100-810
Dallas, Texas 75205
www.goodmediapress.com

Manufactured in USA

Names: Cloke, Kenneth, author.

Title: Politics , dialogue and the evolution of democracy : how to discuss race , abortion , immigration , gun control , climate change , same sex marriage and other hot topics / Kenneth Cloke.

Description: Includes index. | Dallas, TX : GoodMedia Press, 2018.

Identifiers: ISBN 978-0-9911148-9-4 | LCCN 201895429

Subjects: LCSH Conflict management. | Political participation--United States. | Democracy--United States. | Mediation--United States. | Social conflict. | Dispute resolution (Law)--United States. | BISAC POLITICAL SCIENCE / Political Ideologies / Democracy | POLITICAL SCIENCE / Political Ideologies | POLITICAL SCIENCE / Peace.

Classification: LCC JK1764 .C5355 2018 | DDC 323 / .0420973--dc23

The fact is that all the power in the world cannot transform someone who hates you into someone who likes you. It can turn a foe into a slave, but not into a friend. All the power in the world cannot transform a fanatic into an enlightened man. All the power in the world cannot transform someone thirsting for vengeance into a lover.

Amos Oz

If you are neutral in situations of injustice, you have chosen the side of the oppressor. If an elephant has its foot on the tail of a mouse and you say that you are neutral, the mouse will not appreciate your neutrality.

Desmond Tutu

Our lives begin to end the day we become silent about things that matter.

Martin Luther King, Jr.

Here is my secret. A very simple secret. It is only with the heart that one can see rightly. What is essential is invisible to the eye.

Antoine de Saint-Exupery

INTRODUCTION

DEMOCRACY, DIGNITY, DIALOGUE AND DOMINATION

Words like 'freedom,' 'justice,' and 'democracy' are not common concepts; on the contrary, they are rare. People are not born knowing what these are. It takes enormous, and above all, individual effort to arrive at the respect for other people that these words imply. —James Baldwin

The 20th century has been characterized by three developments of great political importance: the growth of democracy, the growth of corporate power, and the growth of propaganda as a means of protecting corporate power against democracy. —Alex Cary

The fire, the energy, and the life of democracy is popular pressure. Democracy itself is a government constantly responding to continuous pressures of its people. The only hope for democracy is that more people and more groups will become articulate and exert pressure upon their government ... Can there be a more fundamental, democratic program than a democratically minded and participating people? Can man envisage a more sublime program on earth than the people having faith in their fellow men and themselves? A program of co-operation instead of competition? This, then, is the job ahead ... —Saul Alinsky

INTRODUCTION

OVER THE COURSE OF CENTURIES, WE HAVE BECOME IMMENSELY POWERFUL, unimaginably wealthy and highly advanced in technology, medicine and health care delivery — yet many people on the planet live in poverty, without electricity, rudimentary medical care, sanitation or running water. In math and science, we have achieved more in the last three decades than in previous millennia, yet we have hardly advanced at all in our ability to get along, to communicate about our differences, or to solve our social, economic and political problems without slaughtering each other.

Human populations have skyrocketed, social media has proliferated and the world has shrunk, connecting diverse cultures and conflicting social traditions that previously had little connection with one another, thereby exacerbating social, economic, political and environmental problems that can no longer be solved locally, even by the most powerful nation states.

So, on the one hand, we have advanced rapidly in knowledge, skills and capacities; on the other, we remain mired in ancient enmities and antiquated methodologies. Nowhere is this clearer than in the attitudes and behaviors, processes and relationships, skills and capacities we bring to resolving our social, economic and political conflicts.

While it has long been considered preferable simply to destroy or vanquish our opponents, it is no longer possible to do so without simultaneously harming ourselves. In the first place, these "opponents" are simply *people*, who see things differently, with whom it is possible to talk, negotiate and solve problems. In the second, we increasingly think and act, communicate and relate, touch and are touched, *internationally*, bypassing borders that once sheltered us and intensified our isolation, encouraging us, at least in our imagination, to separate ourselves from those who looked, thought and acted differently.

As a result of these changes, without our fully realizing it, the *form* of our society, economics and politics has shifted, forcing us now to consider how we will respond to racial, religious, gender and other forms of diversity; requiring us to learn how to cooperate in solving global environmental, health, migration and other complex problems; and driving us to do so in ways that are at least as complex, diverse, intricate, far-reaching, multidimensional and multifaceted as the problems themselves.

What is clear at the outset is that divisive win/lose approaches, hostile biases and stereotypes, adversarial assumptions and antagonistic zero-sum methodologies unnecessarily pit us against each other, mistakenly cause us to identify each other as the problem, and diminish our ability to work together and collaborate in resolving issues that impact all of us.

Rather than tracing our political system's ills to the immorality, or flawed personalities or evil of individual politicians, any genuinely democratic process requires us to consider the political system as a whole, in which the characters of individual politicians do not distract our attention from joint problem-solving, or discovering deeper, underlying issues and unnoticed opportunities, including how it might be possible to:

- Reimagine the ways we organize and exercise political power
- Respect our differences and discuss our conflicts in ways that promote learning and keep us connected as human beings
- Collaborate and use our differences to design richer, more complex and effective problem-solving strategies

What Is Democracy?

We have thought of democracy as consisting largely of casting votes for representatives in periodic elections and come to accept the adversarial campaigns and brutal competitions for power, money and prestige that seem to inevitably accompany them. Yet as James Baldwin eloquently points out in the epigraph at the opening of this introduction, the *implications* of democracy are far deeper and more essential, and require enormous effort to preserve. It is increasingly clear that democracy requires a number of *higher order* attitudes and intentions, processes and relationships, skills and capacities to be successful, and that these include respect for other people, as Baldwin suggests — but also respect for their diverse *ideas*, beliefs and interests, and for the right of each and all of us to have a voice in every part of the political process — not merely through our elected representatives, but *directly*, as owners of an inalienable right to govern ourselves.

More deeply, the political impact of prejudice and unresolved conflict is always to enfeeble democracy and empower autocracy, leading in extreme cases to fascism and dictatorship. A shocking recent study by professors Steven V. Miler and Nicholas T. Davis found that intolerant white people's fears that democracy benefits immigrants and other races led them to support authoritarian ideas, including military rule, or a strongman or dictator who would ignore legislatures and election results. Similarly, the World Values Survey found that while 92 percent of more than 73,000 people in 57 countries thought democracy was a good way to govern, there has been a significant loss of trust in government and increase in support for a strong leader "who does not have to bother with parliament and elections."

Dignity and Democracy

As Naomi Klein declared in a disarmingly simple, yet profoundly far-reaching phrase, "Democracy is not just the right to vote, it is the right to live in dignity." Dignity, diversity and democracy are in fact inseparable, and those who do not have the ability to participate in discussing or making decisions about the issues that impact their lives inevitably, in some measure, lose both self-respect and the respect of others. More profoundly, the denial of dignity and respect for others tacitly legitimizes unjust social, economic and political systems that tolerate domination, oppression and exploitation, and permit the powerful to prey on and subordinate the powerless.

The difficulty is that democracy is *not* the simplest form of government, in part because it requires a higher order of skills to be exercised by its citizens, who not only need to be educated and capable of critical, independent thought so as to make intelligent decisions, but also to know how to communicate, negotiate and solve problems collaboratively with their opponents; how to welcome those who are different or disagreeable; and include even those who would exclude others.

Among the skills required of those who would practice democracy is therefore the ability to use systems and processes that are *inherently* respectful and dignifying — not just toward those who are like us or agree with us, but critically and especially toward those who aren't and don't — especially toward those with whom we are in conflict. More broadly, the attitudes, skills and capacities required of citizens in any genuine "government of, by and for the people," *necessarily* include a number that are crucial in conflict resolution, especially these:

- Active, empathetic and responsive listening
- Appreciative inquiry
- Non-violent communication
- Emotional intelligence
- Collaborative, mutual gain and interest-based negotiation
- Consensus building
- Prejudice reduction and bias awareness
- Support for diversity and cross-cultural communication
- Team and community building
- Mediation
- Restorative justice and circles
- Open heart-to-heart conversations
- Apology and acknowledgment
- Forgiveness and reconciliation
- Dialogue facilitation
- Informal problem-solving
- Conflict coaching

- Conflict resolution consulting
- Participatory feedback and evaluation
- Conflict resolution systems design

In short, for democracy to evolve, adapt to current conditions and live up to its promise, we need to develop and significantly improve our attitudes and behaviors, processes and relationships, and skills and capacities in using a broad range of communication, diversity, collaboration and interest-based conflict resolution methods, some of which are ancient and common to all cultures, and others that have been invented, discovered, practiced, critiqued or extended only in the last few decades.

We also need to develop enhanced attitudes and behaviors, processes and relationships, and skills and capacities in reducing resistance, overcoming impasse, building trust, encouraging participation, valuing diversity and dissent, redressing injustices, community organizing, reducing bureaucracy, supporting political honesty and transparency, encouraging feedback and evaluation, educating people in critical thinking, and understanding and accepting ambiguity and complexity.

In part because we have lacked these skills, democracy has been constrained and constricted, as Alex Cary describes in the second epigraph listed above, through the use of power- and rights-based adversarial processes, which include not just crude forms of political propaganda, but vicious campaign advertising, soft money bribery, and the corruption that is encouraged by lobbying and campaign contributions. These combine to reduce politics as a whole to hostile power contests between elected representatives funded and controlled by wealthy contributors. It is as true today as it was decades ago, as Justice Louis Brandeis warned: "We may have democracy, or we may have wealth concentrated in the hands of a few, but we can't have both." And at the same time, as another Supreme Court Justice, Robert Jackson, observed, "It is not the function of government to keep the citizen from falling into error; it is the function of the citizen to keep the government from falling into error." Only an active, collaborative, educated and skilled democratic citizenry can make this happen.

Because of the debasement and corruption of the political process by money, normal adversarial, power- and rights-based, incremental approaches to reform inevitably confront a barrier or limit in the unwillingness of the wealthy to surrender their prestige, wealth and power; and in their ability, through ownership of the media and financial sway over politicians, to block, channel and forestall efforts to bring about essential, transformational, systemic change.

We therefore require a different, innovative set of attitudes and behaviors, processes and relationships, skills and capacities that will allow us to bypass and remove these barriers, in ways that do not reinforce the unequal, adversarial assumptions that gave rise to, and continue to justify them. In short, we require a revolution in the way we engage in social, economic and political conflicts, in the forms of problem-solving, decision-making and conflict resolution, — a non-violent revolution, whose principle methods are those of communication, dialogue and mediation — or what I have described as a *conflict revolution*.

The third epigraph by Saul Alinsky that opens this introduction fittingly identifies what I believe is the road to this revolution; that is: a shift from isolating, adversarial, power- and rights-based forms of political activity to participatory, collaborative, *interest*-based forms that seek to strengthen dignity and respect toward others, along with the interactive, collaborative attitudes and behaviors, processes and relationships, skills and capacities that are needed for direct, participatory forms of democracy to evolve and flourish.

To initiate this transformation and allow it to percolate, replicate and expand throughout our social, economic and political systems; to shift our focus from power and rights to interest-based forms of problem-solving, decision-making and conflict resolution; to move from representative to direct, participatory forms of democracy, will require: first, a clear understanding of the nature of both the problem and the solution; second, the kind of popular pressure for which Saul Alinsky was well-known; and third, a new set of conflict resolution attitudes and behaviors, processes and relationships, skills and capacities that can help make the transition easier, more likely and sustainable.

The level of skills and capacities needed to change individual politicians or selected social, economic or political policies are significantly less complex and challenging than those required to alter the nature of power itself, or to introduce new forms of political dialogue and democratic governance that do not legitimize or rely on domination, but seek its eradication.

DOMINATION VS. DEMOCRACY

Domination generally means being at the mercy of the arbitrary will or power of another and controlled by them, regardless of whether that control is exercised directly or indirectly, and regardless of who is subject to it. Domination implies the end of democracy, as it grants a monopoly of social, economic and political control to those who govern — but it also, on an interpersonal level, signifies the loss of genuine relationship, as can be seen in couples and families, schools and workplaces. As a result, it triggers resentment, resistance and revolt, and permits the use of only a limited, inferior, one-sided form of problem-solving. Worst of all, it constricts our capacity for empathy, openness, honesty and awareness, and our ability to feel genuine love or affection for others.

Politics, as will appear more clearly in the chapters that follow, has always consisted of two parts, pitted and warring against each other. On the one hand, it is a form of social problem-solving. On the other hand, it is a method of domination, designed to defend the status, wealth and power of a few over the many they seek to rule or control.

The proposition of this book is that it is possible for us, by developing higher order attitudes and behaviors, processes and relationships, skills and capacities, especially in dialogue and conflict resolution, to improve our ability to resolve chronic political conflicts, by turning our differences into improved relationships and more successful problem-solving, strengthening democracy and reducing the need to dominate others politically.

The key component in producing this shift is public dialogue, which invites people to come together and constructively discuss their differences. For this reason, much of what follows is focused on developing dialogue techniques and searching for ways of applying them to difficult and dangerous political topics, and the chronic conflicts that lie hidden beneath their surface.

ABOUT THE BOOK

My intentions in writing this book have been fivefold: first, to consider the way we think about politics and political conflicts from a conflict resolution perspective; second, to identify some of the skills that may be required for democracy to take a more collaborative, interest-based form, focusing on dialogue, diversity and conflict resolution as core democratic skills; third, to explore the application of these ideas to global issues; fourth, to survey the forms, evolution and limits of social, economic and political democracies; and fifth, to consider throughout how we might design more effective approaches, interventions and processes that could propel us forward, or prevent us from moving backward toward barbarism.

The chapters are of differing lengths and purposes, some concentrating on practical skill building and others attempting to clarify the way we think about and address complex social, economic and political issues, and what may lie hidden beneath their surface. Some of the chapters take the form of essays, a few of which have been published in *ACResolution*, online at *Mediate.com*, or in previous books and articles I have written, but felt important to reproduce here in order to offer a more complete description of some essential piece of a larger puzzle, as with the mechanics of the dialogue process, or to express some core idea that is central to understanding democracy or political conflict.

INTRODUCTION

My Reasons for Writing It

I come to this topic through a lifetime of experience in political activity and conflict resolution that for many years felt disparate and disconnected, but appear to me now to require each other, as I attempt to demonstrate in the pages that follow. Initially, I was an activist in many of the movements of the 1960s, which led me to appreciate the importance of democracy, not merely as a means of bringing about social change, but as a requirement for and a byproduct of our desire for dignity and respect from others. Years later, I became a full-time mediator, dialogue facilitator, conflict coach, trainer and conflict resolution systems designer, giving me many opportunities to design, organize and facilitate courageous conversations and dialogues over difficult and dangerous political issues, including between Israelis and Palestinians, Ukrainians and Russians, Armenians and Azerbaijanis, immigrants and Greek citizens, Sandinistas and the opposition, and many others.

Over the last 38 years, I have mediated and facilitated thousands of dialogues between people who did not like or trust one another, or whose political or personal beliefs were antithetical to each other, or who were on opposite sides of some important issue, or who were simply in conflict over how to solve a problem that touched both of them. These have been little laboratories in which the core ideas in this book were tested under radically democratic and demanding conditions.

Out of these experiences has come my recognition of the amazing, extraordinary and quite beautiful capacity for open and honest communication that is ever-present in dialogue and mediation, even when it seems to have been lost, along with an appreciation for the subtle, layered and incredibly evocative dualities, connections and transformational possibilities that emerge whenever opponents come together and talk.

Most recently, I have been engaged, under the auspices of Mediators Beyond Borders International (MBBI), with Combatants for Peace,

INTRODUCTION

composed of former soldiers for the Israeli Defense Force, Hamas, Fatah, etc.; and with Women Wage Peace, consisting of Jewish and Muslim women who come together against enormous odds and with great courage to advance the idea that peace is possible — not by remaining silent about things that matter, but by fearlessly exploring their differences, without ever forgetting what they have in common. It is simply stunning to watch groups like these, or Hutus and Tutsis in Rwanda, Catholics and Protestants in Northern Ireland, and many others around the world daringly engage in dialogues with each other.

In the end, I believe there is no alternative other than to learn how to live together on this shrinking, vulnerable, endlessly captivating and challenging planet, and to develop the attitudes and behaviors, processes and relationships, skills and capacities we need to survive without killing each other, or ourselves and to sustain democracy, which is the *only* political system that makes these ends possible. Yet both in the U.S. and around the world, we are divided into deeply hostile political camps, slipping backward in our commitment to equality, equity and democracy, and increasingly threatened in our ability to participate in relationships that are shared, voluntary, diverse, collaborative and egalitarian. To keep these relationships alive, we need to develop the attitudes and behaviors, processes and relationships, skills and capacities that enable us to talk about our political differences, and across our seemingly intractable conflicts.

None of this will be easy, and will require enormous collaborative efforts, starting with ourselves, our families and the communities where we live, and extending outward to include everyone. This challenge is uniquely ours and much hangs in the balance. We need to accept and embrace it, using all the skills we have, and leaving no one behind.

Wishing you a useful and enjoyable read, and wonderful conflicts,

Kenneth Cloke, Santa Monica, CA

www.kencloke.com

OVERVIEW OF POLITICS AND POLITICAL CONFLICT

You need power only when you want to do something harmful. Otherwise, love is enough to get everything done. —Charlie Chaplin

Every exercise of power incorporates a faint, almost imperceptible, element of contempt for those over whom the power is exercised. One can only dominate another human soul if one knows, understands, and with the utmost tact despises the person one is subjugating. —Sandor Marai

My weapon has always been language ... but it has changed. Instead of shaping the words like knives now, I think they're flowers, or bridges.
—Sandra Cisneros

Time and again I have been persuaded that a huge potential of goodwill is slumbering within our society. It's just that it's incoherent, suppressed, confused, crippled and perplexed — as though it does not know what to rely on, where to begin, where or how to find meaningful outlets. —Vaclav Havel

ONE

HOW TO THINK ABOUT POLITICS
AND POLITICAL CONFLICT

Genuine politics — politics worthy of the name, and the only politics I am willing to devote myself to — is simply a matter of serving those around us: serving the community, and serving those who will come after us. Its deepest roots are moral because it is a responsibility ... [T]here is only one way to strive for decency, reason, responsibility, sincerity, civility and tolerance and that is decently, reasonably, responsibly, sincerely, civilly and tolerantly. I'm aware that, in everyday politics, this is not seen as the most practical way of going about it. —Vaclav Havel

Nearly everywhere ... instead of thinking, one merely takes sides: for or against. Such a choice replaces the activity of the mind. This is an intellectual leprosy; it originated in the political world and then spread through the land, contaminating all forms of thinking. This leprosy is killing us; it is doubtful whether it can be cured without first starting with the abolition of all political parties. —Simone Weil

You can rule with a firm hand, or you can rule through consensus. Those with neither the strength for firmness nor the courage for consensus take refuge in the belief that they can remain somewhere in between. But that is an illusion.
—Ivan Klima

WE HAVE ALL WATCHED POLITICAL CONVERSATIONS DEGENERATE INTO angry quarrels, pointless personal attacks and antagonistic power contests. We have seen people sink into screaming matches, shaming and blaming, and personal viciousness, often over the loftiest ideas, deepest passions and most profound political principles. We all know that these tirades can easily descend into senseless violence and appalling acts of brutality. And we have all participated in them, or fanned their flames, or stood passively by and done nothing.

Yet, political conversations matter. They concern our future, our values and integrity, our ethics and morality, our beliefs and behaviors, not only as individual citizens and nation states, but as human beings who are responsible for the world our grandchildren and our grandchildren's grandchildren will inherit.

Successful political decision-making requires not silence or pointless rage, but dialogue; not apathy or aggression, but collaborative negotiation; not passivity or accommodation, but courageous, constructive and creative contention. Silence in the face of critical issues signifies not merely the absence of speech, but the loss of integrity and opportunities for learning, and therefore also the loss of *self*, of values, of citizenship, of democracy, of community, of humanity.

As mediators and conflict resolvers, we have largely been silent about political events. In part this is because we do not know how to express our political views without slipping into adversarial attitudes and assumptions that define most political communications — yet we know from practice that they can be transformed and overcome.

In a recent issue of *ACResolution*, magazine of the Association for Conflict Resolution, two opposing positions on escalating political conflicts in the U.S. were taken by highly experienced, deeply intelligent leaders in the field of dispute resolution. The first was by Lawrence Susskind, founder of the Consensus Building Institute at MIT and a professor in the Program on Negotiation at Harvard Law School, writing:

Neutrality is central to the value we add as ADR professionals. Our neutrality allows us to earn the trust of all sides in a dispute ... My contention is that many ADR professionals are so upset by what is happening in the Age of Trump that they are ready to risk their neutrality. While I understand their motives, I am convinced this would be a disaster for the profession ... If you sign a petition, march peacefully, write op-eds, or lobby for your point of view, there is no way anyone who disagrees with the positions you have taken will accept you as a dispute resolution professional they can trust. I promise you that whatever actions we take in our personal lives will be noted.

A second, contrasting view was authored by Bernie Mayer, a professor at Creighton University and writer of several brilliant, profound and far-reaching books on conflict resolution:

We are, sadly, experiencing the rise of open and unconstrained racism, misogyny, anti-Semitism, and homophobic behavior in our public lives, abetted and even provoked by our President and his associates. Are we obligated to remain silent about this in order to maintain our status as credible neutrals? On the contrary, I think one of the great contributions we can make as conflict interveners is to call out unacceptable behavior, which is making it increasingly difficult for us to talk across our differences or to deal with the most important challenges we face as a society. We need to find constructive and effective ways to confront unacceptable behavior both in our capacity as conflict professionals and as citizens of our world. But we must do this in a way that recognizes that people can change, that interactions make a difference, that people who behave in an abusive manner still have genuine concerns that ought to be addressed, and that we ourselves are fallible.

There is something accurate in both of these statements, yet there is also something I find missing. It should not, I think, be necessary to surrender one's political ideas, beliefs, values, ethics and morality in order to mediate or facilitate dialogues between people with opposing views. Being "neutral" in these conversations should not mean relinquishing the freedom to think or have opinions on important political issues. Otherwise, we capitulate to bullying, blackmail and intimidation, and end up, in the incisive critique of anthropologist Laura Nader, "trading justice for harmony."

On the other hand, "calling out unacceptable behavior" and engaging in polarizing confrontations, while useful in disincentivizing behaviors, pressuring politicians and calling attention to social injustices, can quickly devolve into pointless name-calling, excessive personalization of political differences, distraction from problem-solving, cyclical backlash and oversimplification of complex issues, and leave people's hearts and minds unchanged.

What is missing in this discussion is the deeper *mediative* truth that lies beneath both these statements: that it is possible for us to be open and unbiased without being neutral on issues that matter — i.e., to transcend both bias and neutrality, and work to transform conflict generating attitudes and behaviors, processes and relationships, skills and capacities, without slipping into unnecessarily apathetic or adversarial thinking.

Doing so requires us to think more deeply about the nature of politics and political conflict, and recognize that we need to shift our dialogues and discussions away from the language, limitations, logic and attitudes of neutrality and bias, which are an outcome of power- and rights-based processes that distance us from one another, and toward the *omni-partial* interest-based language, creativity and attitudes of empathy and collaboration, which are fundamental aspects of dialogue and mediation that can change people's hearts and minds and connect us through a commonality of caring and honest, courageous conversation.

Whatever our justifications for remaining silent when political ideas are discussed, or treating each other as enemies and traitors, our ability to address the highly complex, increasingly challenging issues that characterize modern life is no longer optional, as the adversarial assumptions that fuel political debate increasingly fail to capture what

6

is shared by all, and can be resolved or collaboratively negotiated between us.

What happens in the world politically clearly has an impact on our capacity for conflict resolution, by expanding or contracting the trust and willingness of people on opposing sides of an issue to seek peaceful outcomes. But is it possible that the converse might also be true? Could mediation, dialogue and interest-based approaches to problem-solving, negotiation and conflict resolution have an impact on politics and improve the quality and strength of our democracy?

POWER, RIGHTS AND INTERESTS

From our earliest beginnings, we have resolved disputes in three fundamentally divergent ways. The first is based on *power*, relying principally on war, violence, force and duress. Power contests are "zero-sum games" that inescapably produce winners and losers, destroy important relationships and generate a great deal of "collateral damage." Power encourages corruption in those who use it and blind obedience, resistance and revolt in those it is used against. Resorting to power-based solutions therefore routinely leads to future disputes and makes it difficult to change, adapt or evolve without experiencing major upheavals and confrontations.

As a result of these difficulties, a second way of resolving conflicts has arisen based on *rights*, relying primarily on legislation, litigation, adversarial forms of negotiation, bureaucratic coercion, rules and regulations, contractual agreements and policies and procedures. Rights are *limitations* on the exercise of power, yet depend on power for their enforcement, yet are correctly perceived by those in power as reducing their exclusive and otherwise unlimited control and ability to dominate.

Rights-based processes are also zero-sum games that generate winners and losers, undermine relationships and result in collateral damage, but less so than power-based solutions. Since rights rely on legally

7

interpreted and enforced rules, change is discouraged, individuals are seen as obstacles, conflicts are mostly settled rather than prevented or resolved, and nothing significant or systemic is transformed or transcended without careful vetting by those in positions of power or authority. Uniquely, right-based methods give rise to bureaucracies, which are needed to promulgate, interpret, define and selectively enforce competing, "one-size-fits-all" rights, and shield them to some extent against power-based incursions.

Because both power- and rights-based approaches are zero-sum games, they distribute social status, economic wealth and political power hierarchically, competitively and disproportionately, with most going to the least at the top, less going to more in the middle, and least going to most at the bottom. As a result, there is unending competition, chronic conflict and an unbridgeable schism between the few at the top, the more in the middle, and the most at the bottom.

The smallest group at the top, because they are fewest, will predictably favor the most violent and autocratic power-based methods in order to hold on to their disproportionate and precarious share of status, wealth and power. Those in the middle will predictably favor the use of more moderate, legal and bureaucratic rights-based methods in order to maintain their intermediate, but precarious position against competing forces at either end, hoping always to join those above, yet fearing those below.

This unstable, constantly shifting balance of power gives rise to temporary alliances and coalitions between these competing classes and the political factions that claim to represent them, producing an apparently endless cycle of chronic social, economic and political conflict. Wherever status, wealth and power are fixed by heredity, *caste* conflicts appear and become chronic and sometimes political; wherever they are defined by employment, *class* conflicts arise and also turn chronic and political; wherever they are determined by race, gender, religion, nationality, disability, etc., chauvinistic conflicts emerge, and so on, with different kinds of power and rights being used to support the domination of the few over the many.

While power-based processes rest on hierarchy, operate by command and result in obedience, rights-based processes rest on bureaucracy, operate by control and result in compliance. Power-based approaches encourage open attitudes of domination, resulting in personal arrogance, elitism and contempt. Rights-based approaches encourage *covert* attitudes of domination, resulting in social alienation, cynicism, apathy and uncaring. Neither seeks to prevent or transcend chronic conflicts, or to evolve by dismantling them at their systemic source.

As a result of these dynamics, power- and right-based systems have gradually begun giving way to a third approach to resolving conflicts, which is based on *interests*. Interests reflect not merely *what* people want, but the reasons *why* they want it. Interest-based processes are "win/win," and do not *require* a winner or a loser. Consequently, they are better able to encourage informal problem-solving, facilitation, dialogue, collaborative negotiation, consensus building and mediation and to prevent, resolve, transform and transcend chronic conflicts by dismantling them at their systemic source. This allows them to support more collaborative, democratic relationships and encourage continuous adaptation, peaceful evolution, and personal and systemic change.

Interests are unique and diverse, yet compatible and synergistic. They invite people to communicate at a deeper level, learn from each other, and work jointly and collaboratively to solve problems. They encourage conflicted parties to redesign the dysfunctional power- and rights-based systems and structures that have caused, aggravated and sustained their disputes.

Interest-based processes rest on direct democracy, operate by consensus and result in ownership. For these reasons, they are able to invite deeper levels of resolution, more complex, collaborative interactions and democratic relationships, and invite people into more poignant and profound levels of caring, intimacy, connection and community.

Chronic social, economic and political conflicts commonly result from win/lose, competitive, hierarchical allocations of status, wealth and power — as well as from the *ways* status is measured and assigned, wealth is created and distributed, and power is apportioned and exercised. Because power- and rights-based approaches are win/lose, they are inescapably competitive, creating hierarchical divisions between privileged and downtrodden, haves and have-nots, rulers and ruled, few and many, routinely favoring the former over the latter.

Rights-based approaches, because they flow from and are ultimately grounded in power, adopt a *formally* neutral stance and impartial attitude toward these chronically conflicted groups, yet replicate them simply by paying no attention to their underlying assumptions and inequities. In any system or environment where prejudice and bias operate, being colorblind and gender-neutral will *always* mean that equality is professed publicly and in principle, while discrimination is permitted privately and in practice.

Interest-based approaches, on the other hand, because they require collaboration and consensus, are inherently democratic and egalitarian, and seek to unify socially, economically and politically divided groups, while at the same time appreciating their diversity and individuality, in order to take advantage of their unique perspectives in a search for synergistic solutions to complex problems.

What Is Politics?

More than two millennia ago, the Greek statesman Pericles warned its citizens, "Just because you do not take an interest in politics does not mean politics won't take an interest in you." It is important to begin, therefore, by recognizing that politics is a way of changing *ourselves*, as well as the world we live in, and that it does so in vastly different ways, depending on who participates and how.

Politics has been defined as "the art of compromise," based on Max Weber's notion that, "Politics is the art of compromise and decision making based on social benefits weighed against costs." But what if we defined politics instead as the art of *conflict resolution*, in which compromise, as in mediation, is merely one of many possible outcomes, and a lesser one at that? What if we regarded political conflicts as a large-scale variant of ordinary, everyday conflicts, triggering emotions and behaviors similar to those we find in other disputes, making them amenable to interest-based methods such as mediation and dialogue? What, then, might a *mediative*, interest-based, participatory and collaborative form of politics look like?

In its democratic form, politics began over two thousand years ago in Athens, and it is there that our search for a comprehensive definition of politics needs to begin. Aristotle was the first to think deeply about these issues, defining politics as "a search for the highest common good," reasoning as follows:

> Every state is a community of some kind, and every community is established with a view to some good, for mankind always act in order to obtain that which they think good. But, if all communities aim at some good, the state or political community, which is the highest of all, and which embraces all the rest, aims, and in a greater degree than any other, at the highest good.

Aristotle also defined politics as a way of providing for the general welfare, and as a method for making sure that the laws would be fairly conceived, wisely interpreted and justly enforced. These sound fine as definitions — the only difficulty is that none of them can predict the kind of politics we experience today, or witness throughout history.

In his book, *Politics*, not long after the passage quoted above, Aristotle expresses the view that, of course, none of this applies to women, children, slaves or barbarians, who are rightfully excluded from political participation, in spite of the fact that they constituted the overwhelming majority of Athens. And it is this passage, combined with the first, that begins to come closer to what we have seen throughout history, and still experience today.

If, on the one hand, politics is a search for the highest common good, while on the other hand, it belongs exclusively to a minority of men, adults, slave owners and native-born citizens, it will always be compromised and partisan, and the project and purpose of politics will *necessarily* become one of domination, giving rise to a fear that the majority of women, children, slaves and barbarians who have been suppressed, oppressed, exploited and dominated may someday decide to exercise their majority and use democracy to assume power themselves, and either eliminate domination or become dominators themselves.

Other approaches to understanding the role of politics can be traced back to the dialogues of Socrates, who argued that the chief goal of politics was to increase virtue in order to make the citizen "as good as possible." Politics should be regarded as a core method for increasing virtue because it encourages people to take responsibility for each other, address their conflicts and common problems, and share in the work of governing.

Politics encourages people to become less self-centered by developing their capacity for empathy with others and strengthening socially constructive skills. But, as with Aristotle, while these definitions are useful, it is impossible to predict the highly self-centered, negligibly empathetic, socially destructive history or present state of politics, unless we recognize the ways that domination saps and undermines virtue.

In a similar vein, Plato professed that politics could be defined as "a search for justice" and should support "... not the disproportionate happiness of any one class, but the greatest happiness of the whole." In *The Republic*, Plato also argued that democracy was systematically flawed and would degenerate into a vulgar, lawless, undisciplined, despotic state of "extreme democracy" leading to tyranny — in part as a result of frustration over unresolved conflicts between diverse factions and classes, and a need to reconcile their goals and interests — but again, without acknowledging the role of domination in generating those chronic conflicts, and fueling resistance to sustain them at their systemic source.

Plato believed that liberty, freedom and equality would inevitably lead to an overindulgence of selfish desires and interests, which would in turn create disrespect for political and moral authority. As a result, conflicts would emerge between factions who each want to fulfill their distinct desires and interests, causing the common good to be replaced by selfishness and the good of the faction. Plato believed this would happen because ordinary people are easily manipulated and can be ruled by those who are foolish, vicious and brutal. Strong leaders in a deeply divided democracy will readily turn politics over to demagogues and tyrants who use fear and anger over unresolved conflicts to instill obedience and consolidate control.

Populism can therefore be defined as a rejection of rights-based forms of democracy, with those on the right moving backward toward tyranny and power-based solutions, and those on the left moving forward toward participation and interest-based solutions — in both cases, because rights-based democracies lack the higher order skills and capacities needed to resolve political conflicts successfully, or use informal problem-solving, collaborative negotiation, dialogue and mediation to soften conversations about political differences.

In *Gorgias,* Plato offers a useful illustration of the dilemma of conflicting interests: while cooks aim to bring pleasure to those who will eat their food, doctors aim to increase their health. Cooks are thus like politicians who seek votes by promising to fulfill desires, while doctors are like philosophers who consider only what will benefit the health of society. Hence, only philosophers, as a result of their orientation and rigorous acquisition of knowledge, are able to transcend selfish interests and search for the common good, and are therefore uniquely qualified to exercise political power.

Certainly, the dangers Plato warned of are real and have been experienced throughout history, yet the "epistocracy" of "philosopher kings" he favored have also been known to turn into dictators and tyrants, and there is no reason why, using interest-based techniques, factions cannot be brought to negotiated agreements or consensus, or why politics cannot include both cooks and philosophers, Eros and Logos, pleasure and knowledge. More deeply, beneath each of these factions and interests lie competing claims for status, wealth and power, together with a win/lose, domination-oriented, power- or rights-based process for deciding between them.

To promote virtue and diversity without dictatorship or tyranny, we require *interest-based* approaches that enable us to discuss and reconcile the desires of competing factions, and uncover ways of combining the diverse self-interests of cooks and doctors, Eros and Logos, pleasure and knowledge through open, honest, constructive dialogues that acknowledge the importance and legitimacy of both by designing outcomes in which food is both healthy and delicious. To do so, we require philosopher-cooks, i.e., politicians who are skilled in using dialogue and mediation to synthesize the interests of diverse factions and constituencies, while upholding the highest moral and ethical principles. With regard to Plato's description of the innate bigotry, corruptibility and cupidity of the electorate, as Eleanor Roosevelt wrote, "In the final analysis, a democratic government represents the sum total of the courage and the integrity of its individuals. It cannot be better than they are." It is therefore essential in any direct, participatory form of democracy that politics and virtue be viewed as interdependent; that politics not consist solely of electing representatives or cravenly appealing to the selfish interests of adversarial factions; that the use of politics to dominate others be systemically dismantled; and that a broad range of philosopher-like skills, including moral introspection, ethical reflection, shared values processes, restorative justice processes, dialogue facilitation, mediation, and education in the development of personal and social virtues, be regarded as essential in the education of citizens.

Henry Adams wrote that "Politics, as a practice, whatever its professions, has always been the systematic organization of hatreds." Yet conflict resolution, as a practice, consists of surfacing and discussing, acknowledging and reframing, transforming and transcending hatreds — not only internally, but relationally and systemically. Dialogue and mediation have been highly successful in exposing the sources of hatred in caring, explaining why political conflicts become so bitter, and exploring ways of handling hatred and hostility in political discourse.

SLAVERY AND THE STATE

If we return to Aristotle's definition of politics as "a search for the highest common good" in light of the exclusion of women, children, slaves and barbarians, and regard it for a moment exclusively from the standpoint of slavery, it is apparent that the "highest common good" of the slave is antithetical to that of the slave owner, who is able to reduce slave revolts and conflicts by creating an *apparently* neutral state that uses its monopoly over the means of force and violence to punish slaves for not working, prevent them from escaping and return them to their owners when they do. Centuries later, Anatole France wryly observed how "the law, in its majestic equality, forbids the rich as well as the poor to sleep under bridges, beg in the streets, and steal bread."

The only solution to these chronic conflicts lies not in short-term political compromises that offer slaves minor protections against the worst forms of abuse by their owners, but in the complete abolition of slavery. From a conflict resolution point of view, slavery as a *system* will predictably generate chronic conflicts wherever and whenever it exists, precisely because it is based on domination and exploitation, and therefore grounded in the inequality, disrespect and indignity of the slave, who will never entirely accept these conditions.

If we imagine ourselves as mediators or dialogue facilitators in the period immediately before the U. S. Civil War, what role might we have played that, with foresight, could have reduced the severity and persistence of conflicts over slavery? If we take into account all the chronic conflicts that flowed from slavery, together with the continued impact of racial domination and discrimination into the present, it could only have been by attempting to build bridges between Blacks and Whites; initiating open, honest dialogues with both on the basis of their common interests, capacity for empathy and mutual desire for freedom and equality; and advocating complete abolition.

Yet even the smallest efforts at dialogue would have clearly been seen at the time as supporting abolition, and would have been considered by both sides as a far-from-neutral bias or favoritism directed against the legally sanctioned, widely accepted institution of slavery. Indeed, it was partly the unwillingness, lack of skills and vigorous opposition to any form of dialogue or conversational equality that made all other solutions impossible and civil war inevitable.

In *The Dance of Opposites*, I offered a different example, showing how a seemingly minor and apparently neutral procedural issue could reflect, reproduce and potentially resolve a much larger conflict:

As an illustration, consider the Fugitive Slave Act that allowed Southern slave owners before the Civil War to claim that ex-slaves living in a Northern free state were runaways and petition the courts to have them returned to servitude. At issue was whether, in federal courts, the slave had a right to speak and raise objections, as any citizen of a free state might, to being returned to slavery. If not, slavery was recreated procedurally within the courts, even in Northern abolitionist states. But if the slave could speak freely, slavery was abolished procedurally, even in courts in slave owning states. What appeared on the surface to be a simple procedural rule took on a transformational character and challenged the justice of slavery as a legal institution. In this way, the Fugitive Slave Act threatened to turn the entire nation into a slave state and abolish the rights of Northern states to grant manumission.

THE EVOLUTION OF POLITICS

From these examples, we can see that the development of more advanced forms of politics depend in part on the rise of more advanced approaches to conflict resolution, which in turn encourage the elimination of more primitive, archaic and outmoded methods of domination. Chronic social, economic and political conflicts based on slavery had to end at their systemic source so that more advanced conflicts based on capitalism, together with correspondingly advanced approaches to democracy, conflict resolution and domination, could take their place.

The project of domination has thus evolved over centuries, altering the form of social, economic and political systems and continually creating both chronic conflicts and new approaches to resolving them that shifted from slavery to feudalism, in which the aristocracy used power-based absolutist monarchies to control the state and dominate serfs; and from feudalism to capitalism, in which corporations and wealthy individuals used rights-based electoral democracies to manipulate the state and dominate employees and foreign competitors. We can then ask, what would the use of interests look like in relation to domination, democracy and the state?

To begin with, the essence of any interest-based approach to democracy will necessarily and primarily consist not of electing political representatives and voting for or against political options, but of ending the *project* of dominating others, and recognizing that we are all in this world together and equally entitled to make decision about its future and be treated with dignity and respect.

More profoundly, domination takes place not just physically, mentally and emotionally, but in our language and the ways we communicate with each other. It consists certainly in the use of physical violence, mental intimidation and emotional trauma, but also in the use of hostile rhetoric, adversarial personal attacks, racial and gender stereotyping, and deceitful propaganda to bully, cajole and coerce

17

others into thinking only approved, conventional, orthodox, safe and acceptable thoughts.

Any non-dominating political system must therefore emphasize interest-based methods of communication in order to break up coercion and uniformity in thought, create connections between diverse views and dissenting ideas, explore underlying concerns that simmer beneath the surface and search for collaborative options that do not require anyone's humiliation or defeat.

SOME ADVERSARIAL DEFINITIONS OF POLITICS

Most definitions of democracy focus on popular elections and participation in selecting representatives to government who make political decisions for us. Yet at the heart of democracy is a complex problem-solving, conflict resolving process that today requires egalitarian relationships between citizens who have the ability, not simply to pick the representatives who will decide for them, but decide for themselves and become *owners* of the political process as a whole. Doing so demands the development of higher order attitudes and behaviors, processes and relationships, skills and capacities that enable people to identify issues, brainstorm options, facilitate and participate in dialogues, critique and analyze alternatives, select appropriate criteria, dissent, build consensus, offer feedback and evaluate ways to improve future effectiveness.

Yet, over the course of centuries, politics has been defined instead as unavoidably adversarial. Here is a small sample of some interesting definitions of politics, some humorous, that highlight its hostile, violent and recurrently corrupt character:

- "Politics: A strife of interests masquerading as a contest of principles. The conduct of public affairs for private advantage." —Ambrose Bierce
- "Politics is the art of looking for trouble, finding it everywhere,

diagnosing it incorrectly and applying the wrong remedies."
—Groucho Marx

- "Political language is designed to make lies sound truthful and murder respectable." — George Orwell
- "Politics is almost as exciting as war, and quite as dangerous. In war, you can only be killed once, but in politics many times." — Winston Churchill
- "Politics is the art of preventing people from sticking their noses in things that are properly their business." — Paul Valery
- "Politics is war without bloodshed, while war is politics with bloodshed." — Mao Tse Tung
- "In general, the art of government consists in taking as much money as possible from one class of the citizens to give to the other." — Voltaire
- "Politicians are the same the world over, they promise to build a bridge even when there is no river." — Nikita Khrushchev
- "In politics, stupidity is not a handicap." — Napoleon Bonaparte
- "Government is the great fiction through which everyone endeavors to live at the expense of everyone else." — Frederic Bastiat
- "Practical politics consists in ignoring facts." — Henry Adams
- "Without alienation, there can be no politics." — Arthur Miller
- "Politics is the entertainment division of the military industrial complex." — Frank Zappa

With these interesting insights, it is possible to offer a few additional, somewhat overlapping adversarial, dominating, win/lose power- and rights-based ways of defining politics — for example, as:

- Ways of organizing and exercising power over and against others
- A monopoly by those in power over the means of war, violence, force, intimidation and coercion
- A set of adversarially negotiated, legally sanctioned,

legitimized forms of domination and control enforced by
the State
- A way of unifying in-groups by pitting them against out-groups
- A gradual narrowing of options through bullying, hostility, bribery and personal disparagement
- A top-down method of problem-solving and conflict resolution that consistently favors one group of people over another
- Rules designed by a minority of the propertied to exercise control over a majority of the propertyless
- A patriarchal system of control over decision-making by women and gays
- Rules for collecting taxes, protecting private property and distributing power, wealth and status unequally to those who are rich and powerful
- A process for resolving disputes by means of laws that are passed, implemented and interpreted by officials who are selected by those in power to safeguard their interests
- A battle over competing, one-sided visions of the future, only one of which will win
- A hierarchical method of control that permits some behaviors and prohibits others, where either everything that is not prohibited is permitted, or everything that is not permitted is prohibited
- An exercise of domination and hegemony within a geographical area
- An ability to imprison or ostracize minorities and dissenters, allowing some in and keeping others out
- A way of uniting some people by dividing and pitting them against others

The consequences of defining politics in these and similarly adversarial ways include, most critically, the creation of *chronic* political conflicts and enduring resentment, resistance, rebellion and revolt on the part of those who feel power-down, defeated, excluded, dominated and disrespected. A somewhat subtler consequence is that truth and falsity, along with science and logic, art and creativity, may also become adversarial, and be turned into weapons or subordinated to political advantage.

TRUTH AND FALSITY IN POLITICAL CONFLICTS

It is typical for political advocates on opposing sides to label each other's factual claims as false, or more recently as "fake news," and dismiss entirely what they have experienced as obviously and irrefutably untrue. Even the most rigorous fact-checking, however, seemingly fails to convince anyone, or change their minds or political conclusions in the slightest. In mathematics, where there is far greater clarity about what can be proven to be true and false than in politics, Godel's "Incompleteness Theorem" nonetheless holds that, within certain mathematical systems, there are true statements that cannot be proven, together with false statements that cannot be disproven within the system, forcing truth and falsity to lie at least partly outside the realm of provability. In response, mathematician Ian Stewart writes:

> Classical logic, with its sharp distinctions between truth and falsity, with no middle ground, is two-valued. Godel's discovery suggests that for mathematics, a three-valued logic would be more appropriate: true, false, or undecidable.

A similar three-valued or "multi-valued logic" would be equally appropriate in discussing a number of political differences. "Paraconsistent" forms of logic, for example, offer ways of assessing statements that are both true and false, and would be described as paradoxical in traditional logic. Dov Gabbay at King's College, London, for instance, is attempting to develop rules for reasoning that capture emotional arguments, including those that arise in political conflicts.

As an illustration, in politics, there are factual assertions, such as:

"President Obama was born in Kenya," that can easily be proven to be false, while the underlying reasons these statements became popular and gained a wide audience: i.e., the view of a Black President as "foreign," or the desire to diminish his power and popularity by labeling him as inferior without using explicitly racist epithets that might be more easily dismissed, can be regarded as at least tactically and *emotionally* true.

Yet the fundamental political issues that separate left and right and gave rise to this demonstrably factually false assertion — the issue, for example, of what course the United States ought to follow with regard to race, abortion, immigration, gun control, climate change, same sex marriage or any proposal for action, must be regarded as far more complex, multidimensional and difficult to decide than a simple separation into true and false facts will allow.

Similarly, though equally controversially, global warming, climate change and human contributions to both through the use of fossil fuels, CO2 and methane emissions, deforestation, and similar activities have been scientifically verified by innumerable in-depth studies; yet again, the underlying reasons for their denial, including financial contributions to politicians by fossil fuel companies, dependence on automobiles, distrust of science, and similar factors require deeper dialogues and more complex conversations.

Indeed, it is the very complexity of social problem-solving and political decision-making that gives rise to the desire for simplistic, adversarial solutions. The conversion of complex problems into simple scapegoating assertions allows people to channel their rage and confusion into authoritarianism, war, genocide and adversarial political practices. As Adolf Hitler wrote, without apology:

> I will tell you what has carried me to the position I have reached. Our political problems appeared complicated. The German people could make nothing of them. ... I, on the other hand, reduced them to the simplest terms. The masses realized this and followed me.

The simplest way we describe any conflict or problem is: "It doesn't exist." The second simplest is: "It's your/his/her/their fault." The third simplest is: "It isn't true/clear/proven." And the fourth is: "It's been/being taken care of." If we try to disprove any of these assertions factually — not just politically, but in any conflict, we rapidly discover that we have slipped into a self-defeating, non-disprovable argument, one that turns in a vicious circle, forcing us to realize that the desire to deny that there are problems, or find someone to blame, or disregard them as untrue, or assume someone else will handle them are far more convincing than logical or rational discourse concerning a complex set of facts.

Yet, in response to "birther," "climate change denial," "flat earth" and similarly untrue and illogical assertions, it is possible to direct people's attention to, and openly discuss, the underlying *emotional* truths that are revealed *metaphorically* in the reasons they offer, and in the precise accusations and "factual" allegations that typically pepper their adversarial communications. We can invite them into more nuanced, complex exchanges in which these assertions, which never last and are hard to pin down long enough to be refuted, are simply *bypassed* in favor of deeper, more "truthful" conversations about the concerns that gave rise to them, *without* surrendering scientific accuracy or legitimizing falsehoods. The danger is that we can easily slip into a "pseudo-dialogue" that presents, for example, round and flat earth ideas, or evolution and "intelligent design," as equally *factual*, when scientific truth unambiguously establishes that only one of them is true. Yet beneath these controversies lies a hostile attitude toward science that exaggerates emotional truths and places them on the same level as scientific truth, whereas facts and feelings are fundamentally different and require their own unique form of dialogue to discover what is true with respect to each. (For more on "varieties of truth," see my book, *Conflict Revolution: Designing Preventative Systems for Chronic Social, Economic and Political Conflicts*.)

Exaggeration, in all conflict conversations, is used to communicate the *priority* and personal importance of emotional, as opposed to factual truths, so that if we are offered a choice between factual accuracy and emotional accuracy in telling a conflict story, we will nearly always opt for emotional accuracy, because it is only emotionally compelling stories that induce empathy and allow others to easily understand what we *felt* happened, and why we are so upset.

Consider, for example, commonly used phrases, like "You always," and "You never," to which the other person nearly always counters with "Yes I do," or "No I don't," which are denials and not at all the responses we were looking for. As a result, we can realize that these statements were not *meant* to be factually correct, but instead can be understood as consisting of a combination of two statements:

1. You are doing this too often/too little for me; and
2. I am getting seriously emotionally upset about the number of times this has happened, and the fact that you haven't heard or responded to my requests to do it less/more often, so I am going to exaggerate how often you do it so you will understand that I am upset and respond to my emotional request, rather than to the factual assertion that justifies it

The difficulty, of course, is that the words "You always," and "You never," are *heard* as accusations, factual assertions and adversarial responses, prompting denials, counter-assertions and counter-accusations. It is possible, however, for mediators to tease apart these statements and ask questions that invite the underlying *meaning* of the assertion to be expressed, acknowledged and addressed. For example, we can see that, merely by using these words, we have:

- Camouflaged our requests as statements of fact
- Exaggerated the truth
- Stereotyped the other person as unreasonable
- Not taken responsibility for communicating our needs
- Ignored others' needs, explanations, or reasons for acting in their own self-interest

- Failed to accurately describe what we really want from others
- Missed opportunities to become vulnerable and invite others into more intimate conversation and relationship
- Suggested that it is not acceptable to express deeper emotions directly
- Infused frustration and disappointment into the conversation
- Converted desire into anger and hurt feelings into annoyance
- Missed opportunities to collaboratively negotiate the satisfaction of mutual needs and diverse interests
- Created a source of chronic conflict within our relationship

Even with simple assertions like these, it is possible to avoid getting caught up in assessing the truth or falsity of pseudo-factual statements, for example, by separating factual from emotional communications, identifying what is taking place beneath the surface, clarifying the consequences that flow from using that form of communication, reframing the statement to avoid misunderstanding, acknowledging both parties' emotions, surfacing their underlying interests, inviting apologies and deeper acknowledgments, etc.

These techniques help people gain perspective on their problems, pinpoint their underlying sources, invite them to work together to solve them, and prevent future conflicts from occurring. Mediators routinely do this in cases of interpersonal misunderstandings and miscommunications, and we can see how these techniques might easily be adapted to shift political conversations as well.

Indeed, emotionally charged distortions of facts can be found in nearly every political argument, and a similar set of interventions can allow us to bypass what merely *appear* to be factual assertions, but are actually emotional markers and *requests*, indicating that there is some issue the speaker cares deeply about, and at the same time, does not have the skills to discuss in a non-adversarial, emotionally intelligent way.

What Is Wrong with "Politics as Usual" — A Summary

Here then, by way of summary, are a few things we can say are "wrong," costly, conflict-generating and ineffective about the way we discuss and conduct "politics as usual," from an interest-based conflict resolution perspective. Politics, in its power- and rights-based forms, is thus:

- Unnecessarily divisive and adversarial
- Nearly always win/lose and winner take all
- Controlled by wealthy individuals, military and industrial elites, corporations and special interests
- Grounded in domination, inequality and disrespect
- Easily corrupted by money and controlled by bureaucrats
- Discouraging and dismissive of popular participation
- Fearful of diversity, dissent, "alien" cultures and unorthodox ideas
- Opposed to openness and direct democracy, and in favor of secrecy and hierarchical control of information
- Drawn to manipulate electoral processes and fake outcomes to gain short-term advantage
- Too time consuming, too costly and exercised too personally
- Increasingly ineffective in solving global problems
- Able to transition easily into autocracy and authoritarianism
- Resistant to evolution, adaption, improvement and change
- A systemic source of chronic conflict

Toward an Interest-based Language of Politics

What kinds of attitudes and approaches to politics are most likely to reduce violent, hostile and adversarial behaviors? What kinds of words, phrases and processes are most likely to clarify communications and increase trust? What kinds of relationships are most likely to encourage constructive and collaborative behaviors? The answer, as suggested above, lies in the core distinction between power, rights and interests.

Reconsidering this distinction from a somewhat different perspective and framework, it is clear that the language and communications that inform our political conversations, negotiations, dialogues and mediations is grounded in power-, rights- and interest-based approaches to problem-solving and decision-making, each reflected in a different set of words and phrases, as well as in attitudes and behaviors, processes and relationships, skills and capacities, regardless of whether they occur between individuals or systems, couples or families, organizations or nation-states. To reiterate, these are:

1. Power-based words and phrases, attitudes and behaviors, processes and relationships, skills and capacities that routinely produce winners and losers, destroy important relationships and encourage corruption in those who use them, while encouraging blind obedience, resistance and revolt in those they are used against.
2. Rights-based words and phrases, attitudes and behaviors, processes and relationships, skills and capacities that use legislation, litigation, adversarial forms of negotiation, bureaucratic coercion, rules and regulations, contractual agreements and policies and procedures to resolve differences.
3. Interest-based words and phrases, attitudes and behaviors, processes and relationships, skills and capacities that use informal problem-solving, facilitation, public dialogue, collaborative negotiation and mediation to resolve disputes.

To make this distinction clearer, imagine how it is translated into language. Thus, the language favored by power-based organizations such as the military, police and monarchical states requires clarity, simplicity, and uniform interpretation in order to encourage unthinking obedience. The communications that emanate from these institutions therefore take the form of declarations, pronouncements and orders, which reinforce hierarchy and command, and imply punishment and contempt for those who disobey.

The language favored by rights-based organizations like legal institutions, bureaucracies and formally democratic states requires narrow distinctions, exceptions and adjudicated interpretations in order to maintain control by permitting some behaviors and forbidding others. The communications that emanate from these institutions therefore take the form of rules and regulations, policies and procedures, legislative definitions and legal interpretations, which reinforce bureaucracy and control, and imply coercion and censure for those who do not fit in.

The language favored by interest-based organizations such as teams, civil society and direct, substantively democratic states, requires affirmation of diversity, dissent and dialogue in order to encourage collaboration and participation. The communications that emanate from these institutions therefore take the form of open-ended questions, public dialogues, value-driven rules and consensus decision making, which reinforce social equality, economic equity and political democracy. Here are some trivial examples of each, often overheard in families, couples and relationships, as well as in schools and workplaces:

- *Power:* "You must ..." "You shall ..." "You will ..." "... or else." "... because I said so, that's why."

- *Rights:* "You should ..." "You ought to ..." "You need to ..." "You have a right to ..." "You are entitled to ..."

- *Interests*: "You could ..." "You might consider ..." "What would happen if you ..." "What would you like to have happen?" "Why?" "What do you think will happen if you ..."

WHY INTEREST-BASED POLITICS ARE DIFFERENT

While these language choices are revealing, the development of an interest-based approach to political conflicts rests on a deeper understanding of the nature of the political process. The brilliant essayist and author Isaiah Berlin wrote about politics in a way that helps us understand how it might be done differently:

> So long as only one ideal is the true goal, it will always seem to men that no means can be too difficult, no price too high, to do whatever is required to realize the ultimate goal. Such certainty is one of the great justifications of fanaticism, compulsion, persecution ... If there is only one solution to the puzzle, then the only problems are first how to find it, then how to realize it, and finally how to convert others to the solution by persuasion or by force. But if this is not so ..., then the path is open to empiricism, pluralism, tolerance, compromise. Tolerance is historically the product of the realization of the irreconcilability of equally dogmatic faiths, and the practical improbability of complete victory of one over the other. Those who wished to survive realized that they had to tolerate error. They gradually came to see the merits of diversity, and so became skeptical about definitive solutions in human affairs.

Movement in this direction will require a profound, transformational shift in the methods for realizing our ideals or goals, from violence, autocracy and the exercise of power; to coercion, law and the enforcement of rights; to dialogue, democratic participation and the satisfaction of interests. To do so, we require not merely compromise, but a rich infrastructure of collaborative interest-based words and phrases, together with methods and techniques, attitudes and behaviors, skills and capacities, arts and sciences that lead people who disagree and do not trust each other to discover that they can actually solve their problems together.

In contrast to the list of adversarial definitions of politics cited above, here are a few, somewhat overlapping ways of thinking about politics that draw our understanding of adversarial, power- or rights-based politics in a more collaborative, interest-based direction. Politics in this sense can be defined as:

- A process of social problem-solving
- A collection of ideas, beliefs, interests and desires regarding the future
- A group of conversations and dialogues about what ought to be done and why
- A set of stories and beliefs about the past that shape the future
- A group of words and phrases that convey respect and inclusion
- A collection of processes and relationships organized around a shared set of values and ideals, ethics and morality, goals and objectives
- A diverse group of people uniting to achieve a common goal
- A system for making decisions that are accepted by nearly everyone
- A living, evolving expression of collective identity
- An egalitarian attitude, culture or mindset about people, power and privilege
- A way of owning, fixing and sharing responsibility for social decisions
- A compact, agreement or contract reconciling competing interests
- A mixture of unspoken expectations, desires, needs and interests
- A continually evolving set of creative ideas and social purposes
- A way of resolving chronic conflicts and mediating between diverse interests

More concisely, I believe there are three simple, interest-based ways of defining politics that discourage domination, not only as an attitude, but as a goal, a process and a relationship. These definitions are:

1. *Politics is a social problem-solving process.* As a result, a diversity of views about the nature of the problem and multiple, alternative ways of solving it will predictably result in better, more sustainable solutions.
2. *Politics is a large group decision-making process.* As a result, the greater the consensus, the stronger the democracy, the more apt people are to agree with a decision and the more likely it is to be effective.
3. *Politics is a conflict resolution process.* As a result, the amount of chronic, on-going, systemic conflict can be dramatically reduced by assuming that there is more than one correct answer; by adopting a complex, egalitarian, interest-based approach to conflict resolution; and by allowing no one to lose so that that others are able to win.

Toward a Mediative, Interest-based Approach to Political Conflicts

If we ponder the nature of political conflicts over long stretches of time, without regard to their specific content, we can see that they can be greatly simplified, revealing their constituent parts and enabling us to develop more effective approaches to resolving the important issues that lie beneath their surface. Doing so suggests methods we can use to shift political communications in more constructive directions and highlight their deeper significance.

What makes an issue *political* is therefore, in the first place, the presence of a disagreement over choices, or future direction or values, ethics and morality, any of which can, in a variety of ways, mutate into conflict. Politics can therefore be defined as a process for making social choices, and a way of responding to chronic conflicts that arise as a consequence of the choices we make and the ways we make them.

If we say that politics consist of choices about the direction in which we need to be moving based on a set of shared values, ethics or morality, several questions rapidly arise: Whose choices? Which direction? Why that one? What values, ethics and morality? Who says? Politics is conflicted by definition, because even consensus or unanimity on an issue means that *some* choice has been made, some specific direction has been charted and some group's values, ethics or morality is being implemented.

The problem is not merely that we disagree with each other about political choices, directions or values, ethics and morality, but that the *ways* we disagree also produce conflicts. Political disagreement is an essential aspect of diversity and citizenship, and an important element in successful social problem-solving. But a belief that ours is the *only* truth routinely triggers personal hostilities, hatreds and enmities, and moves us beyond mere disagreement, transforming our differences into conflicts, which produce emotional responses that diminish our ability to accurately evaluate complex choices, decide which is the best direction, and live together with differing values, ethics and morals.

What, then, turns productive disagreements into unproductive conflicts? It is possible to simplify and abstract political conflicts by breaking them down into sub-components or elementary parts, and seeing them as a recipe or set of instructions that tell us how to *create* political conflicts wherever and whenever we wish, but that equally tell us how to dismantle them. Thus, if we ask: what are the minimal requirements for any political conflict, I believe there are three:

1. *Diversity*: In the first place, there must be two or more distinct individuals or groups of people, each with diverse beliefs, ideas, opinions, needs, values and interests. Without this, there cannot be conflict.
2. *Inequality*: In the second place, there must be an inequality in power between these individuals or groups, reflecting their differing abilities to implement their diverse beliefs, ideas, opinions, values, etc. Without this, the conflict will not take a political form.

3. *Adversarial, win/lose process*: In the third place, there must be an adversarial, win/lose process for political problem-solving or decision-making that pits diverse individuals and groups against each other, allowing only one to prevail. Without this, the conflict will not become polarizing or chronic.

While conservatives and those on the right commonly seek to reduce the level of political conflict by decreasing diversity, boosting respect for accepted or conventional ideas and buttressing established authority; liberals and those on the left seek to do so by increasing equality, drawing attention to new and diverse ideas and championing the freedom to dissent, articulate, argue for and implement them. Neither group, however, focuses on the adversarial win/lose nature of the political process, without which diversity and inequality do not regularly and predictably result in political polarization.

The question then arises: is politics *necessarily* an adversarial, win/lose process that cannot help but result in polarization? To some extent, the answer is yes, because politics is a social problem-solving, group decision-making process that requires diverse constituencies to make choices between what are often mutually exclusive alternatives, and there is sometimes a fixed sum that needs to be divided and is not enough to support all the options.

But this answer is overly simplistic, as it focuses only on outputs and does not adequately take into account the ways that inclusive, consensus building, collaborative, mediative and interest-based processes are able to "expand the pie," or produce a "positive no," or generate new options by listening, assessing criteria, brainstorming creative alternatives, building consensus, soothing injured feelings, resolving underlying disputes and maximizing constructive outcomes.

Effective political problem-solving and decision-making consists partly in using processes that avoid pointless personal insults and unnecessary demonizations, and redirect conflicts toward *genuine* differences in direction. These require us to recognize that there are three distinct sets of concerns that form the basis for political analyses, problem-solving, conflict resolution and decision-making:

1. *Content*: The substance or content of the problem must be successfully identified, discussed, addressed and resolved.
2. *Process*: The process of solving problems and making decisions must be inclusive, transparent, effective and fair.
3. *Relationship*: The relationship between the people who are impacted by the problem, or trying to solve it, or make decisions about it, must be respectful, constructive, trusting and collaborative.

If the content of the problem is successfully addressed and the relationship is constructive, but the process is ineffective and unfair; or if the content and process are successful and effective, but the relationship is competitive, adversarial and untrusting, chronic conflicts will arise that can prevent even the best solutions from being implemented. Yet nearly all of our focus in solving political problems and making decisions is on the *content*, and comparatively little is devoted to improving either the processes or the relationships.

While these three are intricately interconnected, it is important to periodically set aside disagreements over content in order to focus our attention exclusively on improving processes and relationships. Doing so makes it possible to achieve content goals far more effectively in the long run by learning to act fairly, repair trust and work constructively, even when there are disagreements over content.

This is especially important in political conflicts, where nearly everyone is focused on substance, even to the point of being willing to sacrifice processes and relationships entirely, thereby allowing deeply desired ends to justify the use of undesirable means, without realizing that by using hostile, adversarial means we routinely produce hostile, adversarial ends. And it is precisely our willingness to achieve results at the expense of fairness in processes and trust in relationships that fuels most of our political conflicts and makes them intractable.

TWO

THE NEUROPHYSIOLOGY AND MORALITY OF POLITICAL CONFLICTS

All power dynamics — all instances of repression and authoritarianism and manipulation — are just failed metaphors for the ways our own brains interact with us. —Camilla Shamsie

The whole aim of practical politics is to keep the populace in a continual state of alarm (and hence clamorous to be led to safety) by menacing them with an endless series of hobgoblins, all of them imaginary. —H. L. Mencken

[T]he difficulty of achieving the simple is infinitely more complicated than any other task or skill, that is, it is less difficult to conceive, create, construct and manipulate an electronic brain than to find in our own the wherewithal to be happy ... —Jose Saramago

POLITICS, OF COURSE, IS AN ACTIVITY OF THE BRAIN. IT MAKES SENSE, therefore, to consider how political messages are received, interpreted, crafted and responded to by various parts of the brain. Our brains also separate experiences into distinct categories, like pleasant and unpleasant, right and wrong, positive and negative, good and evil, and partly as a result, politics is widely regarded as a method for solving moral problems, usually by forcing people to conform their behaviors to hotly disputed opinions about what is perceived to be right and wrong, moral and immoral.

In *The Dance of Opposites: Explorations in Mediation, Dialogue, and Conflict Resolution Systems Design*, I wrote about the neurophysiology of conflict, and will not reiterate here most of the research I cited there, except to cite some of the studies that help us understand how the brain sculpts and shapes our responses to political conflicts.

The brain is awash in chemicals, including hormones and neurotransmitters that accentuate and dampen its responses to conflict and influence its organization, plasticity and operations. Neurotransmitters are chemicals that relay, amplify or modulate signals that are sent between neurons and other cells. There are many different hormones and neurotransmitters, of which the most important are glutamate and GABA, which excite and modify synapses. With regard to conflict, the following compounds seem to be most active:

- Adrenalin, which triggers the fight or flight response
- Testosterone, which stimulates aggression
- Oxytocin which instills trust, increases loyalty and promotes the "tend and befriend" response
- Estrogen, which triggers the release of oxytocin
- Endorphins, which reinforce collaborative experiences with pleasure
- Dopamine, which generates a reward response and fortifies addiction
- Serotonin, which regulates moods
- Phenethylamine, which induces excitement and anticipation
- Vasopressin, which encourages bonding in males in a variety of species

These neurotransmitters stimulate areas of the brain that are responsible for organizing the body's response to perceived threats and conflicts, which may be expressed physically, mentally or emotionally, and can be triggered by perceived antagonisms or differences that are entirely moral or ethical, procedural or relational, metaphoric or ideological.

Recent research has revealed a number of connections between political beliefs and areas of the brain responsible for emotional responses such as fear and disgust. Here is a summary of a few of many recent studies that reveal interesting and unexpected connections and associations between neurophysiology and politics:

- Using data from MRI scans, researchers at University College London found that self-described liberals have a larger anterior cingulate cortex, associated with understanding complexity, while self-described conservatives were more likely to have a larger amygdala, associated with fear and anxiety.
- A team at MIT ran tests to see if objects could influence judgments and decision-making. Passers-by were asked to judge a job candidate by looking at their resume. Half were given the resume on a heavy clipboard and half on a light one. Those with the heavy clipboard rated the same candidates more serious than those with the light one.
- Volunteers who sat on a hard seat were less willing to change their price in a hypothetical car purchase than those sitting on a soft seat. Textures associated with tactile metaphors have been shown to trigger linguistic links to related behaviors.
- University of Southern California researchers asked male and female volunteers to put their hands in ice water, raising their levels of the stress hormone cortisol. They then looked at angry or neutral faces in a brain scanner. Men showed *less* activity in key face-processing regions of the brain and their ability to evaluate facial expressions declined. In women, on the other hand, this region became *more* active, as did an area of the brain linked to empathy and the ability to recognize others' emotions.
- Israeli researchers, writing in the journal *Fertility and Sterility*,

found that women undergoing in vitro fertilization were almost twice as likely to conceive if they had been made to laugh by a hospital "clown" who entertained them as soon as their embryos were implanted.

- A University of British Columbia researcher in Canada found that "the mere thought of having money makes people less likely to help acquaintances, to donate to charity, or to choose to spend time with others — precisely the kind of behaviors that are strongly associated with happiness." Spending as little as five dollars on someone else has been shown to promote greater happiness than spending money on oneself.

- When people have just seen an organic fruit salad, they think a cheeseburger has 1,041 calories, but only 780 calories after seeing a "decadent cheesecake."

- In offices with an honor system for coffee, people are more likely to pay on days when a photograph of human eyes is discretely posted above the coffee machine.

- People tip waiters an average of 140 percent more if the waiter repeats the order *verbatim*, as opposed to paraphrasing it.

- Sociologists at Tilburg University in the Netherlands interviewed travelers at a train station during and after a strike by janitors, and found that people in messy environments were more likely to accept negative stereotypes of Muslims and homosexuals. Travelers were asked to sit while filling out the survey, and those in messy environments chose to sit farther away from a black man than a white man.

- The *Swiss Journal of Psychology* reported a study in which women asked male passersby for directions to Valentine Street or Martin Street (neither exists). A moment later, they encountered a different woman struggling to retrieve her cellphone from a group of threatening guys. Those asked about Valentine Street were more likely to offer help than those asked about Martin Street.

- Yale University psychologists met volunteers and casually asked them to hold a hot or iced coffee while writing down their names. They later read a description of a fictitious person and answered questions about their character. Those who held an iced coffee rated the person as less warm and friendly. In a similar experiment, just thinking about being socially excluded can make a room feel about 3° C cooler.

- People who watched an upsetting film or sniffed a disturbing smell as opposed to a neutral one were more judgmental and severe about unethical acts. Those who read about an unethical act expressed a greater preference for cleaning products, while offering people an antiseptic wipe afterward reduced their willingness to volunteer to help out a desperate student.

- Harvard University researchers created a "public goods" game in which players choose whether or not to contribute money to a common pool that was to be redistributed equally. They divided participants into three groups, one that could punish freeloaders, one that could reward contributors, and one that could do either. Rewarding people always gave the largest return, and when those who could chose opted to reward they received larger payoffs.

- Oxytocin and vasopressin are known to promote collaborative social behaviors in humans and primates, and were recently shown to relax spontaneous social interactions and reduce differences in social behavior between dominant and subordinate monkeys, flattening status hierarchies and increasing synchrony and empathy by stimulating the anterior cingulate gyrus, which is linked with empathy.

POLITICS AND RISK

Dr. Darren Schreiber at the University of Exeter, with colleagues at the University of California, San Diego, measured brain activity as participants played a simple gambling game. They found that Republicans and Democrats did not differ in the risks they took, but there were striking differences in the participants' brain activity during the risk-taking portion of the experiment. Specifically, liberals and conservatives use different parts of their brains when making risky decisions and these regions can be used to predict which political party they prefer. Thus, when given a gambling task, Democrats showed significantly greater activity in the left insula, a region associated with social and self-awareness, while Republicans showed significantly greater activity in the right amygdala, a region involved in the body's fight-or-flight system.

Brain activity in these two regions alone was enough to predict whether a person was a Democrat or Republican with 82.9 percent accuracy. By comparison, a longstanding model in political science that used the party affiliation of a subject's mother and father to predict the child's affiliation was only accurate 69.5 percent of the time. Another model based on differences in brain structure distinguished liberals from conservatives with 71.6 percent accuracy. These results suggest that liberals and conservatives engage in very different cognitive processes when they think about risk.

Politics and Vulnerability

It has been shown in a number of studies that people who self-identify as politically conservative have a larger and more active right amygdala, associated with fear and anger. A 2011 study looked at MRI scans of self-described conservative young adults and found they had more gray matter volume in their right amygdalas than their liberal counterparts. In 2013, another team of scientists expanded that research to show that conservatives display greater activity in their right amygdala when taking risks than liberals do.

Recently, Yale professor John Bargh asked a group of participants to imagine that they had been granted a superpower by a magic genie and were as invincible as Superman — bullets would bounce off them, fire couldn't scorch their skin, and "a fall from a cliff wouldn't hurt at all." A control group was simply told to imagine that they could fly. Researchers then asked them political questions, including whether they "would be reluctant to make any large-scale changes to the social order," and whether "it's okay if some groups have more of a chance in life than others." Liberal participants' attitudes on social issues didn't shift at all. Conservative participants, on the other hand, began adopting more liberal views on social issues (though not on economic ones.) Those who imagined themselves with the ability to fly experienced no significant changes in their political views.

POLITICS AND DISGUST

Another recent study suggests that it is possible to determine whether someone is liberal or conservative simply by the way they respond to pictures of objects that commonly induce disgust, such as blood, feces or vomit. The study found that socially and politically conservative students responded physically by looking away from "disgusting" images more rapidly than their liberal peers, but the same response did not hold true for people with fiscally conservative beliefs. Self-reported social conservatives stared longer at images of faces reacting in disgust to the same images. This was not true for sad or scary images, however, and there were no significant differences in how people reacted to these images based on their political beliefs.

Self-identified conservatives have been shown in several studies to be more hostile to "outgroups" and to people (or animals, or objects) that don't come from the places they do or behave like them. For example, conservatives were more likely to tell researchers that they had more empathy for family members over friends, endorse fellow countrymen over foreigners, and take the side of humans over nonhuman subjects.

In another study, conservatives tended to agree with statements like "I often have tender, concerned feelings for my family members who are less fortunate than me," but less so toward people in general. Liberals more frequently reported feeling tenderness toward less fortunate people in general, beyond those in their own families.

Jonas Olofsson and his team at Stockholm University in Sweden have shown that disgust helps explain why people lean toward right-wing thinking.

> We thought body odor disgust might be related to authoritarian ideological attitudes, because inter-group contact and social change is minimized in authoritarian societies, which might make disgust-sensitive individuals feel that those societies are more 'safe' from contamination. ... Across three studies, we found that body-odor disgust was indeed associated with the degree to which persons reported authoritarian attitudes.

Olofsson's team concluded that body odor is a kind of shorthand people rely on when gauging how riddled with germs someone might be. They believed it was more a person's fear of disease rather a dislike of sweat that explained why some people became more authoritarian. This same aversion response and correlated conservatism applied to their own body odor as well as that of others.

An earlier related study found that women make decisions about male attractiveness based on chemical indicators in their body odor and sweat that indicate they have immunities to diseases the women lack, as measured by differences in their genes for the "major histocompatibility complex" or MHC. Men also seem to prefer women who have dissimilar MHC genes, specifically human leukocyte antigen or HLA genes.

In a series of studies in Europe, poverty, deprivation, a harsh childhood and exposure to stress were shown to increase the likelihood that people would prefer strong, dominant, authoritarian leaders. One study included 66,281 people living in 46 European countries and controlled for participants' levels of education, income, current stress and childhood exposure to literature and politics, yet still found a significant correlation of childhood poverty with preference for authoritarian leadership.

POLITICS, INTERNET, ALCOHOL AND AMBIGUITY

In an effort to assess the impact of the internet on politics, researchers looked at 3.5 billion comments from 25.3 million people between 2007 and 2017 on reddit, a social network that is built around discussion groups that were then used by more than 230 million people a month, including ultra-conservative and right-wing advocates, and looked at the frequency of offensive words and phrases in both political and non-political groups.

They found that while non-political comments were fairly civil, people were 35 percent more likely to use offensive language in political discussions, and these comments became significantly more offensive between May 2016 and May 2017 than during any previous period over the last 10 years. Moreover, political comments dropped in their level of language and intelligence on average from a seventh grade (age 12) to a first grade (age 6) level after 2007.

Alcohol use also moves political views to the right, researchers have found, presumably because it strips away complex reasoning. People can also be more easily moved to the political right by distracting them, or putting them under time pressure or telling them not to think too hard. Those asked to deliberate more deeply or for a longer period of time or to concentrate on solving a problem shifted their political thinking to the left.

Researchers have also found that right-wing and pro-fascist supporters hold views that are strongly correlated with a dislike of ambiguity and cognitive complexity, and represent on average the lowest 10 percent in intelligence. The highest 10 percent in intelligence, they found, are inclined either to the left or to libertarian political views.

PRIMING AND POLITICS

Several studies have revealed that the brain is highly responsive to suggestion. In a series of remarkable experiments it has been shown that the performance of simple, seemingly unrelated tasks can be increased or decreased merely by placing a briefcase or piece of sports equipment nearby, triggering unconscious associations with work or play.

In an interesting study, subjects were made happy or angry, then shown happy and angry faces, then friendly and hostile interpersonal scenes in a stereoscope. Happy subjects perceived more happy faces and friendly interpersonal scenes while angry subjects perceived more angry faces and hostile interpersonal scenes.

In addition, it has been shown that relatively small favors or bits of good luck (like finding money in a coin telephone or receiving an unexpected gift) induce positive emotions in people, and that these emotions increase the subjects' inclinations to sympathize, empathize or provide help to others.

Equally dramatic, test results can be predictably raised or lowered merely by asking people of color — or those who have been discriminated against in their country of origin — to identify themselves by their race, gender or discriminatory category beforehand; by giving indirect racial, gender or stereotypical emotional cues; or by priming teachers falsely in advance of a test regarding the level of innate intelligence or stupidity of their students, producing conformity with expectations in a well-established "Pygmalion effect."

In one remarkable study, when 12- and 13-year-old African-American students were asked to spend 15 minutes indicating which values, such as friendship or family, they upheld, the achievement gap between them and white students decreased by 40 percent. Similarly, when female college students read passages before a test arguing against gender differences in mathematical ability, their scores on a math test increased by 50 percent.

At a very subtle level, Yale University psychologist John Bargh found that when volunteers were "primed" with words associated with the elderly, like "wrinkle," they took significantly longer to walk down a hall than those who had not been primed. And interestingly, Alex Pentland of the MIT Media Lab found that even without priming, watching body language and tone of voice for only a few minutes allowed researchers to predict with 87 percent accuracy the outcome of subsequent negotiations between strangers.

Here are some additional results, culled from a large number of fascinating priming studies:

- Integrating words such as "cooperation" and "fairness" into sentences can result in a higher occurrence of these behaviors in negotiations and conflicted conversations.
- When subjects were asked to think about the lowest and highest *fair* price for a car before negotiating, they made conciliatory moves more quickly, were happier with the results, reached agreements in half the time and were willing to negotiate again.
- Students primed with the word "rudeness" interrupted speakers more quickly than others.
- People using a public bathroom were more willing to pay a fee on the honor system if the word "honesty" was posted, or to pay for coffee if a picture of a face or an eye was posted nearby.
- Scores in Trivial Pursuit® were increased by thinking of a professor and decreased by thinking of a soccer hooligan.
- People who were primed with the names of their friends were more willing to help others, including strangers.
- Researchers at the Interdisciplinary Center Herzliya in Israel conducted a study involving 76 Israel-born Jews, 59 Israeli Arabs and 53 Palestinians living in the occupied Palestinian territories. Each individual was randomly assigned a reading — one portraying groups as having a fixed nature and the

other describing them as flexible and open to change. Those primed to believe their adversaries were changeable were significantly more optimistic about their ability to reach a negotiated peace, suggesting they would be more willing to compromise to reach agreement.

- Group members primed with the words *dependable, helpful, share* and *support* were more cooperative within their group than others, even to their individual economic detriment.
- U.S. participants who listened to and mouthed the words of the national anthem "O Canada" together showed increased feelings of being "part of the group," and consistently made more cooperative decisions in an economic game.
- William Cox has shown that when presented with a depressed patient who "self-stereotypes herself as incompetent a therapist can find ways to prime her with specific situations in which she had been competent in the past. … Making memories of her competence more salient reduce[s] her self-stereotype of incompetence."

Nobel Prize winner Daniel Kahneman cites a number of fascinating studies of priming in his outstanding book, *Thinking, Fast and Slow,* among which are these:

- Exposure to a word makes it easier for people to recall it later. If you have recently seen or heard the word EAT, you are temporarily more likely to complete the word fragment SO_P as SOUP than as SOAP. The opposite occurs if you just saw the word WASH.
- The same is true if the word is presented in a whisper or a blurry or hard to read font.
- Subjects asked to complete the word fragments W_ _H and S_ _P were more likely to complete them as WASH and SOAP if they had been primed to think about an action of which they were ashamed, and as WISH and SOUP if they were primed to think of food.

- Merely thinking about stabbing a co-worker in the back leaves people more inclined to buy soap, disinfectant or detergent than batteries, juice or candy.
- This also connects to body parts. People who were asked to lie to an imaginary person over the telephone preferred mouthwash over soap, while those who lied on email preferred soap.
- An entirely different set of associations and memories occur to us if we are asked "Is James friendly?" than if we are asked "Is James unfriendly?" In each case we easily slip into "confirmation bias" that leads to memories and associations that confirm what the question primed us to think. The same is true for other negative and positive priming associations.
- Students were asked to walk around a room for five minutes at a rate of 30 steps per minute, about one-third their normal pace. Afterward, they were much quicker to recognize words associated with old age, like "forgetful, old and lonely." *Acting* old reinforces ideas and thoughts about old age.
- Similar reciprocal links show that being happy makes you smile, but also that smiling makes you happy — even if it is only achieved by holding a pencil sideways in your teeth.
- People asked to squeeze their eyebrows together showed enhanced emotional responses to upsetting pictures.
- Nodding (yes) increases acceptance of editorials while shaking one's head (no) reduces it.
- A study of voting patterns in Arizona in 2000 showed that support for school funding propositions was greater if the polling station was located in a school rather than in a business.
- A different experiment showed that people exposed to images of classrooms and school lockers also increased their tendency to vote for school funding initiatives. This difference was greater than that between voters who were parents and voters who were not.
- On the other hand, words and images of money caused people

to become more selfish, sit farther apart, and become less willing to help someone who pretended to be confused about a task, or to help pick up pencils after a researcher dropped them on the floor.

- Reminding people of their mortality has interestingly been shown to increase the appeal of authoritarian ideas.

These studies suggest that our brains can be influenced, shaped and programmed by consciously selected practices that result in differing political outcomes. Even at a seemingly trivial and subtle level, it has been shown, for example, that the ventromedial prefrontal cortex (which is responsible for empathy, compassion, shame and intuitive emotional responses to moral dilemmas) can be significantly strengthened by the practice of meditation, or merely thinking compassionately for a few moments about the well-being of others. Research also reveals that a variety of cognitive biases directly influence political thinking. A new study of 2,600 U.S. participants has shown, for example, that those who score low on political knowledge tend to overestimate their political expertise, and do so even more when greater emphasis is placed on political affiliation, thereby confirming the "Dunning-Kruger Effect," in which people with little expertise or ability assume they have superior expertise or ability because they don't know enough to *know* that they don't know.

From these studies we can see that while a great deal of seemingly rational political thought is concerned with facts and ideas and principles and values, beneath their surface, a number of complex neurophysiological responses are taking place to perceived risk, uncertainty, fear, body odor, disgust, disease, technology, alcohol and similar influences.

These studies also suggest that it is possible to design creative approaches to the methodology and organization of dialogues and conversations between political opponents that accentuate areas of mutual understanding and agreement, or at least minimize and relax the fight and flight reflex. Yet this research also raises the possibility of manipulation, gaming, and misuse of this data for malevolent or immoral purposes. As a result, it is imperative that we look more closely at the relationship between politics and morality.

POLITICS AND MORALITY

While these neurophysiological studies imply that facts and logic are useful in rationalizing and justifying political opinions, and convincing ourselves we are right, they also play a role in forming political views and persuading others that they are correct. Consequently, it is easier to understand how the intense, instinctual, even primordial physical, mental and emotional responses to fear and disgust translate *directly* into morality, as a heuristic, a shorthand, a set of simple rules or an easy to follow algorithm for avoiding danger and disease.

Accordingly, as the cognitive linguist and philosopher George Lakoff argues, these subconscious neurophysiological responses coalesce into thoughts and feelings, leading not only to political ideas and opinions, but to underlying moral ones as well. In his book *Moral Politics*, Lakoff describes how a conservative world-view emerges from what he calls a "Strict Father" model, giving rise to a set of moral overtones and injunctions.

According to this "*mid*-20th century model, the basis of conservative politics is the traditional nuclear family, with the father primarily responsible for earning income to support the family and for protecting it, largely from outsiders who are feared, by establishing and enforcing rules they are expected to obey. The mother does not work outside the home but takes care of the children and the house, and upholds the father's authority through love and obedience. The children are expected to respect and obey their parents, and if they don't, the father disciplines and punishes them, encouraging self-reliance in the boys and supportive nurturance in the girls.

On the other hand, a liberal world-view emerges from what Lakoff calls a "Nurturant Parent" model, which gives rise to a different set of moral overtones and injunctions. According to this *late* 20th century model, love, empathy and nurturance are primary and children become responsible, self-disciplined and self-reliant — not through the external authority of the father, but by being cared for and respected, and by caring for and respecting others, especially those who are weaker or less fortunate. Fathers and mothers and boys and girls are equal, and may or may not follow a gender-based division of labor. Instead of obedience, children are encouraged to question, decisions are made more democratically, and their values, ideas and wishes are taken seriously.

Each of these archetypal world-views gives rise to a different set of beliefs about how to behave, which become self-fulfilling prophecies that produce their own unique set of moral injunctions and justifications. When children grow up respecting and obeying the external authority of their fathers they are more likely to be patriotic and obedient to the external authority of a political leader and adopt adversarial attitudes toward outsiders, which cause them to behave adversarially in return. This allows them to backward-engineer and justify their original obedience and adversarial assumptions.

And when children grow up learning empathy, respect for others and democratic decision-making, other people behave more collaboratively in return, similarly encouraging them to backward-engineer and justify their original liberal assumptions and translate them into collaborative moral principles.

Thus, while democracy flows from one set of neurophysiological responses and moral assumptions, autocracy and dictatorship flow from a different set of neurophysiological responses and moral assumptions, each moving outward from the family to assume a political form, and mediated through a set of metaphors that express an underlying set of needs, desires, interests and attitudes toward oneself and others. The first are oriented primarily to risk and family, while the second are oriented primarily to empathy for others and wider social relationships. And implicitly, by understanding these responses and metaphors, it becomes possible to influence political opinions and choices.

Thus, in a recent study at Stanford University, participants were given brief passages about crime in a hypothetical city named Addison. Half of the participants read passages in which a few words were changed to describe crime as a "virus infecting the city," while for the other half, crime was described as a "beast preying on the city." Otherwise, the passages were the same. Yet changing these few words dramatically shifted people's ideas of how crime should be handled. When asked to come up with solutions for crime, those who read the passage with the "beast" metaphor supported more punitive solutions, such as longer jail time, while those who read the passage with the "virus" metaphor supported more reformative measures that addressed the root causes of crime. Shifting these metaphors led to greater differences in opinion than pre-existing differences between Republicans and Democrats.

Lakoff and others hypothesize that *all* thinking, especially political thinking, is fundamentally metaphorical, with moral overtones and behavioral consequences that precede and follow their use. For example, a study at the University of California found that describing cancer using warlike metaphors, such as "fighting" cancer, made people less likely to say they planned on engaging in preventative behaviors like quitting smoking, yet framing the effort to stop climate change as a "war" rather than a "race" led people to feel there was greater urgency in reducing carbon emissions.

From Morality to Ethics, Values and Integrity

A somewhat different view of the relationship between morality and politics emerges from the writings of Jean Piaget, and later of Lawrence Kohlberg, whose analysis of the six stages of moral development, based on Piaget's work, proceeds from lower to higher orders, as follows:

1. Orientation to obedience and punishment, and deference to superior power and prestige (*"How can I avoid punishment?"*)
2. Orientation to self-interest and a *"You scratch my back, and I'll scratch yours"* relationship to others (*"What's in it for me?"*)
3. Orientation to good intentions ("golden rule"), social consensus and peer group conformity (*"What do I need to do to be a good boy or girl?"*)
4. Orientation to obedience to law, people in authority and maintaining the social-order (*"What if everyone did that?" Law and order morality*)
5. Orientation to social contract, respect for diverse opinions and values, and majority rule (*"The greatest good for the greatest number"*)
6. Orientation to universal ethical principles, seeing justice as superior to law, and a moral obligation to disobey unjust laws (*Principled conscience: "Do only what you are willing to make into a universal law."*)

While there are a number of critiques of Kohlberg's stages, they are useful in understanding political conflicts because it is easy to see how different varieties of political conflict emerge at each stage, and indirectly identify what is needed to move to the next stage. It may be, however that a slightly modified version of Kohlberg's sixth stage can be used to describe the evolution and metamorphosis of political morality, by drawing a distinction between morality and ethics or values. On a simplified level, we can define these terms, plus a few others that are relevant in political dialogues, as follows:

- *Morality* = Objective ideas about what is right in general
- *Ethics* = Subjective ideas about what is right for oneself and others
- *Values* = Integrity-based choices for oneself
- *Norms* = Commonly accepted standards of behavior in a group
- *Mores* = Ideas about correct behavior within a given culture
- *Manners* = Rules to avoid offensive behavior

Kohlberg's sixth stage of moral development can then be reconfigured and made applicable to political conflicts by mapping our transition from morality to ethics and shared values, and considering these ideas in relation to the final step in Abraham Maslow's hierarchy of needs, as forms of self-actualization — in this case, political self-actualization, which is an essential element in direct, participatory, interest-based forms of democracy, as described in Chapter 10.

The first five of Kohlberg's stages track the movement from obedience to external moral authority, to the development of an internal set of moral principles that are not just abstract and general, but practical and personal. A revised sixth stage of moral development would describe the shift from abstract moral precepts that are regarded as objectively true, to individualized ethics and shared values that are regarded as subjectively true, yet socially discussable.

In this stage, we begin to think for ourselves, yet respect the views of others and are able to engage in non-absolutist, consensus-building dialogues with them. We achieve political self-actualization, not by creating an isolated, moralistic self that knows the One Truth and is superior to and separated from others; but a self that is empathetic, connected and caring, that knows many truths, and is in respectful, collaborative relationship both with itself and with others.

Certainly, our ability to recognize that justice is morally superior to laws, which after all, may be enacted by those in power for the purpose of permitting domination or perpetuating injustices, is an essential element in the development of a higher stage of moral sensibility. But equally important is the transition from objective moral principles that are preached and imposed on others to their subjective internalization in the form of ethics and values that are personally adopted and discussed with others. It was for this reason, perhaps, that Simone de Beauvoir wrote, "To be moral is to discover fundamentally one's own being."

While morality and objective rules can be preached and imposed on others, as well as on oneself, ethics, values and integrity are subjective, personal, open to change, always improving and defeated by imposition, coercion and preaching or exhortation. When morals are preached and externally imposed, just as when they are unexamined, they easily turn contradictory, violent and hypocritical.

Political institutions are notorious for encouraging leaders to preach one thing in public and practice another in private. In order to minimize hypocrisy and duplicity in politics, it is essential to shift our conversations from objective, abstract, external, conformist, moral condemnations to subjective, practical, internal, diverse dialogues over ethics and shared values; and that we transition from the use of self-righteous preaching, violence and shaming, which force obedience and compliance, to the use of ethical self-examination, values-based communication, inclusion and empathy, which encourage mutual understanding, kindness, personal responsibility and consensus.

Ultimately, each of us needs to identify for ourselves the areas where our walk does not match our talk. Instead of being frightened by these discussions, we can use them to bring our daily practices into conformity with our ethical principles, shared values and integrity. In truth, no one can dictate or manage the morality, let alone the ethics, values or integrity of another person, and in the end, each of us needs to accept personal responsibility for doing what we believe is right.

Politics, as a *methodology*, systematically attempts to reduce inherently complex, un-decidable questions to simple, decidable ones, and then decide them without necessarily listening to input or advice from others, even those who are closest to the problem. By doing so, we collapse metaphysical choices into logical contentions, and ethics into morality. Worse, we disregard important information that could significantly improve the quality of our decisions.

CREATING A CONTEXT OF ETHICS, VALUES AND INTEGRITY

In *The End of Management and the Rise of Organizational Democracy*, Joan Goldsmith and I wrote about the importance of moving from abstract notions of morality to creating a *context* of ethics, values and integrity. The difficulty is that, as opposed to morality, ethics and values require higher order skills, significantly more time and effort, and are often paradoxical and uncertain, and as a result, sometimes difficult to comprehend, articulate, agree on or actualize.

Yet the search for ethics, values and integrity poses a rich set of complex questions that can initiate and encourage ethical growth. Here are a few I find helpful, especially in dialogues that are concerned with exploring shared values:

- Why do we *not* act according to our values? What motivates us to act in ways that lack integrity? Why do we have to struggle to maintain them? If we stop struggling, are they still values?
- What is the value of admitting that we do not always act according to our values? What values do we affirm when we acknowledge that acting according to our values is a struggle? What is the effect of moralizing or preaching to others about how they ought to behave? How do we acknowledge our common effort to live up to our highest expectations in ways that encourage learning?
- What is the strategic importance of the reasons we offer for not living up to our values? What is the value of clearly articulating a value to which we are not conforming, or the reasons we are unable to do so? How can we use values lapses to encourage self-awareness and integrity? Can the reasons we do not live up to our values help us set more powerful goals and become more strategic in our choices as individuals, organizations and societies?
- How do we teach values without preaching or moralizing or turning them into dogmas? Where and how do we learn values? What would a values-oriented education look like? Which values are learned through experience, dialogue or contemplation? How can political groups structure

experiences, or review them once they have occurred, so as to encourage values-based learning?

- What do we do when values clash or pull us in opposite directions? What determines the outcome of a clash of values? What are the mechanisms by which we choose one value over another? How do we identify high-priority values when we are being pulled in opposite directions by competing choices? How do we go about rationalizing our choices? What then happens to our values?

- What do we do when values are changing? What do we say when new values appear in politics, such as valuing racial, cultural and gender diversity? Are there better ways of teaching new values than through blame, punishment and loss of face or career?

- What do we do when behaviors do not match values? How do we know if someone is not acting according to his or her values? How do we avoid imposing values, and at the same time offer honest feedback about how behaviors are out of sync with shared or declared values and personal or social integrity? How do we shift the context of our conversations about values from threats to opportunities and learning?

- How do we continuously improve our values? How can political groups and individuals clarify their values priorities? How can they articulate and define higher levels of improvement? How can they learn to accept new challenges and continuously improve, rather than rest on their laurels?

- How do we create a culture of values? How can we support political cultures in encouraging ethics, values and integrity, and build awareness and acceptance? How can we improve motivation, acknowledgment and support for values-based behaviors? How can we institutionalize values without violating what made them values in the first place?

The point of these questions is not to suggest answers, but to encourage honest introspection, open dialogue over values and a search for answers that enhance the integrity of every person and group. Their purpose is to reveal an essential truth: that integrity is increased by a shared process of grappling with open-ended ethical and values-oriented questions that reveal the complex, paradoxical nature of their formation and implementation, rather than slipping into political pronouncements that simplistically seek to impose moral or political ideas on others.

THREE

HOW TO DISCUSS RACE, ABORTION, IMMIGRATION, GUN CONTROL, CLIMATE CHANGE, SAME SEX MARRIAGE AND OTHER HOT TOPICS

People fail to get along because they fear each other; they fear each other because they don't know each other; they don't know each other because they have not communicated with each other. —Martin Luther King, Jr.

A dialogue is very important. It is a form of communication in which question and answer continue till a question is left without an answer. Thus the question is suspended between the two persons involved in this answer and question. It is like a bud with untouched blossoms … If the question is left totally untouched by thought, it then has its own answer because the questioner and answerer, as persons, have disappeared. This is a form of dialogue in which investigation reaches a certain point of intensity and depth, which then has a quality that thought can never reach. —Jiddu Krishnamurti

Intelligence is not what you know but what you do when you don't know. —Jean Piaget

IF WE STOP AND THINK FOR A MOMENT ABOUT ALL THE MYRIAD ARGUMENTS we have had or witnessed over these and other hotly contested political issues, and if we consider all the yelling and screaming, heated debates and diatribes, accusations and insults, we are inescapably yet unsurprisingly drawn to several conclusions regarding political conflicts:

1. Nearly all of us have deeply held, intensely passionate, highly emotional, staunch and unswerving beliefs about political issues.
2. Rarely are we able to listen deeply, with open minds or hearts to those who disagree with us, or to change our minds based on their logical consistency, factual accuracy or emotional intensity.
3. Instead, political arguments make us *more* argumentative, adversarial, insulting, fractious, dismissive, obnoxious, stubborn, aggressive, insensitive, uncaring and reactive.
4. As a result, political arguments often end up rupturing our relationships, destroying our trust and alienating us from one another.
5. Consequently, we often elect to remain silent, or suppress our true beliefs and feelings, or pretend to agree when we really don't, or leave rather than risk a loss of intimacy and connection with people we care about.

Whatever our justifications for treating each other as enemies, or alternatively, remaining silent when political ideas are discussed, our ability to address the highly complex, intricate and increasingly challenging issues that characterize modern political life is less and less optional. As our world shrinks, these issues impact us in significant ways, allowing distant social, economic and political decisions, environmental choices and technological changes to profoundly impact our lives and the lives of those we love.

Indeed, it is conceivable that in the absence of improved communications and the development of more advanced dialogue, problem-solving, negotiation and conflict resolution skills, it will be difficult to weather the violence and nuclear devastation that could easily happen, simply as a result of the adversarial ways we respond to political disagreements — not just as democracies or technologically advanced societies, but as a species.

Political issues have become so costly, destructive and global that there is really no alternative other than for us to learn how to discuss these issues constructively and work together across our political differences to address them. Fortunately, significant improvements in communication, dialogue, problem-solving, negotiation and conflict resolution techniques offer us a number of powerful and effective ways of doing so and developing the higher order skills and capacities we need for democracy to evolve and succeed.

Yet to succeed in political dialogue, as in mediation and all of conflict resolution, it is necessary for us to surrender the idea that there is a single, all-encompassing political truth, which is ours, and recognize instead that *every* political argument is an effort to establish the truth, validity, value and importance of *some* personal, emotional or social experience; and at a deep level, it is not necessary to deny one in order to affirm another.

This does not mean that what people want or say is always correct, or appropriate, or best for them, or that what other people say and want isn't equally important, but that the reasons why they want and say it invariably contain and reveal some deeper truth about their feelings and experiences that can be shared, acknowledged, discussed and satisfied — though not always in the way they want or say.

Politics, despite its linguistic assumptions and orientation to power and rights, need not be treated as a zero-sum game in which one side is completely right and all others are completely wrong, but can instead be considered an effort to learn from, acknowledge, investigate and integrate multiple, diverse, contradictory interests and emotional truths in order to come to a deeper understanding and appreciation of each others experiences and formulate a common policy and direction.

It is important to keep dissent, diversity, dialogue and debate alive, and at the same time to recognize that condemning both sides as equally responsible for political conflicts, or trying to appear neutral when neutrality has ceased to exist, are common forms of conflict avoidance. The middle ground in politics, as in life, is usually overly simplistic and sometimes cowardly, like advocating a middle ground between equality and slavery, honesty and lying, diversity and genocide, fairness and bigotry.

As I see it, dialogue and mediation, considered simply as *processes,* are inescapably aligned with equality, honesty, dignity and fairness, in opposition to slavery, lying, genocide and bigotry, largely because they seek to reveal what is genuine and human *beneath* the anger and fear, defensiveness and hostility, distortions and cover-ups that are triggered by conflict. The same can be said about conflicts between peace and war, democracy and fascism, and similar divides. Conflict resolution, as a process, is not "neutral" on these issues, but favors peace and democracy, simply because they are essential for dialogue and mediation to work, and demonstrably less likely to result in chronic costly and destructive conflicts.

Conflict resolution processes, at their core, represent an approach to resolving disputes that is based on the *essential equality* of diverse interests, and the absence of a need to choose between them. They are therefore inherently democratic, egalitarian and collaborative because they bypass power- and rights-based win/lose assumptions; because they encourage diverse desires, feelings, experiences and truths to coexist; because they search for synergistic combination, catalytic integration and consensus; and because they welcome everyone to the conversation and invite them to work together to solve their common problems.

The difficulty is that political differences can easily be turned into personal divides, and the desire to open a dialogue or mediate differences may appear to one side or the other or both to suggest concession or defeat. As a result, we need to find better ways of responding to growing polarization over political differences that do not slip into false assumptions of superficial equality between adversaries, or cause us to cease being "omni-partial," and lose our capacity to express empathy and draw both sides into dialogues that elicit their deeper interests and reveal *potentially* transformational common ground. Palestinian Attorney Jonathan Kuttab has identified a number of common pitfalls in dialogues and mediations over political issues that need to be acknowledged and addressed in designing political conversations. These include:

1. *False Assumption of Symmetry:* It is mistaken to assume that oppressor and oppressed, occupier and occupied, powerful and weak are the same or that they can be treated as equally aggrieved.

2. *Tendency to Ignore Underlying Conflicts:* People in mediation often behave reasonably and want to reach agreements, and may ignore or avoid issues that could be disruptive.

3. *Acceptance of the Status Quo:* There is a tendency in mediation to accept and take for granted what is or have been the case for years, even when this is perceived by some to be wrong.

4. *Pressure to Compromise Principles:* People in mediation often feel pressured to surrender or compromise on points of principle in order to reach agreement, even when there are moral reasons not to.

5. *Dialogue as a Substitute for Action:* There is a tendency to substitute talk for action, especially for those who seek to change the status quo. Many see mediation as an end in itself, rather than as an effort to secure justice.

6. *Pressure to Renounce Allies and Practices:* Members of out-group and oppressed groups are often pressured to renounce violence, yet in-groups and oppressors are permitted to continue.

7. *Danger of Co-Optation:* Government authorities can misuse and co-opt mediation for their own purposes.

It is possible to address these issues in designing political dialogues and mediations, partly by eliciting and acknowledging the unique history and experience of each side, by encouraging honest and principled conversations about differences, by seeking to change conditions through joint action, and by reducing resort to power- and rights-based approaches and prioritizing interest-based ones.

POWER- AND RIGHTS- VS. INTEREST-BASED APPROACHES TO POLITICAL DISCUSSION

In power- and rights-based political debates, opponents often issue loud protestations and harsh denunciations of moral lapses and transgressions by others, along with simplistic claims of uncompromising toughness and unyielding stands regarding complex, subtle, multilayered problems. Each of these undermines political discourse and makes dialogue and agreement much more difficult.

The language, syntax, metaphors and narrative assumptions that are common to power- and rights-based political speech make it more difficult to prevent or de-escalate violence, or transform debates into genuine dialogues, or come to grips with the exhausting, often painful issues that underlie our most important political choices. Power- and rights-based conversations are fundamentally competitive, and therefore turn into power contests, while rights-based approaches incite each side to claim the moral high ground, act unilaterally, trivialize discussions, manipulate processes, dominate relationships, seek legalistic solutions, control decision-making and duck responsibility for outcomes.

Interest-based approaches, on the other hand, design processes and foster relationships that support social equality, economic equity and political democracy, and are inherently respectful because they are able to benefit diverse constituencies simultaneously. They dismantle domination and control in large and small ways, aiming at their sources in anger, fear and disgust, and for this reason, make it possible to shift the language of political dialogue by reframing the metaphors that define their meaning, the processes that guide them and the relationships they nurture.

It is possible, for example, even with hardened political adversaries, to identify ground rules, agree on forms of communication and reach process agreements that invite everyone to constructively share their experiences and perceptions about the issues. It is possible to break up highly adversarial advocacy groups, put them into small diverse teams, ask them to identify and analyze aspects of the problem that need to be addressed, and brainstorm possible solutions; to meet as separate or mixed groups and agree on the words that describe the kind of relationship they most want to have with each other, then list the obstacles that stand in the way of achieving it, or the behaviors *their* side engaged in that they think may have been counter-productive or disrespectful to the other side, present these to their opponents to see how accurate they were and discuss how to move their communications and behaviors in a more constructive direction.

Mediation has demonstrated in countless disputes between feuding neighbors, divorcing couples, entrenched litigants, labor-management adversaries and advocates for hostile political constituencies that people can stop yelling, insulting, blaming and accusing each other and start listening — not by advancing hostile and adversarial political arguments, which are nearly always experienced personally as confrontational, disrespectful and ineffective, but by being honest, authentic, empathetic and open to exploring both sides' issues.

Dialogues often take the form of stories, empathetic questions, searingly honest discussions, emotionally vulnerable revelations, admissions, acknowledgements, confessions and openhearted apologies. These, in turn, commonly lead to listening, informal problem-solving, collaborative negotiation, personal requests, sincere promises, honest disagreements, acceptance and heartfelt declarations.

The shift from single to multiple truths happens *automatically* when we ask questions that do not require a single correct answer. If we ask, for example, who is the oldest person in the room, there will be a single correct answer, but if we ask instead, "What does your age mean to you?" or "What issues are you facing at your age?" there will be multiple correct answers that are not mutually exclusive or in conflict, but additive and multiplicative. In political conflicts, there are many such questions, including these, which I find useful:

- What life experiences have led you to feel so passionately about this issue?
- What is at the heart of this issue, for you as an individual?
- Why did you decide to participate in this dialogue?
- Why do you care so deeply about this issue?
- Do you see any gray areas in the issue we are discussing, or ideas you find it difficult to define?
- Do you have any mixed feelings, uncertainties, or discomforts regarding this issue that you would be willing to share?
- Is there any part of this issue that you are not 100 percent certain of or would be willing to discuss and talk about?
- Even though you hold widely differing views, are there any concerns, principles or ideas you think you may have in common?
- What underlying values or ethical beliefs have led you to your current political beliefs?
- Do the differences between your positions reveal any riddles, paradoxes, contradictions or enigmas regarding this issue?
- Is it possible to view your differences as two sides of the same coin? If so, what unites them?
- Can you separate this issue from the person you disagree with?
- Is there anything positive or acknowledging you would be willing to say about the person on the other side of this issue?
- What processes or ground rules would help you disagree more constructively?
- Instead of focusing on the past, what would you like to see happen in the future? Why?

- Are you actually disagreeing over fundamental values, or over how to achieve them?
- Are there any facts or arguments that could convince you that the other side has a valid point, or that there is more than one way to address this issue?
- Is there a way that both of you might be right? How?
- What criteria could you use to decide what works best?
- Would it be possible to test your ideas in practice and see which work best? How might you do that?
- What could be done to improve the *other* side's ideas?
- Could any of the other side's ideas be incorporated into yours?
- Is there any perspective or aspect of this issue that either or both of you have left out?
- Are there any other alternatives to what you are both saying?
- Do you think it would be useful to continue this conversation, to learn more about each other and what you each believe to be true?
- How could you make your dialogue ongoing or more effective?
- What could you do to improve your process for disagreeing with each other in the future? For encouraging future dialogue?
- Would you be willing to do that together?
- What are some next steps you might take together to better understand the issues and how you each see them?

In these ways, interest-based processes such as dialogue, collaborative negotiation and mediation make it possible for people to discuss difficult, dangerous and complex issues, and to reach consensus on common approaches in spite of significant differences in their political beliefs, values, cultures, races, genders and other types of diversity. They make it possible to bridge the gap between ordinary language and political discourse by shifting the communication process from debates over who is right, to dialogues over what is best; and focusing on what needs to be done and how to achieve it, without destroying each other in the process.

Once people accept an invitation into authentic, interest-based dialogue or mediation, their lives are nearly always touched and transformed, often in small ways. They enter an interactive, collaborative, mutually defined space that invites them to surrender their stereotypes, biases, assumptions and preconceptions — even their sense of an entirely separate and exclusive self -- and discover truths that seemingly lie outside them, and may even feel foreign, yet resonate and reverberate deeply inside them. They begin by creating a conversation, a joint understanding of the problem and a search for meaning that synchronizes their diverse interests, moderates their identities as opponents or adversaries, and subtly unifies and transforms their antagonistic, divided views about themselves, each other, the issues, and even the world they live in.

BENEATH ARGUMENTS ABOUT ABORTION AND GUN CONTROL

Political arguments follow similar forms and patterns, in which someone typically begins by expressing a belief, concern or interest, often in the form of a one-sided assertion, unambiguous opinion, personal accusation or self-evident pronouncement about a politicized topic, which is then taken personally by the listener, who disagrees, defends and responds in kind. The argument then grows increasingly heated, driving out all possibilities for listening, empathy, understanding, acknowledgement, search for deeper issues, learning, negotiation, problem-solving or agreement.

If we map power- and rights-based political arguments moment-by-moment and step-by-step, we can see how these conversations quickly turn counter-productive and end up convincing no one. But if we map them instead in their interest-based form, we can watch new information emerge that transforms their understanding of what the conflict or disagreement is actually about.

What I find most interesting about arguments over abortion and gun control, as well as over a number of other hot political topics, is that beneath the facts and logic, the accusations and arguments, a remarkable symmetry can be observed, leading to a deeper understanding of what is at stake in these discussions, and how they might be moved in a more constructive and useful direction.

Arguments about abortion, for example, commonly divide people into two camps: "right to choice" and "right to life." Those who favor the right to choice assert the primacy of personal freedom and the individual's right to choose; while those who favor the right to life assert the primacy of protecting life and the need for social control and regulation of individual decisions that impact the rights of others, in this case, the fetus.

On the other hand, in arguments about gun control, the same people commonly divide into *exactly* opposite camps, with those against gun control asserting the primacy of personal freedom and individual rights, while those who favor it assert the primacy of protecting life and the need for social control and regulation of individual decisions that impact the rights of others, in this case, students and members of the public.

In mediation, when we observe this kind of mirror symmetry and polarity reversal, it is often an indication that there are deeper and more complex issues lying beneath the surface of the dispute that have not yet been recognized, openly acknowledged or honestly discussed. For example, beneath the issue of abortion lie a number of deeper, intensely emotional, polarizing issues involving in varying degrees, for example: women's right to sexual freedom and/or sexual pleasure, gender roles in child rearing, clarity and confusion over gender definitions, decline of patriarchal power and control, commercialization of sexuality, attitudes toward teenage sex, unspoken sexual thoughts and desires, profound changes in the nature of marriage and the nuclear family, fears of sexual license and promiscuity, etc.

These connect to still broader social issues involving the status and pay of women, support for single parents, the presence or absence of low-cost medical care, the role of the state in controlling sexuality and protecting personal privacy, the role of religion in regulating sexual morality, the cost of raising children, the loss of career opportunities as a result of parental responsibilities, the availability of maternal and paternal leave, the presence or absence of free, quality education, attitudes toward rape and spousal battering, openness in discussing sexuality, responses to sexual harassment, the right to tell others how to live, etc. Rarely are any of these topics discussed in arguments over abortion, yet each of them may directly influence people's attitudes, beliefs and choices.

Similarly, deep beneath the surface of arguments over gun control lie a series of unspoken, unacknowledged and un-discussed topics that connect these conversations with far-ranging interests and concerns, including fear of others, overt and covert racism, degree of comfort and familiarity with firearms, desire for personal or political domination through the use of force, bullying and the experience of being bullied, personal experiences with violence and crime, fear of race war or retribution by Blacks for decades of mistreatment, loss of well-paying jobs and job security by impoverished or underpaid workers, social alienation, repressed rage, unresolved personal conflicts, military experience, increased fears of war and terrorism, opposition to conspiracies and tyranny, attitudes toward restrictions on people who are mentally ill, sensational fear-based journalism, dependence on hunting for food, decline of macho-based masculine ideals, violence in movies and television, attitudes toward global violence, etc.

Indeed, the history of the Second Amendment to the U.S. Constitution reveals that guns and "well-regulated militias" were often used not only to oppose British and other tyrannies, but in the South to suppress slave revolts and capture runaway slaves; in the North to control indentured servants and suppress organized labor; in the West to drive Native Americans and Mexicans off land that could be claimed by settlers; and in all those places to hunt and feed families.

At the same time, there are many countries in the world and many locations in the U.S. where there are lots of guns yet low levels of violence, suggesting again that there are deeper issues that have been obscured by simplistic or superficial definitions of the problem, and that more complex, nuanced, interest-based approaches to discussing it are possible between people on opposing sides.

Similarly, a history of abortion reveals a connection between birth control and the domination and unequal status of women, financial dependence on men, rape and sexual harassment, opposition to women's right to vote, suppression of women's economic and property rights, and a lack of social or government support for poor and working families. At the same time, it is possible to agree that both choice and life are precious, suggesting again that the issue is deeper, more emotional and more grounded in ethical and personal choices than any purely political debate or unilateral solution is likely to acknowledge or accept.

None of this is meant to imply that there are not aspects of abortion and gun control that properly belong to governments and political decision-making, or that there are not significant differences between these issues, or that people ought to surrender their beliefs and values, or that they should avoid openly and honestly discussing their disagreements and conflicts.

A majority of people might agree, for example, that late-term abortions and access by people who are mentally ill to assault weapons are legitimate topics for governments to regulate or prohibit, and that access to birth control and the use of rifles to hunt for food are not, or at least less so. For example, a 2018 survey of over 2100 gun owners and non-owners published in the *American Journal of Public Health* showed broad support for universal background checks, safe handling tests, improved mental illness reporting and similar gun regulations. The difficulties, I think, are: first that there are significant ambiguities, gray areas and disagreements between these opposing poles of opinion; second that there is an unclear but important tension and need for balance between majority rule and minority rights in any democracy that cannot be finally or completely eliminated, and fluctuates widely between cultures and moments in history; and third that voting on these issues will not eliminate the need for both private ethical choices and public dialogues regarding the deeper issues that lie beneath their surface.

We can therefore acknowledge that these issues are deep, subtle, intricate, complex, dialectical, multi-determined, multidimensional, highly personal, intensely emotional, layered and lasting. We can also recognize that, in many respects, they are not political issues at all, but have been made into political issues for partisan purposes, because they help mobilize adversarial political factions and motivate them to vote, because they appear morally simple and because they impinge on deeper political issues, as they have throughout history.

The Political Dialectic of Order and Anarchy

At least by the time of ancient Athens, and likely before, there were major, chronic conflicts between order and anarchy, freedom and control, individuality and conformity, centralization and decentralization, domination and self-determination, Eros and logos, and what have come to be known as Apollonian and Dionysian principles, interacting through what the Greeks called a dialectic, an eternal cycle of opposition and integration, negation and synthesis, repetition and transformation.

In an organizational setting, I think of these conflicts as a "dialectic of direction," leading to two very different kinds of synthesis and outcomes, as depicted in the diagram at the end of this section, which suggests an ongoing interactive relationship within organizations and workplaces between leadership and self-managing teams.

Applying these ideas to political conflicts, including those over abortion and gun control, it would make sense to reword this diagram, especially the circles in the bottommost center, by inserting the words: "personal freedom" and "social responsibility," with the overlapping center between those circles creating a Venn diagram with the words "ethical dialogue" in the center, in order to suggest that these issues are inherently without a single, one-sided, *permanent* political or ethical solution, but instead represent an unending conversation between complementary truths.

Instead of being centralized politically or decentralized personally, I find from my experience as a mediator and dialogue facilitator that these and similar political issues need to be *simultaneously* struggled through by each individual, and at the same time discussed and debated by society generally, without ever extinguishing personal freedom or social responsibility, but continually re-examining the ethical dilemmas they present through open and honest dialogue.

Addressing these complex issues through public dialogue *and* ethical reflection encourages people to discuss their differing experiences, ideas and beliefs, and at the same time not regard them as *having* a single, universal, final or permanent, moral or ethical, social or personal, public or private solution, which has always, and can only end in suppressing personal freedom *and* social responsibility, silencing public discussion, grossly simplifying important ethical issues, and being condemned, no matter what the outcome, to repeated reversal, simply because these are issues that *do not have* a single, eternally correct answer.

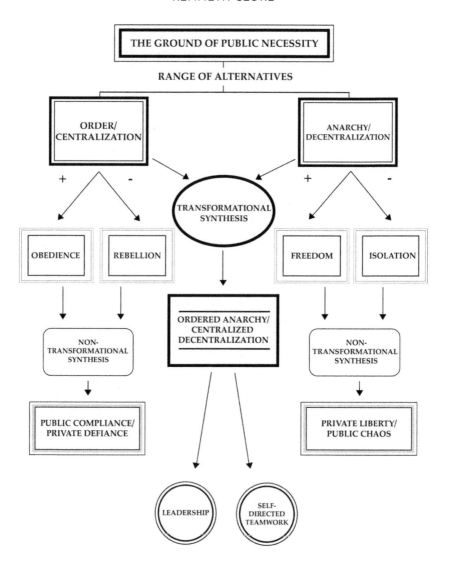

20 Ways to Talk About Political Differences

How, then, can we discuss divisive political issues in ways that achieve these ends, preserving opposing truths and encouraging open and honest communication, learning and transformational syntheses? I believe we can work to achieve these goals by:

1. Creating an atmosphere, attitude, intention, shared value and context of dignity and unconditional respect for each other, regardless of our opinions or positions on divisive issues
2. Being sure to invite into the conversation people who do *not* agree with each other
3. Reaching consensus on a set of ground rules or shared values that can guide these conversations
4. Agreeing to use skilled facilitators to keep the dialogue open, honest and on track, and skilled mediators to intervene if necessary
5. Agreeing not to suppress anyone's experiences, reflections, ideas, beliefs, passions or emotions, while at the same time focusing on the problem as an "it" rather than a "you," and striving not to personalize disagreements
6. Asking questions that do not have a single correct answer, and inviting everyone to offer their own unique answers
7. Consistently coming from a place of curiosity and learning, and probing to discover the deeper meaning of the issues to each person
8. Acknowledging and validating everyone's deepest emotions and ideas, interests and concerns, intentions and experiences
9. Expressing gratitude and thanking people for their dissent and diversity, for their courage and willingness to learn
10. Breaking large groups up into smaller groups where everyone can participate
11. Sharing responsibility for group process and modeling openness and honesty, empathy and compassion, listening and acknowledgement

12. Asking small groups to select volunteers to perform important tasks such as facilitation, recording, process observation, critique of content, presentation to other groups, timekeeping, etc.
13. Stopping the process when it isn't working, talking openly about whatever isn't working, and agreeing on what each person can do to improve it, starting with ourselves
14. Designing questions that will draw people on opposing sides into deep, direct dialogue with each other
15. Asking people in small groups to brainstorm possible solutions and present them to each other
16. Reaching consensus on recommendations for personal and political action, setting aside for future dialogue all points on which there is no consensus
17. Seeking ways for people on opposite sides of an issue to agree on specific, practical steps they can take to improve their communications and relationships in the future
18. Inviting people to consider how they might continue and expand the dialogue
19. Applauding everyone's efforts and acknowledging their contributions
20. Eliciting feedback, jointly evaluating the process and making improvements

For democracy to work, more advanced skills in conflict resolution, including informal problem solving, consensus building, collaborative negotiation, dialogue facilitation, mediation, restorative justice, impasse resolution and what I think of as "the collaborative arts and sciences," are increasingly essential. At the heart of all these skills is the realization, grounded in experience that people can disagree over important issues and not lose their capacity for human empathy and understanding.

To do so, it is important to separate *political* forms of problem-solving from *personal* ones, and to rethink the nature and role of governments and individuals in any genuine, substantive, direct, participatory and interest-based form of democracy, where citizens do not merely vote for candidates (who will not, in an event, address the underlying personal or historical issues described above), but join together to solve social problems and make political decisions using collaborative, interest-based attitudes and behaviors, methods and techniques, skills and capacities, processes and relationships.

How to do so in the middle of difficult and dangerous dialogues and courageous political conversations requires a deeper examination of the nature of dialogue and its relationship to the evolution of democracy, together with a consideration of actual experiences and examples using these techniques to design, organize and facilitate political dialogues and conversations, as described in the following section.

HOW TO DESIGN, ORGANIZE AND FACILITATE POLITICAL DIALOGUES

If you talk to a man in a language he understands, that goes to his head. If you talk to him in his language, that goes to his heart. —Nelson Mandela

There is more than a verbal tie between the words common, community and communication ... Try the experiment of communicating, with fullness and accuracy, some experience to another, especially if it be somewhat complicated, and you will find your own attitude toward your experience changing.
—John Dewey

Dialogue cannot exist without humility. —Paulo Freire

We have to face the fact that either all of us are going to die together or we are going to learn to live together and if we are to live together we have to talk.
—Eleanor Roosevelt

FOUR

WHY DIALOGUE IN POLITICS?

We live in terror because dialogue is no longer possible, because man has surrendered entirely to history, because he can no longer find that part of himself, every bit as real as history, that sees beauty in the world and in human faces. We live in a world of abstractions, bureaucracies and machines, absolute ideas, and crude messianism. We suffocate among people who think they are right in their machines as well as their ideas. For those who can live only with dialogue, only with the friendship of men, this silence means the end of the world. —Albert Camus

If the future of mankind is not to be jeopardized by conflicting spheres of civilization and culture, we have no alternative but to shift the ray of our attention from that which separates us to that which unites us. Mine is a vision of a United Nations consisting not — as happens so frequently today — of divided nations but of united people, belonging to a world in jeopardy which can be saved only by uniting all human forces. —Vaclav Havel

Being right can stop the momentum of a very interesting idea. —Robert Rauschenberg

THE MOST DIFFICULT ISSUES WE FACE IN LIFE, WHETHER AS COUPLES, families, organizations, societies or nations can rarely be resolved by individuals acting alone, or elites acting autocratically, or factions acting in their exclusive self-interests, but only by coming together across our differences, listening and talking to each other, discussing our disagreements, working collaboratively, deciding what to do democratically, mediating our conflicts, and acting in concert in the interests of all.

Yet working collaboratively with those who are different, those we dislike, those with whom we disagree, even those whose actions we find repellent, requires higher order listening, dialogue, negotiation, collaboration and conflict resolution skills, each of which demands more time and greater effort than simply acting alone. It can be exhausting, irksome, messy and galling to listen openly and empathetically, or engage honestly and constructively with opinions and interests that diverge sharply from our own. As a result, we often act unilaterally, ignoring the needs and desires of those who do not agree with us.

But when we act unilaterally, in our own exclusive self-interest, in matters that directly and significantly impact others, often without including or even informing them, they feel disrespected, just as we would, and are more inclined to resist, undermine our proposed solutions and create costly chronic conflicts. Indeed, our history as a species is replete with examples of problems made worse by refusals to listen, failures of communication, exclusions from decision-making, rejections of dialogue, oppositions to participation and denunciations of collaboration.

If we could add up all the costs we've incurred as a result, including the repeated, sometimes violent conflicts sparked by these failures of communication and collaboration, the results would be staggering, and vastly outweigh the increased time, effort, expense and skills required to overcome the obstacles and complexities of learning how to talk and act together. To avoid these costs, we need to develop more advanced skills and capacities in dialogue and mediation, which in turn require higher order proficiencies in listening, empathy, emotional intelligence, informal problem-solving, group facilitation, prejudice reduction, consensus building, collaborative negotiation, reducing resistance, overcoming impasse, etc., all of which are indispensable if diverse groups are going to engage in collaborative problem-solving and interest-based forms of decision-making.

WHY WE NEED DIALOGUE

We need dialogue because without it we drift apart, our differences become untenable, our fears grow palpable and our distrust circles without end. We need it because the smallest human unit is not one, but two; because it is how learning occurs in all relationships; because it invites us to open our hearts to each other, as well as to pained parts of ourselves; because it resets our priorities and reveals the beauty and symmetry of our differences; because we need each other, and die a little inside without it; because, in it's absence, we are expelled over and over from the Eden of our capacity to love one another; because it seems easier to turn each other's lives into a living hell than to apologize, rebuild trust and restore intimacy and collaboration in conflicted relationships.

On-going relationships of all kinds require *continual* efforts to communicate and reconnect, because only by doing so can we overcome our differences and reunite after our conflicts have ended. At a much deeper level, it is these very differences and conflicts that teach us how to solve more complex and intractable problems by enabling us to envisage and explore a wider range of potential solutions.

If we imagine our diverse communities, combative factions, contested political ideas, divergent values and beliefs, and dissimilar cultures, religions, races and genders as scaled-up versions of the conflicted relationships we see in marriages and families, we might ask: "What would happen in your marriage or family if everyone behaved as hostilely and disrespectfully toward each other as they do in political conflicts?" And, "What would happen, in your marriage or family, if everyone stopped listening, engaging in dialogue, discussing and negotiating differences, collaborating or resolving conflicts, as political adversaries repeatedly do?" Clearly, the outcome would be disastrous. Would it not be better then, to behave in politics as we do, or ought to, in our marriages and families, rather than the other way around? The difficulty facing every political community and nation is ultimately not *whether* to engage in dialogue over political issues, but *how* to do so successfully and sustainably, especially where the issues are complex and contentious; where the stakes are high; and where the accumulated pain, loss, grief, guilt, shame and suffering experienced by each side has not been recognized, acknowledged or rectified by the other side — often because the other side's experiences have *also* not been recognized, acknowledged or rectified. But how do recognition, acknowledgement and rectification begin when *both* sides feel unheard? Not through more and sterner refusals to communicate, or violence and aggression, or blame and punishment, which only add to the problem and make communications and relationships worse, just as they do in couples and families. Instead, it is by listening to both sides as they describe their experiences; by acknowledging and assuaging their pain; by facilitating open, honest and empathetic dialogue; by creatively exploring issues together; by collaboratively negotiating and mediating the most pressing issues to each person; and by engaging in committed, combined, coordinated actions aimed at solving their common problems.

HOW TO THINK ABOUT AND DISCUSS POLITICS

In thinking about how to discuss political differences, the essayist Isaiah Berlin offered a useful way forward, proposing that we regard political ideas, rhetoric and communications as "inherently un-philosophical," in the sense that they are based on values over which people naturally disagree because they flow from dissimilar interests, orientations and experiences, and therefore on entirely different sets of facts. As a result, political communications should be regarded as factually diverse, unscientific, effectively un-falsifiable and philosophically inexact, leading to an acceptance of different, co-existing "alternative" truths, each representing unique personal and group experiences, *all* of which can be regarded as valid from the particular personal and subjective point of view of the individual or group that experienced it.

In other words, it is possible to view political statements not as adversarial, win/lose, true or false propositions (which is how they are generally stated and heard), but rather as idiosyncratic indicators of experience and perception, personal stories of pain and injustice, declarations of disagreement and desire, appeals for solidarity and support, requests for listening and improved relationships, wishes and hopes for the future, none of which are *necessarily* mutually exclusive, in that they do not *require* other truths to be false in order to be true themselves.

This is the essence of all interest-based approaches to conflict resolution, which routinely reframe positions as interests and desires, accusations as confessions and requests, and criticisms as suggestions for improvement and invitations into deeper communications, connections and relationships. Most interestingly, from a conflict resolution perspective, Berlin asked, "In what kind of world is political philosophy — the kind of discussion and argument in which it consists — in principle possible?" He answered, "Only in a world where ends collide." In other words, only where there is an adversarial, win/lose outcome — or, we may add — process for deciding which truth will be implemented going forward.

In this way, we can see that political speech *is* conflict speech, and that the question "What should be done?" is inherently unanswerable as a complete, comprehensive or universal solution for everyone. As Berlin explains:

Not because it is beyond our powers to find the answer, but because the question is not one of fact at all, the solution lies not in discovering something which is what it is, whether it is discovered or not — a proposition or formula, an objective good, a principle, a system of values objective or subjective, a relationship between a mind and something non-mental — but resides in action: something which cannot be found, only invented — an act of will or faith or creation obedient to no pre-existing rules or laws or facts.

From this proposition, Berlin concludes that *no* political argument powerful enough to convince large numbers of people can be *entirely* wrong. Thus, *every* powerful political idea represents some important piece of personal or political truth, based on some genuine socially and historically bounded experience, even if it is presented in a distorted, adversarial, dogmatic, false and misguided way.

Berlin was not referring, of course, to *factual* truths, which can often be determined scientifically, but to subjective or emotional truths that have been transformed into and disguised as objective political statements, visions of the future, proscriptions, creeds, moral injunctions and calls for action. In an insightful passage, Berlin wrote:

> The social contract is a model which to this day helps to explain something of what it is that men feel to be wrong when a politician pronounces an entire class of the population ... to be outside the community — not entitled to the benefits conferred by the State or its laws. So too, Lenin's image of the factory which needs no supervision by coercive policemen after the State has withered away; Maistre's image of the executioner and his victims as the corner-stone of all authority; Locke's analogy of government with trusteeship; ... all these illuminate some types of social experience.

Political philosophies are therefore not by nature solitary, scientifically provable, factual or exclusive, but compound, poetic, metaphoric, emotional and shared — concerning, for example, the desire for freedom from tyranny, domination and oppression; or the fear of chaos and search for security. What is important in analyzing political arguments and positions in dialogue is therefore to probe *beneath* the formal, factual arguments and rationalizations people offer for their views and beliefs, and elucidate the deeper stories and experiences, interests and emotions, metaphors and analogies, syntax and grammar that gave rise to them.

To do so, as in all conflict resolution undertakings, we need to surrender the idea that there is a single, permanent, universal political truth, which is ours, and recognize instead that *every* political argument is an effort to establish the truth and validity, value and importance, of someone's subjective social or political experience. This implies that politics, despite its linguistic assumptions and orientation to power or rights, need not be a zero-sum game in which one side is right and must win, while all others are wrong and must lose, but can instead be transformed by dialogue into an effort to acknowledge, investigate, integrate, catalyze and *synthesize* multiple, diverse, contradictory truths, in an effort to formulate a common policy and direction over a protracted period of time, where interests are various and consequences and impacts are unclear.

The recognition that there is more than one kind of truth contradicts an ancient idea about logic that dates back to Aristotle, which I describe in my book, *Conflict Revolution: Designing Preventative Systems for Chronic Social, Economic and Political Conflicts* (Second Edition). Aristotle wrote that three basic laws are essential in creating a consistent rational system, each of which can be seen as incomplete or limited:

1. *The Law of Identity:* A statement is what it is. In other words, A is identical to A. Yet we know that there are times when A is not entirely A, as in quantum physics where position and momentum are uncertain and particles are only *probably* at any given location. Or using a more familiar example, someone may be frightened and courageous at the same time.

2. *The Law of Non-contradiction:* A statement and its contradiction

cannot both be true. If A is true and B is the opposite of A, then both A and B cannot be true. Yet we know that there are times when A and B are both true and opposites, as in relativistic physics where no single reference frame offers a truer version of reality than any other. Or more commonly, it is possible to both love and hate another person.

3. *The Law of the Excluded Middle:* A statement is either true or false and cannot be true and false at the same time. For example, A must either be true or false and cannot be both simultaneously. Yet we know that there are times when a statement is true and false at the same time. For example, light is both a wave and a particle. Or more recognizably, the stories we tell about our conflicts are often true and false at the same time.

Indeed, this is precisely what interest-based conflict resolution at its core represents: the use of storytelling, emotional intelligence, empathy, consensus building, power-balancing, dialogue facilitation, mediation and other tools to include everyone, dominate no one, search for commonalities and synergies, and not reject anyone's personal or emotional truth just so someone else's can be heard and acknowledged.

THE IMPLICIT TRANSFORMATIONAL APPROACH OF CONFLICT RESOLUTION

Mediation, dialogue and other interest-based processes, as described earlier, themselves possess an *implicit* political orientation that is innately democratic, egalitarian and collaborative, as they invite a variety of interests and truths to compete, contend and search for synergistic combinations. They reduce prejudice and hatred — not by personally attacking those who are prejudiced or hateful, but by building empathy through storytelling, reframing insults as requests, including others as equals, acknowledging both sides' emotions and interests, and working together to solve common problems — in other words, by searching beneath the hostile veneer of both sides' adversarial positions for the hidden, unsatisfied, heartfelt interests that gave rise to them; and discovering new and creative ways of combining, transforming and transcending them.

In this way, we can see that there are two fundamental approaches to combining things. First, there is the "lower middle way" of compromise and settlement, in which, for example, we take hot water, combine it with cold water and create lukewarm water. This is exemplified in the non-transformational technique of compromise. Or second, there is the "higher middle way" of resolution and transformation, in which we take water, combine it with flour and heat, and produce bread. This is exemplified the transformational technique of creative collaboration, in which new, emergent phenomena arise out of complexity, which were not present and could not have been anticipated beforehand.

As physicist David Bohm argued, dialogue is not just a simple exchange between two monologues, but a catalyst and precondition for synthesis, the surfacing of more effective solutions and the principle way that new, creative, holistic ideas emerge in conflict. It is therefore not only a critical skill in social problem-solving, but the basis for collaboration and democracy, and illustrative of what Bohm saw as a higher form of intelligence:

What is needed is a dialogue in the real sense of the word, which means 'flowing through,' amongst people, rather than an exchange like a game of ping-pong ... The basic idea of ... dialogue is to be able to talk while suspending your opinions, holding them in front of you, while neither suppressing them nor insisting upon them. Not trying to convince, but simply to understand. The first thing is that we must perceive all the meanings of everybody together, without having to make any decisions or saying who's right and who's wrong. It is more important that we all see the same thing. That will create a new frame of mind in which there is a common consciousness. It is a kind of implicate order, where each one enfolds the whole consciousness. With the common consciousness we then have something new — a new kind of intelligence.

Dialogue is therefore a *condition* for the realization of democracy, not only politically, but in all relationships, from couples and families to organizations and nation-states. It is a methodology of inclusion and participation, and the most effective process for supporting collaboration and achieving consensus on solutions to complex problems.

Perhaps most importantly, it is a way of accessing group or "swarm" intelligence that turns differences to advantage by combining them and searching for emergent, synergistic, higher order solutions that allow us to leverage the wisdom that resides — not simply in one isolated part, but holistically and *holographically* — i.e., in each of them and in their combination.

How Dialogue Transforms Emotions, Expectations, Intentions and Attitudes

While much of our focus in dialogue and mediation is on substantive issues that divide people, most of what actually occurs in conflict is a consequence of unacknowledged emotions, un-communicated expectations, undeclared intentions and avoidant, accommodating or aggressive attitudes. If these deeper sources of conflict remain unspoken, negative and hostile, they will instigate intransigence, distrust and resistance that will distort the issues, making them appear more important and less amenable to solution than they actually are. Whereas, if our emotions, expectations, intentions and attitudes can be communicated openly, honestly and in ways that are positive and constructive, people will become more trusting and the same issues will be transformed into clues and gateways to catalytic, synergistic, higher order outcomes.

For example, people in conflict are often reluctant to talk to each other or engage in dialogue or mediation, and commonly cite a rich variety of rationalizations for *not* communicating. Yet when we search beneath these reasons we generally discover injured feelings, false and unmet expectations, frustrated caring and collaborative intentions, and attitudes of conflict avoidance, accommodation or aggression, along with a subconscious belief that they lack the skills they need to initiate genuine listening and collaboratively negotiate positive outcomes.

Yet surfacing and clarifying these rationalizations allows us to identify more precisely what they are *actually* angry about and reframe our message so they can hear it without becoming unnecessarily angry, frightened or defensive. We can then plan strategically what we are going to say and how; set the stage, timing, mood and location for our conversation; anticipate their objections; listen empathetically and responsively; summarize, validate and acknowledge what they said; tailor our responses to meet their concerns; offer concessions that satisfy their interests; and reveal how to develop these skills through dialogue, *without* minimizing our interests or watering down our message.

If we merely rationalize our reluctance to speak directly with them and avoid meeting or discussing our concerns with them, we will not improve our skills and the conflict will remain unresolved. If we charge into the conversation without recognizing the validity of their emotions or listening to their expectations and experiences, we are likely to trigger more anger and defensiveness than necessary, and be less able to respond constructively.

More deeply, if we do not engage in dialogue, we will find it nearly impossible to develop the skills we need to lovingly and caringly re-connect with people who have upset us, or release ourselves from the pain created by our conflict. And it is these skills that we discover and practice in dialogue and mediation, as we learn how to participate in open and honest conversations, how to listen empathetically to other people's stories, acknowledge their emotions, recognize and satisfy their interests and collaboratively negotiate solutions.

Factual and Emotional Truths in Dialogue

Many people refuse to engage in dialogue with others because "they are lying," or "not telling the truth," or "acting dishonestly." What we do not understand initially is that the consequences of factual distortion, duplicity and exaggeration in the stories we tell about our conflicts extend far beyond the obvious impact they have on others. It is therefore important for us to look more closely at the nature of "lying" in conflict stories, and its relationship to dialogue.

In the first place, we all learn to tell stories as children, and to distort what happened or lie in order to protect ourselves and avoid punishment, mostly by making up excuses that erase or minimize our culpability and assuage our injured vanities. We grow up in families where people lie about all sorts of things. We watch grownups lie about their work, beliefs, thoughts and feelings — even about who they are. We grow up in societies where corporations lie about their activities and intentions, and fund advertising and commercials that are one continuous lie. We listen to political candidates and government officials lie about their mistakes and failures, and to political speeches that consist largely of lies, obfuscations, distortions and hypocrisies.

In conflict, we lie to others and to ourselves, even about whether or not we are lying. We lie because we are afraid, because we don't have the courage to face the truth, because we think others won't know, because we gain momentary advantages, because our self-esteem is fragile and our self-confidence is weak. We tell "white lies" to avoid hurting other people's feelings with the truth and bolster our own self-esteem. And every time we lie we create a divided self, consisting on the one hand, of the part that lied, and on the other, of the part that knows it was a lie.

In dialogue and mediation, we seek to re-integrate and restore this divided self, by surfacing the deeper dishonesties hidden in our adversarial assumptions, by reframing judgments about ourselves and others as subjective experiences, by legitimizing emotional truths, by recognizing that dishonesty is an expression of concern for what is true — or more deeply, as a *request* that one's deepest truths be heard and acknowledged. In this way, "You are lying" can be reframed simply as "What truth do you know that is not included in what s/he just said?"

In these and other ways, hostile attitudes and adversarial assumptions about what is *factually* true and what isn't can lead us to deeper inquiries in dialogue, encouraging us to recognize that few truths are mutually exclusive, allowing many different truths to coexist and combine to create larger, more complex, catalytic and synergistic truths that lead to better solutions and more sophisticated and advanced forms of problem-solving.

In dialogue, as in all stories and conflict narratives, there are two primary forms of truth: objective, or factual truth and subjective or emotional truth. Through stories we learn that it is advantageous for us to reshape, recolor and distort factual truths in order to communicate much deeper and far more important emotional truths. And if we have to choose, we will always tailor factual truths to convey or highlight the emotional truths that make our story compelling. For this reason, conflict stories are simply lies, told in search of a deeper truth.

As a result, nearly all of us tell stories about our conflicts that distort the facts, including who we are, who the other person is, what we experienced, what we felt, what we want, and what the real issues are — partly in order to survive and avoid recrimination, blame and self-loathing; and partly to define and *create* ourselves through stories about other people that mask our own mistakes and failures, and shift the blame for culpable, avoidant or aggressive behaviors, hostile attitudes and vindictive intentions from us to them. (For more on conflict stories, see my book with Joan Goldsmith, *Resolving Personal and Organizational Conflicts: Stories of Transformation and Forgiveness*, or my books, *The Crossroads of Conflict: A Journey into the Heart of Dispute Resolution* and *The Dance of Opposites: Explorations in Mediation, Dialogue and Conflict Resolution Systems Design*.)

An Algorithm for Political Dialogue

A generic description of the steps needed to make dialogue, mediation and other interest-based processes more effective and fair, or to build more constructive, collaborative, democratic relationships, seem to me to include the following 15, which can be regarded as an algorithm for interest-based methodologies and recursive improvement, for turning circles into spirals, and revealing step-by-step how to improve our ability to discuss and learn from political conflicts.

1. All interested parties are included and invited to participate fully in designing and implementing content, processes and relationships.
2. Decisions are reached by consensus wherever possible, and nothing is regarded as final until everyone is in agreement.
3. Diversity and honest differences are viewed as sources of dialogue, leading to better ideas, healthier relationships and greater unity.
4. Stereotypes, prejudices, assumptions of innate superiority and ideas of intrinsic correctness are considered divisive and discounted as one-sided descriptions of more complex, multi-sided, paradoxical realities.
5. Openness, authenticity, appreciation and empathy are regarded as better foundations for communication and decision-making than secrecy, dishonesty, insults and demonization.
6. Dialogue and open-ended questions are deemed more useful than personalized, adversarial debate and cross-examination.
7. Force, violence, coercion, aggression, humiliation and domination are rejected, both as methods and as outcomes.
8. Cooperation and collaboration are ranked as primary, while competition and aggression are considered secondary.
9. Everyone's interests are accepted as legitimate, and acknowledged and satisfied wherever possible.

10. Processes and relationships are considered at least as important as content, if not more so.
11. Attention is paid to emotions, subjectivity and feelings, as well as to logic, objectivity and facts.
12. Everyone is regarded as responsible for participating in improving content, processes and relationships, and encouraged to search for creative solutions, synergies and transformations.
13. People are invited into heartfelt communications and self-awareness, and supported in reaching resolution, forgiveness and reconciliation.
14. Chronic conflicts are traced to their sources, where they can be prevented and their systems redesigned to discourage repetition.
15. Victory is regarded as obtainable by everyone and redirected toward collaborating to solve common problems, so that no one feels defeated.

While these ideas may seem impractical or idealistic when applied to the rough and tumble of political conflicts, they have proven highly successful and produced positive results in countless dialogues, mediations, collaborative negotiations and similar processes over decades in diverse cultures and conditions around the world.

No technique, of course, can be successful at all times and places, in all cultures and with everyone, but finding ways of applying these interest-based principles in political dialogues and mediations will allow us to reduce the level of enmity and hostility in political conflicts and move just a little closer to solving a growing number of global problems that cannot be solved without them.

We may then discover that the *true* work of dialogue is to draw our attention inward, so that we can begin to dismantle the internal adversarial assumptions that feed all our conflicts, with the goal of freeing ourselves from their pointlessly polarizing power-based dynamics. As Michel Foucault wrote:

The real political task in a society such as ours is to criticize the working of institutions that appear to be both neutral and independent; to criticize them in such a manner that the political violence that has always exercised itself obscurely through them will be unmasked, so that one can fight them.

A potential for violence is implicit in every antagonistic, power-based approach to conflict, because it is easy for power--based debates and the diatribes they inspire to turn people who disagree into enemies of everything the other side believes in and stands for. This, however, is not really politics, but in the famous observation by Carl von Clausewitz, simply war by other means.

Similarly, a potential for coercion and manipulation is implicit in every adversarial rights-based approach to conflict, especially political conflicts, because it is equally easy for rights-based political processes and bureaucratic communications to inspire policies and procedures, rules and regulations, laws and legal interpretations that stack the deck in favor of one side over the other.

We therefore need to carefully consider not just *why*, but *how* to design, organize and conduct interest-based communications and dialogues over difficult and dangerous political issues. And rather than create one-size-fits-all rules, models or designs, which can never work because each issue, group and circumstance is different, it is essential that we re-design the process collaboratively, each time, from scratch. Most importantly, we need to think deeply about how to design dialogues and other conflict resolution processes in ways that leave room for complexity and ambiguity, so that when conversations between political opponents take an unexpected turn and head into dangerous territory, we will be able to move with what is happening in that moment in the conversation and the group, and help them frame it in ways that satisfy everyone's desire for connection, participation, collaboration and community. . The dalai lama reminds us:

Non-violence means dialogue, using our language, the human language. Dialogue means compromise; respecting each other's rights; in the spirit of reconciliation there is a real solution to conflict and disagreement. There is no hundred percent winner, no hundred percent loser — not that way but half-and-half. That is the practical way, the only way.

Dialogue supports non-violent approaches and helps them succeed because it elicits respectful communications, invites collaborative processes and encourages interest-based relationships that link and bind us with our opponents, knitting us into a single cloth, and strengthening the capacity for intimacy, caring and connection between couples, families, groups, communities and cultures. It is dialogue that invites us to understand and open our hearts to each other, and dialogue that inspires and sustains our capacity for love and kindness.

Moving from power-based diatribes to rights-based debates to interest-based dialogues, helps us recognize the crucial importance and creative potential of conflict, which require constructive disagreement, healthy dissent, collaborative negotiation and innovative problem-solving, allowing us to return to Aristotle's search for "the highest common good," but this time armed — not with swords and arrows, but dignity and respect, and a rich set of collaborative tools that do not require violence or degradation, subordination or domination.

Only by increasing the use of political dialogue, mediation and other interest-based processes, by building more collaborative political relationships, and by encouraging all of us to do the difficult work of communicating with each other about the things that matter most, will we be able to tackle the complex global problems we are increasingly required to solve. Discovering how is the focus of the next chapter.

FIVE

HOW TO DESIGN, ORGANIZE AND FACILITATE DIALOGUES OVER DIFFICULT AND DANGEROUS ISSUES

An idea that is not dangerous is unworthy of being considered an idea at all.
—Oscar Wilde

We are all partners in a quest. The essential questions have no answers. You are my question, and I am yours — and then there is dialogue. The moment we have answers, there is no dialogue. Questions unite people, answers divide them. So why have answers when you can live without them? —Elie Wiesel

Politics needs new ways of thinking; not the management-style guru garbage of 'outside of the box' or 'blue skies thinking', but an approach to the world as it really is. The bottom line is not profit or loss; the bottom line is people's lives. —Jeanette Winterson

CONVERSATIONS ABOUT DIFFICULT, DANGEROUS AND CONTROVERSIAL ISSUES are minefields, full of hidden traps and camouflaged dangers. As a result, most people assume it is better not to talk about them at all, and avoid participating in conversations that could blow up. Yet silence about difficult problems just guarantees their continuation, and often makes them worse.

So is it possible for us to invent and discover processes that take account of these difficulties, and aid us in avoiding, reducing and overcoming them? Can we design dialogues in which people discuss difficult and dangerous topics in ways that are safe and effective; yet honestly address the issues and help people find solutions? If so, how do we begin?

The information that follows is drawn from a chapter on dialogue in my earlier book, *The Dance of Opposites: Explorations in Mediation, Dialogue, and Conflict Resolution Systems Design,* and is included here with some additions and changes as a guide to those who would like to design, organize and facilitate political dialogues.

DIALOGUE VS. MONOLOGUE

First, it is useful to distinguish dialogue from other forms of communication and identify the principal elements that make it effective. Dialogues are different from monologues, which can take place even when more than one person is speaking. Here are some important distinctions between them:

- **Monologue** is one way. *Dialogue* is two ways.
- **Monologue** is an assertion. *Dialogue* is a responsive conversation.
- **Monologue** is talking at each other. *Dialogue* is talking with each other.
- **Monologue** assumes there is a single truth. *Dialogue* assumes there are multiple truths.
- **Monologue** is announcing "The Answer." *Dialogue* is asking respectful questions and exploring diverse answers.
- **Monologue** is preaching to the choir. *Dialogue* is talking with people who are different about their similarities and differences.
- **Monologue** is about me. *Dialogue* is about us.

- **Monologue** is about power. *Dialogue* is about interests, which are the reasons why people want to accumulate power.
- **Monologue** moves toward opposition. *Dialogue* moves toward relationship.

Monologues tend to advance narrow, self-centered truths that divide us from one another because they are too small, inflexible and simplistic; because they cannot encompass the greatness and complexity of all the possibilities that reside in the problem. For this reason, serial monologues without any engagement, or mutual exchange or responsiveness, do not create a dialogue.

Dialogues, on the other hand, are broader, collaborative searches for synergistic truths that unite us, that are large, flexible and complex enough to include everyone, yet do not make problems simpler than they actually are. Dialogues allow us to cross the divide of our differences and discover what we have in common. They encourage us to communicate and thereby overcome the isolation of individual experience and learn from other points of view.

DIALOGUE VS. DEBATE

We can also distinguish dialogues from debates, which are simply two successive monologues pretending to be a dialogue. Debates define issues and solutions adversarially, in ways that make them automatically unacceptable to the other side. Dialogues, on the other hand, as defined by physicist David Bohm, create "a stream of meaning flowing among, through, and between us." Dialogues define issues and solutions collaboratively and search for ways of making them acceptable to all parties.

Debate is a circular process, in which opponents argue and disagree with each other and are more interested in demonstrating they are right than they are in discovering the truth. In dialogue, truths emerge not from one side winning and the other losing, but from both sides explaining their different perspectives, identifying the meaning of their disagreements and searching for solutions that satisfy their underlying interests. Bohm explained how dialogue achieves these results:

> In ... a dialogue, when one person says something, the other person does not, in general, respond with exactly the same meaning as that seen by the first person. Rather, the meanings are only similar and not identical. Thus, when the second person replies, the first person sees a difference between what he meant to say and what the other person understood. On considering this difference, he may then be able to see something new, which is relevant both to his own views and to those of the other person. And so it can go back and forth, with the continual emergence of a new content that is common to both participants. Thus, in a dialogue, each person does not attempt to make common certain ideas or items of information that are already known to him. Rather, it may be said that two people are making something in common, i.e., creating something new together.

Here are some distinctions between deate and dialogue, developed largely by Bohm and the Dialogue Group for the Boston Chapter of Educators for Social Responsibility:

- **Debate** is oppositional: two sides are opposed and attempt to prove each other wrong. *Dialogue* is collaborative: two or more sides work together to develop a common understanding.
- **In debate**, the goal is to be the only one to win. *In dialogue*, the goal is to find common ground and to find better solutions.
- **In debate**, one listens in order to find flaws and refute arguments. *In dialogue*, one listens in order to learn and find commonalities.
- **Debate** affirms each side's own point of view. *Dialogue* enlarges and transforms both side's points of view.
- **Debate** rarely questions assumptions but defends them against criticism. *Dialogue* questions assumptions and discusses and re-evaluates them.

- **Debate** rarely results in open apology or introspection. *Dialogue* encourages apology and introspection, and openly shares them.
- **Debate** defends one's own position as the best solution and excludes the other side's positions and solutions. *Dialogue* elicits interests rather than positions and reaches better solutions by creatively combining them.
- **Debate** produces closed minds and hearts, a determination to be right, and resistance to change. *Dialogue* produces open minds and hearts, a willingness to be proven wrong, and participation in change.
- **Debate** results in the solidification and entrenchment of beliefs. *Dialogue* results in the modification and re-examination of beliefs.
- **In debate**, one searches for disagreements, mistakes and difficulties. *In dialogue*, one searches for agreements, opportunities and potential synergies.
- **In debate**, one searches for flaws and weaknesses in other's positions. *In dialogue*, one searches for strengths and commonalities in other's positions.
- **Debate** involves opposing the other side without recognizing feelings or relationships, and belittling or deprecating the other person. *Dialogue* involves genuine concern for the other person, acknowledges feelings and relationships, and empathizes with and supports the other side.
- **Debate** assumes there is a single truth or correct answer, only one side has possession of it, and that combining them only weakens them. *Dialogue* assumes there are many correct answers, many people have pieces of it, and that combining them creates much more satisfying and effective solutions.
- **Debate** implies an end or conclusion. *Dialogue* is open-ended and on-going.
- **Debate** assumes that conflict is only resolvable when one side wins. *Dialogue* assumes that conflict is resolvable by both sides winning.

In his book *On Dialogue,* Bohm explains why we need to pay attention to the *process* and design ways of making it more effective:

> Dialogue is really aimed at going into the whole thought process and changing the way the thought process occurs collectively. We haven't really paid much attention to thought as a process. We have ENGAGED in thoughts, but we have only paid attention to the content, not to the process. Why does thought require attention? Everything requires attention, really. If we ran machines without paying attention to them, they would break down. Our thought, too, is a process, and it requires attention, otherwise it's going to go wrong.

Another way of thinking about dialogue is to regard it as a learning process in which participants with diverse ideas, backgrounds and experiences try to understand not only what the other thinks that is different, but more importantly why they think that way and what events and experiences led them to do so. Part of the power of dialogue is its encouragement of personal stories, life experiences and the lessons people draw from them. These induce empathy in the listener and invite deeper levels of listening.

For this reason, it is often useful to open a dialogue by asking people to say something about who they are in relation to the issue. For example, in a dialogue I facilitated, sponsored by Mediators Beyond Borders in Los Angeles about conflicts in the Middle East and attended by more than a hundred Israelis and Palestinians, small groups began conversations with a facilitator asking each participant to briefly introduce themselves and say what personal experiences or connections they have with the Middle East. People were invited to tell stories about their experiences and encouraged to express empathy with each other.

In another dialogue conducted by members of Mediators Beyond Borders in Athens, Greece on problems associated with immigration (for more details, see Chapter 7), small groups of immigrants and Greek citizens began by answering the following questions:

- Have you ever, in a family, neighborhood, school or workplace, been the new one, or felt like an outsider? And have you ever, in a family, neighborhood, school or workplace, been the one who has been there for a while, or felt disrupted by new people coming in?
- What is your name? Does it have a meaning in your family or culture? If so, what is its meaning?
- What is your personal experience with immigration? Your family's experience?
- What stories do you or your friends and family tell about their experience getting here, or living here and interacting with immigrants?
- What has it been like for you being an immigrant, or being a citizen of a country that others have immigrated to?
- What is one thing you would most like others in the group to know about you before we begin?
- What is one wish or hope you have for our dialogue today?

FORMS AND STAGES OF DIALOGUE

It is possible to conduct dialogues between two people, dozens, hundreds, or entire communities and nations, as occurred informally in the U.S. in the days following Sept. 11, 2001. The main difficulty with two-person dialogues is that no one is present to facilitate the conversation if it begins to move off track. The main difficulty with larger dialogues is that people tend to "grandstand," give speeches, and become so distant from one another that they fail to listen empathetically to what is being said, especially by opponents, dissenters, outsiders and critics.

For this reason, the most effective dialogues, in my experience, are those that take place in small, diverse groups of about five to 10 people, led either by a trained facilitator or a volunteer from the group, with a recorder to capture everyone's ideas and discourage repetition, a presenter to report to the large group on what they did, and a "process observer" who can reflect on what worked or didn't in the conversation, and how to improve or get it back on track.

William Isaacs, CEO of Dialogos and author of *Dialogue*, distinguishes four unique stages of dialogue based on Bohm's ideas. He describes, for example:

1. "Shared Monologues," in which group members get used to talking to each other
2. "Skillful Discussion," in which people learn the skills of dialogue
3. "Reflective Dialogue," in which people engage in genuine dialogue
4. "Generative Dialogue," in which "creative" dialogue is used to generate new ideas

As Isaacs sees it, participants in dialogue pass through a number of stages in their ability to listen, process and interact with each other. Dialogue is therefore a continuously changing, *evolutionary* process in which people adapt and modify their ideas and beliefs based on what they are able to learn from each other. This suggests that what is useful and important at one stage may not work when people move to a different stage, which requires considerable presence, awareness, sensitivity and understanding on the part of the facilitator.

How to Organize a Dialogue

To organize a dialogue regarding divisive political issues in a community or organization, it is helpful to break the process down into 15 core steps or elements, and examine each separately:

1. Designing the process
2. Training facilitators
3. Convening participants

4. Setting the stage
5. Agreeing on ground rules
6. Introducing participants
7. Asking questions to encourage dialogue
8. Listening in a committed way
9. Summarizing important and useful points
10. Intervening to encourage listening and resolve conflicts when necessary
11. Breaking into small groups
12. Listening to small group reports
13. Inviting feedback
14. Reaching closure
15. Evaluating the process

Here are a few suggestions on how to go about designing a dialogue using these steps. [Some parts were first published in my book, *Conflict Revolution: Mediating Evil, War, Injustice, and Terrorism*.]

15 STEPS IN DESIGNING A DIALOGUE

1. DESIGNING THE PROCESS

Every dialogue will attract a different mix of participants and cultures, occur in different locations and times, and therefore require different designs to be effective. The steps in organizing a dialogue will vary, depending on the nature and size of the group, the needs of the parties, the character of the issues, the timing of the process, cultural expectations and other considerations. While fine-tuning the process is important, in my experience, the principle elements in the dialogue remain the same, and can be said to consist of these steps, unless more difficult exchanges occur, in which case mediation may be necessary. The design process should take account of the beliefs, cultures and experiences of all the people who are expected to participate, their personal backgrounds, anticipated moods and attitudes, degrees of openly expressed hostility, recent events, willingness to talk to the other side and similar factors. It is important to be flexible and ready to modify the design if it is not working.

2. TRAINING FACILITATORS

It is important to prepare facilitators in advance, including those who will be guiding small group sessions, and make sure they have read and understand the training materials and feel ready to lead the process. It is often useful to have one or two mediators who can "float," listen in on small group sessions, watch for warning signs like raised voices, and be prepared to intervene and help out as needed.

3. CONVENING PARTICIPANTS

The first step is to identify the main parties who will participate in the dialogue, who should include:

- The primary parties to the dispute
- Affected groups in industry, labor, government and community
- Recognized experts and scholars
- Leaders of local community organizations
- Concerned individuals, such as students, teachers and officials
- Anyone who can contribute to the success of the dialogue or undermine it

Next, interview key participants in person in advance of the session to discover their issues and interests, build trust in the process, uncover hidden obstacles to moving forward, gather information to assist small-group facilitators, fine-tune a design for the process, and communicate these to encourage openness and buy-in.

A SAMPLE FLYER TO ADVERTISE "RED STATE/BLUE STATE" DIALOGUES

Here is an example of a flyer you can adapt and use in convening to invite people on all sides of a hot political issue to participate in a political dialogue:

Color This Conversation Purple: An Invitation to Dialogue

We have gone through an exhausting election, filled with anger, hostility and personal attacks, and while half the country is upset and disappointed that they lost, the other half understands that it could have gone the other way, and that *they* might be the ones feeling upset and disappointed.

The problem is, we haven't figured out yet how to talk to each other about our political ideas and beliefs, or discuss our disagreements in ways that lead to learning, increased empathy, mutual understanding, joint problem-solving and win/win outcomes. Yet we are all citizens of this country, and we all care about its future.

How, then, do we begin to talk to each other about difficult and dangerous issues, the ones that we feel strongly about and argue passionately over? The answer is through open and honest dialogues.

What Is Dialogue?

Dialogue was defined by physicist David Bohm as "the flow of meaning between us." It is a learning process in which people with diverse ideas, backgrounds and experiences try to understand not just *what* other people think that is different, but more importantly, *why* they think that way, and what life experiences led them to do so.

How Does Dialogue Work?

Most dialogues start with an orientation and a set of ground rules or process agreements that are reached in a large group, which then separates into small, diverse groups of about 5 to 8 people where most of the conversations take place. These small group sessions are led by an experienced *facilitator*, plus several volunteers — a *recorder* who captures everyone's ideas, a *presenter* who shares the group's ideas with other small groups, a *process observer* who gives feedback to the group at the end about their communications; as well as a trained *mediator* who can step in if the conversations gets stuck.

The goal in dialogue is not to change each other's minds, but to discuss issues in ways that encourage learning and joint problem-solving; to improve our ability to listen and talk to each other; to encourage empathy and understanding, and appreciate our differences; and to explore complex issues without sinking into hatred or stereotyping

Who Are We?

We are a group of experienced mediators and dialogue facilitators who propose to design, organize and conduct a dialogue between those who disagree about the hot political issues that divide us and impact our lives. [insert the specific issue that will be addressed in the dialogue]

How Can I Help?

If you are interested in being trained to facilitate a small group to discuss these issues, or would like to help organize the dialogue, or would like information about how you can help publicize, fund or participate in it, please contact us at: [insert contact and event information]

Please come. You are all welcome!

4. Setting the Stage

Arrange the setting in a friendly, open, neutral location and style. If possible, have chairs arranged in small circles so people can talk to each other. Have flip charts, marking pens, masking tape for hanging them on the wall, paper and pens for note taking, tissues and refreshments available if possible. In addition, it is useful to meet in advance with small group facilitators to prepare them for what they are about to do. Here are some sample instructions that can be used to assist small group facilitators:

SUGGESTIONS FOR DIALOGUE FACILITATORS

Facilitators perform the following functions, or ask group members to do so:

1. Moderate the discussion, if necessary, to keep it on topic.
2. Record key points, preferably on flip chart paper.
3. Keep track of time.
4. Observe and give feedback on the process.

Facilitators should also:

- Ideally arrange chairs in a circle or semi-circle so that each person has eye contact with you and with each other. This seating arrangement encourages interaction and sharing so no one is left out.
- Use each person's name. Nametags or tents are useful to help you remember and make them feel welcome.
- Do not discount, dismiss or minimize participants' ideas or feelings. Stop the process or reframe comments if others do so.
- Be aware of everyone's differences and encourage them to do so as well. Each comes with a different family system, culture, religion, political beliefs and experiences that influence our views.
- Respect requests for confidentiality.
- Show respect, friendliness and interest. Use humor (especially about yourself) whenever appropriate.
- Be fair when you present information or respond to comments or remarks.
- Be less concerned about securing agreement over content and more concerned with reaching agreements over process.

- Focus on positive qualities, and reframe negative ones.
- Discourage individuals from monopolizing the conversation. This helps those who withdraw or refrain from participating who may need encouragement.
- Be a good listener. It is helpful to paraphrase or summarize comments to show that you are listening. It also gives you an opportunity to clarify what was said.
- Be flexible. Go with what is happening.
- Observe how the participants interact and where they seat themselves.
- Listen for words of welcome or hostility, watch for eye contact, observe body language, and especially notice withdrawal and hostility.
- Note the effect on participants of words or actions by others, both positive and negative, and consider giving feedback at the end.
- Take written notes of statements to come back to, group interactions, specific suggestions for follow-up and suggestions for improvement of the process.
- Phrase suggestions for improvement positively, so as to encourage continued improvement.
- Ask participants questions such as:
- "How did it make you feel when s/he said that?"
- "Why did you want to come here today?"
- "Where are you heading with that question?"
- "What are you feeling right now?"
- "How could this dialogue be improved?"
- "What are some other questions you might ask?"
- The facilitator should allow the group time to perform exercises before intervening and not try to manipulate or control the group process.
- If a particular group is not working well, try switching groups so a different person is facilitator, or stop and ask why the conversation is not working.

- If a group is getting sidetracked, ask a question about the original topic.
- Take some time at the end of the session to ask each person how they felt about the discussion, or what they learned from it, or what they will do differently. Encourage participants to report on their experiences and suggestions on how to improve the process.
- Compliment participants on their work.
- Thank everyone for sharing their feelings, experiences and information with the group.

5. AGREEING ON GROUND RULES

Invite participants to discuss and agree on ground rules for the dialogue. Here are some common ground rules, principles or process agreements that can encourage constructive attitudes and help create a trusting environment in which dialogue over difficult issues can be useful:

SOME COMMON GROUND RULES OR PROCESS AGREEMENTS

- We agree to be present voluntarily and that no one will be coerced into attending or speaking.
- We agree that everything we say to each other will be confidential and will not be repeated to others, unless we expressly agree otherwise. (Or: We agree that all statements made during the dialogue are not for individual attribution, unless we decide otherwise.)
- We agree that the process will be completely transparent and open.
- We agree that no group decisions will be made until we have finished discussing the issues.
- We agree to participate in a spirit of learning and open communication.

- We agree to be honest and not withhold our differences or disagreements.
- We agree to communicate respectfully and not engage in personal insults.
- We agree to act with courtesy and not engage in violent or disruptive behavior.
- We agree that we will jointly investigate factual discrepancies.
- We agree that we will not retaliate for anything anyone says or does during the dialogue.
- We agree to publicly support the group's consensus, if there is one.
- We agree that all public announcements, press releases, global emails, bulletins and disclosures issued during these dialogue sessions will be presented in a spirit of collaboration and improving relationships.
- We agree to mediate any disputes we can't resolve ourselves.

6. *Introducing Participants*

As they convene, welcome the participants and invite them to be present in a spirit of inquiry, learning and discovery. Tell them you will review the ground rules, give an overview of the design for the process and present a list of issues to be discussed that has been drawn from the interviews.

You may want to invite people to introduce themselves, either in the large group, or if there are too many, in the small groups they will belong to, as the first or second item on their agenda. If you use self-introductions, asks each participant to state their name, perhaps where they are from, and answer a question that will introduce the dialogue, such as:

- One reason why you decided to be present
- One reason you want to see this issue discussed or resolved
- One thing that, in your life, has led you to feel strongly about this issue

- One outcome you want to achieve
- One thing you believe both sides have in common
- One success you had last year and one thing you are working on this year
- One wish you have for the group or the discussion
- One mistake you made in the past in discussing the issue
- One prejudice or source of hostility you would like to overcome
- One thing that, thinking about the conversation afterward, you will wish you had said or done.

7. ASKING QUESTIONS TO ENCOURAGE DIALOGUE

Thousands of dialogue sessions have been facilitated or mediated over the last three decades between conflicted parties, including communities, political organizations, governments and national minorities. Essential Partners, Common Ground, Mediators Beyond Borders, National Coalition for Dialogue and Deliberation, Dialogos, Alliance for Peacebuilding and similar organizations have developed a rich array of methods for opening lines of communication. Here are a few questions that can be used to open a political dialogue:

- What life experiences have you had that have led you to feel so deeply and passionately about this issue?
- What is at the heart of this issue, for you as an individual?
- Why were you willing to participate in this dialogue?
- Why do you care so much about this issue? What does it mean to you?
- Do you see any gray areas in the issue we are discussing, or ideas you find it difficult to define?
- Do you have any mixed feelings, uncertainties, or discomforts regarding this issue that you would be willing to share?
- Is there any part of this issue that you are not 100 percent certain of, or would be willing to discuss and talk about?

- Even though you hold widely differing views, are there any concerns or ideas you think you may have in common?
- What underlying values or ethical beliefs have led you to your current political beliefs? What values or ethical beliefs do you have in common?
- Do the differences between your positions reveal any riddles, paradoxes, contradictions or enigmas regarding this issue?
- Is it possible to view your differences as two sides of the same coin? If so, what unites them? What is the coin?
- What is beneath that idea for you? Why does it matter?
- Can you separate the issues from the people you disagree with? What will happen if you can't?
- Is there anything positive or acknowledging you would be willing to say about the people on the other side of this issue?
- What processes or ground rules would help you disagree more constructively?
- Instead of focusing on the past, what would you like to see happen in the future? Why?
- Are you disagreeing about fundamental values, or about how to achieve them?
- Is there a way that both of you might be right? How?
- What criteria could you use to decide what works best?
- Would it be possible to test your ideas in practice and see which work best? How might you do that?
- Would you be willing to jointly investigate your conflicting factual assertions?
- What could be done to improve each side's ideas?
- Could any of the other side's ideas be incorporated into yours? How?
- Is there any aspect of this issue that either of you have left out? Are there any other perspectives you haven't described?
- Are there any other ways you can think of to say that?
- Do you think it would be useful to continue this conversation, in order to learn more about each other and what you each believe to be true?

- How could you make your dialogue more ongoing or effective?
- What could you do to improve the ways you disagree with each other in the future? For encouraging future dialogue?
- Would you be willing to do that together?

The purpose of these questions is not to eliminate or discourage disagreements, but to place them in the context of our common humanity and allow genuine disagreements to surface, and be discussed openly and in-depth. These questions reveal that political conversations need not be pointlessly adversarial, but can be transformed into authentic engagements by allowing opposing sides to come to grips with difficult, complex, divisive issues without being hostile or abusive.

These questions also demonstrate that it is possible, even in small ways, to strengthen dialogue, encourage learning and change, and return to the original purposes of politics. The mere possibility that we might do so is sufficient to encourage us to consider how we might redesign all our political processes and activities so as to draw people together — not over and against others, but with and for them, so as to maximize political clarity, ethical self-improvement and the common good.

8. LISTENING IN A COMMITTED WAY

It is important to begin the dialogue process by listening. Here is what Brenda Ueland says about the importance of listening:

> I want to write about the great and powerful thing that listening is. And how we forget it. And how we don't listen to our children, or those we love. And least of all — which is so important too — to those we do not love. But we should. Because listening is a magnetic and strange thing, a creative force. ... This is the reason: When we are listened to, it creates us, makes us unfold and expand. Ideas actually begin to grow within us and come to life. ... Who are the people, for

example, to whom you go for advice? Not to the hard, practical ones who can tell you exactly what to do, but to the listeners; that is, the kindest, least censorious, least bossy people you know. It is because by pouring out your problem to them you then know what to do about it yourself. ... So try listening. Listen to your wife, your children, your friends; to those who love you and those who don't; to those who bore you; to your enemies. It will work a small miracle — and perhaps a great one.

So listen to those you disagree with, even to those you find abhorrent. We are human beings first, before we are left or right, Black or White, or however you define yourself. By listening in a committed way to each other, we create pathways and connections that hold us together and do not allow us to imagine we are so completely different from one another that we could harm each other without feeling guilty or ashamed. The Chilean journalist Ariel Dorfman, who was tortured by the military junta under General Pinochet, wrote, "How easy it is to kill someone you don't have to mourn because you never dared to imagine him alive."

Committed listening is listening as though your life could change as a result of what you are about to hear. We get there by discussing things that matter in small conversations, by having facilitators to keep us on track and recorders to make sure our voices are heard, by agreeing to take turns, by coming to grips with the difficult things people want to say, by searching for practical things we can say to make a difference.

9. SUMMARIZING IMPORTANT AND USEFUL POINTS

It is useful for facilitators to summarize people's points — not everything that is said, but the most important and useful points, as a way of making people feel heard and reducing repetition. This can be done on a flip chart, by a recorder or orally. It can also be done by asking each side to summarize the other sides' ideas, feelings, priorities or disagreements. Summarization should not be simply verbatim repetition, but capturing its essence and repeating it using different words.

10. *Intervening to Encourage Listening and Resolve Conflicts When Necessary*

Sometimes, the dialogue process goes off track. What do we do then? To begin, try these interventions:

- Draw participants into responsive conversations, defuse tensions, acknowledge divergent points of view, summarize agreements and record "points of consensus and disagreement" on flip charts.
- Ask each side to present its position, offer backup information, detailed explanations and provide ample opportunity for questions and dialogue from all points of view.
- Shift the focus from positions to interests, past to future, personalities to issues and prescriptions to options. Ask why people want what they want and probe for underlying concerns.
- Caucus periodically with each side to encourage them to trust and speak freely with you and to bring their interests and hidden issues to the table.
- Ask representatives of opposing positions to meet in "side-bar" negotiations to come to consensus on recommendations to the larger group. Select the strongest advocates so others will not question their recommendations.
- Transition into small group problem-solving and collaborative negotiation, identify areas of agreement, disagreement, mutual interest and consensus. Re-focus attention on relationships and qualities the parties have in common.
- Summarize points of agreement regularly, to build confidence in the process and limit the range of disagreement.

- As the parties reach full and final agreements, review each point of agreement to ensure consensus.
- If they have not reached full and final agreement, confirm interim agreements, agree to limit the use of destructive methods between meetings and encourage continued dialogue.
- List outstanding disagreements to work on at the next session. Elicit recommendations and agendas for following sessions.
- Hold repeated sessions, picking up where you left off and distribute summaries of the last session before the next one.
- Draw each separate session to a close, not a conclusion. Thank participants, assign homework and encourage continued dialogue over open issues.
- Confirm agreements to meet until the conflict is resolved and to forge a genuine resolution.
- Reach for closure, acknowledge participants and celebrate successes. Make the process transparent throughout, explaining what you are doing and why while you are doing it, so everyone can learn skills to resolve conflicts in the future.

David Bohm wrote that the main problem people offer in refusing or rejecting dialogue is that the other side is prejudiced and unwilling to listen.

> After all, it is easy for each one of us to see that other people are 'blocked' about certain questions, so that without being aware of it, they are avoiding the confrontation of contradictions in certain ideas that may be extremely dear to them. The very nature of such a 'block' is, however, that it is a kind of insensitivity or 'anesthesia' about one's own contradictions. Evidently then, what is crucial is to be aware of the nature of one's own 'blocks.' If one is alert and attentive, he can see for example that whenever certain questions arise, there are fleeting sensations of fear, which push him away from consideration of those questions, and of pleasure, which attract his thoughts and cause them to be occupied with other questions. So, one is able to keep away from whatever it is that he thinks may disturb him. And as a result, he can

be subtle at defending his own ideas, when he supposes that he is really listening to what other people have to say. When we come together to talk, or otherwise to act in common, can each one of us be aware of the subtle fear and pleasure sensations that 'block' the ability to listen freely?

Here are some process interventions that can be used by facilitators to help each side become aware of the ways they are blocking listening, keep the conversation on track and encourage respectful communication:

- *Transparency*: "What just happened in the conversation we were having?"
- *Inquiring*: "What do you think should be done? Why do you think so?"
- *Supporting*: "I appreciate your willingness to speak up and express your opinions. Here is an example that supports your point."
- *Acknowledging*: "You took a risk in making that apology/concession."
- *Refereeing*: "What ground rules do we need so everyone can feel we are behaving fairly? "
- *Concretizing*: "Can you give a specific example?"
- *Exploring*: "Can you say more about why you feel so strongly about this issue?"
- *Summarizing*: "Is this what you are trying to say ... ?"
- *Challenging*: "Is that consistent with the ground rules/what the group has already decided?"
- *Coaching*: "Is there a way you could respond less defensively?"
- *Connecting*: "That point connects directly with what was said earlier ... "
- *Re-orienting*: "I think we're lost. Can we get back on track? Are we talking about the real issue?"
- *problem-solving*: "What do you see as some possible solutions?"
- *Uniting*: "What can we agree on here?

- *Contextualizing*: "Why have we come together to discuss this issue?"

If these do not work, consider taking a break and ask those involved to meet separately with a mediator to see if they can resolve their issues.

11. BREAKING INTO SMALL GROUPS

It is always useful to break large groups into smaller ones to give everyone a chance to participate and reduce the tendency to grandstand and use adversarial styles of speech that trigger conflicts in large groups. As indicated earlier, each small group should have a *facilitator*, and if possible, a *recorder* to take notes, a *process observer* to reflect back to the group how they did and intervene with process suggestions if the conversation becomes too heated, a *presenter* to share with the other small groups, a *timekeeper* to stay on track, and sometimes a *mediator* to help defuse tensions.

12. LISTENING TO SMALL GROUP REPORTS

Ask each small group to select someone who will present the results of their conversation, elicit comments from the large group, draw people into dialogue about possible disagreements, and applaud each small group for its work.

13. INVITING FEEDBACK

At the end, ask if anyone would like to offer oral feedback on how the process went for them, and whether they have any suggestions on how it could be improved next time. Thank them for their comments, make sure someone records them and draw the meeting to a close. Instead, or together with oral comments, it is possible to hand out an evaluation form (see below).

14. REACHING CLOSURE

At the end, ask people to reflect on their experience in the dialogue, what they learned or will do differently as a result, or how they felt about the process. Try to end on a positive note that looks toward common action and continued dialogue.

15. EVALUATING THE PROCESS

Sometimes it will be best to ask the participants to complete a written evaluation. More people will participate and the confidentiality of their comments will produce different feedback. Here is a sample dialogue evaluation form you can modify or ask people to fill in at the end. The most important element is that you take every suggestion seriously and consider what can be done next time to make the process work better.

Sample Dialogue Evaluation Form

Please add your comments for the benefit of the facilitators and future participants.

1. On a scale between 1 and 5, 5 being highest, how would you evaluate the usefulness of your dialogue? Please indicate with the correct numerical evaluation: _____

2. What was the most useful and enjoyable part of the dialogue for you?

3. What was the least useful or enjoyable?

4. What could be done to improve future dialogues?

5. What is the most important thing you learned this evening? Is there anything you intend to do differently as a result?

6. Is there anything you are willing to do to help?

7. Other suggestions and comments:

VARIETIES OF DECISION-MAKING

In *The End of Management and the Rise of Organizational Democracy*, Joan Goldsmith and I wrote about how dialogue and other collaborative, self-managing, interest-based processes require higher order skills in democratic forms of decision-making, because they are more open, egalitarian and inclusive, encourage both disagreement and unity, and support creativity, teamwork and partnership.

Organizational decision making ranges from hierarchical, authoritarian, unilateral, competitive, bureaucratic, centralized processes at one pole, to heterarchical, democratic, collaborative, authentic, decentralized processes at the other. There are six fundamentally distinct decision-making processes from which individuals, teams and organizations can choose. Rather than pick one, we need to become fluent in all of them and be able to choose the right one for each type of decision. These six basic varieties of decision-making are:

1. Notification
2. Consultation
3. Delegation:
4. Voting
5. Consensus
6. Unanimity

As we proceed from notification to unanimity, the time and effort required increase, as do the degrees of unity and ownership that following any decision. As a result, we wrote:

> The choice of process depends on the kind of problem to be solved. Rapid, unilateral decision making works fine when issues are clear and stakes are minimal. But [people who] rarely reach consensus or unanimity experience higher levels of conflict and distrust than [those who] periodically take time to make sure everyone is on board...

> Voting is usually considered the appropriate form of decision making for democracies, but problems arise whenever a significant minority loses an important vote, causing divisions and bad feelings to undermine unity and ongoing relationships. Because voting permits

full participation, it is preferable to notification. Yet it is often competitive, contentious and adversarial, and is not preferable to consensus, which is based on interests, rather than rights or power. ... Processes such as consensus aim to satisfy the underlying reasons people are for or against something, create opportunities to modify ideas to meet a broader set of needs, and include dissenters and resisters in owning the results.

Nevertheless, it is clearly inappropriate to use consensus to decide, for example, what someone else is going to have for lunch. It is equally inappropriate to use notification to decide what employees will do in self-managing teams or to vote on whether to act respectfully toward minorities. Each problem needs to be considered separately ... so that everyone involved in implementing the decision accepts the way it was made.

For example, in convening dialogues, the time and place of the meeting are generally announced, there is consultation with constituent groups beforehand, discussion and recommendations are delegated to small groups, sometime there is a vote on delegates or press releases, consensus is reached on the issues reported out by each small group, and there may be unanimity on recommendations for action. A collaborative, democratic approach to deciding which form of decision-making to use in organizations, or in dialogues or mediations, might begin by identifying the issues and topics that will require a decision, then reaching consensus or unanimity on the specific variety of decision-making that will be used for each issue or topic, discussing its strengths, weaknesses and potential for conflicts or misunderstandings, and what steps will taken next if consensus is not reached.

What to Do if Consensus Is Not Reached

If consensus is not reached, for example, regarding small group recommendations for action, the next options include these:

- Separate out issues over which there is no consensus to return to later
- See if it is possible to brainstorm solutions that address the reasons people offer for withholding consensus
- Return to vision or goals, then develop procedures or guidelines that flow from the vision and goals
- Identify shared values, commonalities, principles, interests and criteria for decision making
- Look at each of the objections to see if solutions can be created to these while moving ahead with the proposal
- Take a break and then return the decision to the group for additional problem-solving
- Break issues down into separate parts and try to reach consensus on each part separately
- Create a team composed of representatives of each side to separately brainstorm, prioritize and recommend solutions
- Refer the issue to a completely uninvolved group to develop compromise solutions
- Look for hidden issues
- Bring in an experienced facilitator to help bring about consensus
- Separate into factions and engage in more dialogue
- Ask each group to meet separately and list five suggestions for compromise
- Bring in an outside expert to advise the group
- Table the decision to research the issue, or until there is greater clarity
- Decide not to decide
- Take a straw vote
- Bring in an experienced mediator to help resolve the dispute
- Prepare majority and minority reports
- Vote based on majority rule, while allowing the minority to continue trying to convince others to change their minds

- Allow the group's primary decision-maker to decide

Tips on Dialogue

Engaging people in dialogue using these steps is simple, but it is not easy. It means that people have to actually listen to one another. They have to accept as authentic and valid *for each person* the underlying subjective truth of whatever that person says, even if it contradicts the listeners' perceptions and deeply held beliefs. Here are some final suggestions to help you facilitate political dialogues:

- Consider yourself an ally of all the participants. If you set out to learn to engage in dialogue together and broaden your knowledge of others' life experiences you can't fail.
- Assume that others are sincere in what they say.
- Listen not only for facts and opinions, but subjective experiences, emotions and the reasons behind them. How and why did the speaker arrive at his or her conclusions?
- Don't take things too literally. Listen for meanings, not just words.
- Be patient. A question that may be easy for you — e.g., "What is your racial and ethnic identity?" — may be difficult for others. Give them time to work their way through their resistance and find the words.
- Use real-life examples as reference points. Tell stories.
- Accept silences as part of the process. Don't rush to fill the space.
- Seek clarification. If something is not clear, or if you want to learn more, ask questions. It helps to restate what you think was said, so the speaker can feel heard, correct wrong impressions and expand on unclear ideas.
- Ask "why" questions, but not in a way that sounds judgmental.
- Avoid questions that can be answered with a simple "yes" or "no." A single-word answer may discourage further conversation.

- Be alert to generalizations, both yours and others. A statement may be true of "some," or maybe "most," but surely not "all."
- Use the identifying terms for people that they use for themselves. There's usually a reason behind their choice of group names.
- Say how an experience or statement affected or is affecting you. Reframe "you" or "they" statements as "I" or "We" messages.
- Be honest, but don't release your own pent-up anger, anxiety, or guilt at the expense of others.
- Try not to be defensive. Few of us are always articulate, precise or perfect in our conversations, and inadvertently step on toes. Keep the big picture and goal clearly in mind.
- Watch your body language. Be sure it doesn't say, "I'm bored," "I'm superior," "I don't believe you."
- Do not doubt the authenticity of what you hear. Each person is the best authority on what she or he feels.
- Support others when they try to say something. They may repeat themselves, stammer or pause a while as they try to get it out.
- Understand that you're getting only a tiny glimpse into peoples' lives. Dialogue happens at a fast pace, and not many of us are adept at organizing our thoughts on the spot.
- Refuse to give up on anyone, no matter how unpleasant, opinionated or difficult they may be to deal with.
- Accept that you and others may hold opposing views. Resist the temptation to find quick solutions, correct, argue or counter.
- Be willing to have your biases challenged.
- Don't be impatient to talk about broader issues and problems. If and when the group moves on to analysis, recommendations and action planning, things will go easier if by that time they know and trust one another.
- Don't dominate the conversation.

- Try to open and close on a note of heartfelt appreciation and unity.

(Based partly on materials from the Los Angeles Commission on Human Relations)

FINAL ADVICE

The most important advice I can offer about dialogue is simply to try it. The process works, and even when it seems impossible to reach people, or when pain and rage begin to rise, someone will say something that turns the entire conversation in a positive, constructive direction. If you continue to hold the thought that it is possible and are clear and collaborative in your *intention* and transparent in your process, people will understand and walk away having learned something important.

SIX

DESIGNING DIALOGUES ABOUT PREJUDICE AND DISCRIMINATION

What we must defend is dialogue and the universal communication of men. Slavery, injustice, and lies are the plagues that destroy this dialogue and forbid this communication, and that is why we must reject them. —Albert Camus

Sometimes ... we destroy one wall only to build another. It could be an actual wall, or an invisible wall that surrounds the mind. There are walls that tell us not to go any further from where we are, and walls that tell others not to come in. One wall finally collapses, the world looks different, and we breathe a sigh of relief, only to discover that another wall has been erected in another part of the world — a wall of ethnicity, or religion, a wall of intolerance, of fundamentalism, a wall of greed, a wall of fear. Are we unable to live without a system of walls? —Haruki Murakami

Few people are capable of expressing with equanimity opinions which differ from the prejudices of their social environment. Most people are even incapable of forming such opinions. —Albert Einstein

WE ARE A SINGLE SPECIES, YET DIVIDED AND HOSTILE TOWARD SUBSETS OF ourselves. We share a common fate, yet we segregate, discriminate and build walls to keep each other out. We love and dream, grow angry and frightened, laugh and cry in similar ways, yet we slaughter each other without compunction over petty differences. We are a single human family, yet we denigrate and pre-judge each other based on race, ethnicity, gender, sexual orientation, religion, social class, disability, political beliefs, appearance, family background and thousand similar distinctions.

What is worse, we use these differences to support nonsensical views about each other and justify treating each other unfairly, even to the point of murder and genocide. All of this we have made up and fashioned into cruel fantasies and corrupt imaginings, fueled by competition for scarce and valued resources, and driven by anger, fear, greed, guilt and pain.

Over the course of millennia, we have rationalized the cruelest and most despicable acts toward those who are different, those we dislike or distrust, and we have suppressed and oppressed them, denying them freedom, dignity and the fruits of their labor. We have imagined ourselves a virtuous "Us" in unending battle with an evil "Them," and failed to realize that *there is no "Them,"* there is only us.

THE SOURCES AND NATURE OF PREJUDICE

Prejudice is global and human, and can be found in nearly every culture. We can spot its telltale traces in every conflict, in the ways we stereotype and pre-judge our opponents, in the words we use to describe them, in the punishments we allow ourselves to inflict on them. Historically, prejudice is a kind of original sin that is deeply engrained in our psyches. It is perhaps our longest lasting, deepest, least resolved and most chronic source of social, economic and political conflict -- impacting our species as a whole.

Prejudice can be obvious or subtle, covert or overt, blatant or disguised. It operates both consciously and subconsciously, interpersonally and systemically, and extends not only to races, genders, religions and nationalities, but to physical appearances and abilities, political beliefs, geographical locations, family backgrounds and personalities, as well as to novel ideas, unpopular beliefs, "foreign" cultures, "difficult" personalities and eccentric behaviors, even to nature and "inferior" species.

Prejudice is painful and debilitating, yet awareness of its personal and social costs, its sources and the exact nature of its methods can bring an extraordinary richness and complexity of insight and a wide range of possible responses — not only to those who are victims of discrimination, but to those who practice it, those who try to ignore it, and those who are impacted by the countless conflicts it generates.

We are all complicit in prejudice, bias and discrimination. Every demeaning comment, put-down and personal insult, merely by being expressed in terms of some negative trait or characteristic, contains the possibility that it will be generalized as an *attitude* and applied to others, including ourselves. In this way, prejudice is implicit in nearly every conflict — sometimes consisting simply of an inchoate, unformed, subtle and subconscious state of mind — yet one that can immediately be recognized, expand swiftly and assume a far-reaching odious and hateful expression. Many recent neurophysiological studies have revealed how widespread racial prejudices are; how they are present even among minorities and people who strongly oppose prejudice; how they are triggered quickly and subconsciously; how they become systemic; and how they easily translate into a willingness to think badly about others, and even harm them. These studies undermine popular ideas about prejudice and discrimination, and help explain why it is sometimes so difficult to recognize and oppose. The first step in doing so is to identify the unconscious and systemic levels on which prejudice operates and the steps needed to distinguish and dismantle it.

How Stereotyping and Prejudice Work

Prejudice occurs and needs to be overcome on at least three levels. First, we need to confront it *personally*, as individuals who are not immune from subconscious biases, bigotries, stereotypes and judgments that can crop up in our own lives and interpersonal conflicts. Second, we need to respond to it *professionally*, as mediators, facilitators, conflict resolvers and those who work with people who harbor prejudices against others. Third, we need to overcome it *systemically*, not just in individuals, families and organizations, but socially, economically and politically — i.e., as citizens who appreciate its strategic importance in blocking our ability to collaborate successfully and solve problems democratically.

Prejudice is not always overt, simple, intentional, grossly repulsive or obvious. It can also be subtle, complex, unintentional, ostensibly benign, and operate well below the level of conscious attention. It can be found in insults, judgments, caricatures and stereotypes, but it can also be recognized in refusals to listen or communicate, in stories of demonization and victimization, in an inability to empathize and commiserate with others, in nearly unnoticeable "micro" acts of disrespect and inhumanity, and in the "color blindness" of procedurally democratic organizations, institutions and systems.

Prejudice often lies hidden beneath distrust, poor self-esteem, personal selfishness and hostile, conflicted relationships. It is present, though rarely recognized, in bullying and aggressive behaviors, and is often camouflaged by ego compensations, as it is by one-sided calls for neutrality, patronizing appeals for tolerance, and self-righteous proclamations of opposition to prejudice. It is expressed through contempt, disregard and domination, as well as through cursory politeness, showy displays of liberality and feigned objectivity.

Prejudice is a heuristic or shortcut, a simplifier that frequently operates by means of stereotyping, by which others are lumped together and found wanting. In general, we can break the process of stereotyping down into eight key steps:

1. Pick a characteristic
2. Blow it out of proportion
3. Collapse the person into the characteristic
4. Ignore individual differences and variations
5. Disregard subtleties and complexities
6. Overlook commonalities
7. Match it to your own worst fears
8. Make it cruel

What is useful about this list is that if these eight steps can *create* a stereotype, they can be reversed to *undo* it; for example, by revealing that people are more complex than their stereotype permits, or distinguishing unique individuals within a group, or recognizing the commonalities that exist between people, or engaging in acts of kindness toward others.

Most importantly, it becomes possible to communicate honestly and empathetically about stereotyping and engage in dialogues that encourage people to understand and appreciate their differences and at the same time empathize with others. As Umberto Eco accurately pointed out, "Trying to understand other people means destroying the stereotype without denying or ignoring the otherness."

It helps in doing so if we acknowledge that everyone forms prejudices; that stereotyping is a common element in all conflict communications; that it shapes the stories we tell about our opponents and ourselves; that everyone can learn to overcome prejudices and stereotyping through awareness, empathy and open communication; that everyone can become more skillful in communicating across stereotypes and the subtle lines of separation created by our fear of differences; and that doing so requires us to dismantle what gives rise to them at a deep, subconscious level in our hearts and minds, or systems and institutions.

It helps if we can appreciate that the differences between individuals are nearly always vastly greater than the differences between races, even when appearances suggest otherwise. Siddhartha Mukherjee, for example, summarizing numerous scientific studies that reject genetic justifications for racial discrimination, writes in his book *Gene*:

> The most recent estimates suggest that the vast proportion of genetic diversity (85–90 percent) occurs *within* so-called races (i.e., within Asians or Africans) and only a minor proportion (7 percent) *between* racial groups ... [Emphasis added]

It also helps, in beginning a dialogue or conversation about stereotyping, to ask each person to reflect on how *they* have been stereotyped — perhaps in their family of origin, school or marriage; perhaps in their workplace or profession; perhaps because of what they look like, or how much they earn, or their religious affiliation or non-affiliation, or their views on hot political topics. It then becomes possible for each of us to recognize and appreciate what it feels like to be stereotyped and perhaps better understand what it might feel like to have that experience every day, for decades.

How to Oppose Prejudice Without Recreating It

It is easy to miss the subtle, subversive power of prejudice, sometimes simply by becoming prejudiced against those who are prejudiced, allowing the elusive algorithm of bias to replicate itself. Our goal should therefore be to design constructive, interest-based ways of responding to stereotypes and prejudices that do not stereotype or pre-judge — or castigate, or blame, or point fingers at those who are honest enough to recognize their prejudicial attitudes. It is important to do so because shaming and blaming merely trigger defensiveness, denial, dishonesty and counterattack, which delay and sidetrack our efforts to openly and honestly address the problem.

Instead, our aim should be to defuse prejudice by assisting those in its grip (including ourselves) to:

1. Develop a knowledgeable, confident self-identity and appreciate who they are without needing to feel superior to others
2. Experience comfortable, empathetic interactions with diverse people and ideas
3. Be curious and unafraid of learning about differences and commonalities
4. Feel comfortable collaboratively solving problems and negotiating differences
5. Be aware of biases, stereotypes and discrimination when they occur
6. Stand up for themselves and others in the face of prejudice without becoming biased in turn
7. Experience diverse affectionate relationships that grow stronger as a result of differences

Based on years of experience working on these issues in countless mediations, dialogues, collaborative negotiations, prejudice reduction workshops and other interest-based practices, there are hundreds of effective ways of confronting prejudice, bias and discrimination constructively that allow us to alter and amend, not only the overt statements and discriminatory behaviors that convey it, but the hidden, covert places in people's hearts and minds where it lies buried and camouflaged.

To begin with, we can acknowledge and speak openly about our own prejudices, how we have struggled to overcome them and what it feels like when others act prejudicially toward us. When confronting other people's prejudicial statements, we can do so in a number of interest-based ways. For example, we can:

- Bring awareness to our own emotional responses and calm ourselves before speaking, so as to encourage listening and not prompt counter-attacks, denials and purely defensive responses

- Acknowledge and speak openly about our own prejudices, how we struggled to overcome them, what we learned from them and how we can achieve better outcomes by working through them
- Assume each other's good intentions
- Try to understand exactly where the prejudice came from; for example, from fear, anger, pain, grief, poor self-esteem, family history, unresolved conflicts or other emotions and experiences
- Ask for permission to offer feedback — if it is denied, ask what the likely results or consequences will be of not discussing the issue openly and constructively, or what is needed to do so
- Discuss the statement directly, one-on-one, privately and honestly, in non-threatening, low-key and non-aggressive ways
- Don't shame, blame, attack or accuse; instead, be friendly and accepting, yet assertive and clear
- Be hard on the problem and soft on the person
- Ask if the effect you created was the one you intended
- Ask them if *they* ever felt discriminated against or harassed themselves for any reason and listen to their stories, noticing commonalities
- Indicate yourself what it feels like to experience or overcome prejudice, using "I" statements and personal stories to help them listen and learn
- Try to assess the costs of prejudice, offering examples from personal experience and research
- Suggest alternative phraseology, approaches or perspectives
- State your disagreements openly, empathetically and honestly
- Suggest bringing in a third party to help discuss, facilitate a dialogue or mediate the issues
- Ask questions and listen to responses, model empathy and compassion, and recognize that among the prejudices that need to be overcome are those directed against people who are prejudiced
- Ask for feedback on your feedback and try to improve next time

INTEREST-BASED APPROACHES TO CULTURAL DIVERSITY

Diversity is a rich source of innovation, creative solutions to complex problems and unique ways of adapting to changing environments, yet it is disappearing — not only genetically, but culturally as well, as local isolation gives way to homogenizing global interactions and relationships. It is therefore essential that we find ways of benefiting from diversity by reducing cultural stereotyping, prejudice and discrimination, and learning to collaborate more effectively in searching for richer, more diverse solutions to transnational problems. To do so, we need to appreciate the importance of diversity, improve the methods and techniques we use to resolve cross-cultural differences and discover ways of applying them on both small- and large-scales.

To begin with, we can recognize and appreciate the ways that culture offers diverse ways for people to learn from and live in the world. It helps people define what is possible, how to meet their needs, what they imagine and dream about, how they communicate and relate to one another, why they do what they do, what they permit and prohibit, how they respond to change, how they resolve their conflicts and how they relate to those who are different.

In this sense, every individual, couple and family, every group, organization and nation produces culture. Culture both shapes and reflects what and how we see and understand, think and feel, and how we attribute meaning to words, acts and events. For this reason, whatever conflicts with our culturally defined assumptions and expectations limits what we are able to perceive and appreciate, blocking us from learning from what feels foreign or unimaginable, even inside ourselves, triggering resistance to diversity, dissent and dialogue.

As a result, most cultures implicitly assume they are superior to others and their ways are "right" or "better," yet there is no absolute scale by which one set of cultural values can be judged better than others, except according to some standard that is itself a product of culture.

This does not mean that all cultures are equally effective or successful, or accurately represent the views of all their members, or able to adapt to new conditions, or good at solving problems, or that there is no such thing as cultural learning, progress and evolution; or that all cultural practices are sacrosanct, beyond criticism, eternal and incapable of being improved. It is possible to avoid the twin problems of "cultural relativism" and "cultural imperialism" by using interest-based processes that respect cultural diversity while encouraging cross-cultural learning, democracy and evolution.

Moreover, cultures also consist of values, and values change over time. Once a given value gains recognition within a culture, it can become a benchmark to judge other cultures, especially those with opposing or contrasting values. All cultures "socialize" their members, teaching them "the rules" and pressuring them to conform by rewarding compliance and punishing deviance, dissent and disobedience. By doing so, culture itself can become an obstacle to recognizing and respecting its own *internal* subcultures, prohibiting not only destructive behaviors, but internal diversity, dissent and dialogue, along with potentially useful ideas, approaches, adaptations and improvements. As Emile Durkheim recognized in connection with religious cultures, "The sacred is what is protected by prohibitions."

Yet these same prohibitions, condemnations and pressures to conform can easily be extended to people in entirely different cultures, conditions and historical circumstances. Indeed, most cultures encourage prejudices and prohibitions of various kinds and tolerate discrimination even against their own members, as a method for ensuring conformity through social pressure. These prejudices are expressed through ridicule, jokes, insults, stereotypes and discriminatory put-downs that end in conformity or ostracism, reduced status and a shrunken capacity for empathy that can easily spill over into chauvinism and genocidal violence.

People in every culture want to be accepted, respected, listened to, acknowledged and seen for who they are, yet at the same time, can easily be drawn into denigrating and disparaging others, especially when they themselves are newly arrived, or somewhat different, or want to improve their status by climbing over others, or are frightened they might be treated similarly.

Among the devices used by cultures to teach, socialize and unify their members are stereotypes and archetypes, myths about heroes or villains, stories about conflict, parables about behaviors and their consequences, metaphors for processing information, judgments for defining self and others, and ready-made "scripts" for all occasions that increase unity, but often at the cost of empathy and understanding. As a result, the stock villains of these pieces are commonly loosely disguised members of other cultures or internal dissenters, whose differences are feared and hated, rather than learned from and admired.

We usually define our own culture by contrasting or differentiating it from other cultures. The greater the differences, the more defined the culture. Yet differences can, through the catalyst of conflict, combine with fear, greed, anger, pain and other uncomfortable emotions, triggering misunderstandings, stereotypes, hostility, discrimination and chronic cross-cultural conflicts. As a result, our tolerance of dissimilarity decreases as the magnitude and emotionality of our differences and disagreements increase. Every culture must therefore develop techniques for responding to conflicts and mediating differences, but often without transforming the stereotypes and prejudices that created them, and linger hidden beneath the surface to emerge full-blown in future disagreements.

In this sense, it is possible to regard *all* conflicts as cross-cultural. Cultural conflicts can easily occur, for example, between those who are precise and those who are ambiguous in their communications, those who are open or closed in personal revelations, those who are formal or informal in processes, those who are demonstrative or restrained in emotional expression. Repeated behaviors of any kind in any group, no matter how small, can lead to the creation of subcultures, including *cultures of conflict* that reflect the diverse ways people interpret and respond to disagreements, as for example, with avoidance or accommodation, defensiveness or listening, ridicule or appreciation, counter-accusation or apology, isolation or collaboration. These cultures of conflict specify which behavioral responses to conflict are acceptable or unacceptable, and which methods and approaches are permissible in seeking to settle or resolve them.

Culture and Context

While all cultures assist people in ascribing meaning to events and communications, especially those that involve differences or conflict, these cultural elements often go unrecognized. The eminent cultural anthropologist Edward T. Hall, for example, wrote in *The Dance of Life* that some cultures are fixed and closed while others are fluid and open, especially in their attitudes toward space and time, but also in their approaches to conflict.

Hall distinguished "high-context" from "low-context" cultures, which differ in the importance of context in ascribing meaning. In high-context cultures, especially those that are fluid and open, such as collaboration, democracy and emotionally intimate relationships — i.e., interest-based cultures — most of the meaning emerges from context. In low-context cultures, on the other hand, especially those that are fixed and closed, such as competition, autocracy and emotionally distant relationships — i.e., power- and rights-based cultures — most, if not all of the meaning is expressed in the precise words that are used and context is less important, often because the context itself is producing conflicting meanings.

It is possible to go further and note that prejudice, stereotyping and discrimination operate precisely by *minimizing* context, which otherwise invite more nuanced understandings of diversity and difference, increasing our capacity for empathy, intimacy and understanding. Additionally, more advanced skills and a capacity to read context and culture are essential if differences in race, gender, sexual orientation, social status, economic wealth and political power are to be understood and addressed *systemically*, rather than being seen simply as personal failures.

Hence, cultures that include dissimilar races, genders, religions and political views require higher levels of skill, not only in understanding the meaning of conflict communications, but boosting empathy between their members and reducing chronic and systemic disputes through interest-based interventions; whereas cultures that are based on domination and discrimination or power- and rights-based approaches rely on simple stereotypes and pre-judgments that block empathy and therefore require little or no skill, systemic awareness or ability to read context or complex information in order to interpret.

This permits people, for example, to uphold the principle of formal or legal equality while ignoring the prevalence and persistence of actual discrimination, which requires both empathy, and historical and social context to understand, thereby generating chronic conflicts, for example, between supporters and detractors of affirmative action programs.

Indeed, nearly all social, economic and political conflicts *appear* purely personal, as adversarial communications nearly always take a private, subjective and emotional form, yet are actually grounded in much deeper systems, as well as in implicit, unspoken cultural contexts, including histories, perceptions, assumptions and expectations, as well as myths, archetypes and stories that reveal hidden fears, desires and biases.

It is often difficult to notice these larger systems and contexts, partly because they operate in the background, or are eclipsed by intense emotions, or are conflated and reduced to personalities, or are dangerous to confront, or seem secondary and inessential. Yet it is these unaddressed systems and contexts that permit prejudice and discrimination to replicate, and like embers, burst into flames long after their fires seem to have been put out.

CLARIFYING THE CONTEXT IN CROSS-CULTURAL CONFLICTS

In facilitating dialogues over prejudice and mediating cross-cultural conflicts, we have discovered that it is possible to significantly increase empathy, reduce stereotyping and prejudice, and acknowledge cross-cultural differences by clarifying the contexts in which they arise, engaging in courageous conversations regarding differences, collaboratively negotiating solutions and making cultural perceptions, assumptions and expectations explicit, variable and negotiable.

We can, for instance, design dialogues and conflict conversations in which we ask people from diverse cultures, including couples, families, communities, groups and organizations to:

- Describe the history, sources and positive aspects of their culture
- Talk about how various kinds of conflict, or diversity or change are handled in their culture
- Discuss how cultural styles of communication, negotiation and conflict resolution impact their attitudes, feelings and relationships
- Meet in same or cross-cultural groups, compare cultural styles and list ways they might work together to find joint solutions, or negotiate more collaboratively by appreciating their differences
- Describe the role of context in their culture, or tell stories that illustrate the way problems are solved or conflicts are handled and relate that information to the issues that require resolution
- Identify what they would like to eliminate, change or add to their culture to strengthen its positive aspects
- Clarify the meaning in their culture of recurrent behaviors, such as silence, criticism, anger, apathy, prejudice and conflict
- Analyze how communications, negotiations and conflicts are handled in relation, for example, to:
- Expressions of emotion and personal sharing
- Aggressiveness and collaboration

- Communication of priorities, interests and "bottom lines"
- Compromises and concessions
- Admission of errors or mistakes
- Techniques for overcoming impasse
- Rituals of release, completion and closure
- Methods of forgiveness and reconciliation
- Changing systems and improving culture
- Ask still deeper questions, like what their goals are for this conversation, or what role they would like the mediator or facilitator to play, or what would help them have a really useful conversation, or how success and failure are defined in their culture, or how people in their culture go about forgiving each other and opening their hearts again

SOME QUESTIONS ON LABELING AND LANGUAGE

In addition to these questions, it is possible to interrupt cross-cultural dialogues and conflict conversations in which people are labeling one another, or using language in hostile or adversarial ways, by asking questions that direct their attention to the subconscious choices they made about the ways they describe each other, and to consider alternative ways of speaking that can transform their communications and relationships. Here are some examples:

1. What words would you use to describe your opponent?
2. Have you ever encountered anyone else in your life who matched those words?
3. When was the first time you experienced that kind of person? Who was it? What happened?
4. Do you see any connection between that earlier experience and what happened with the other person in this conflict?
5. What words would you most *like* to use to describe the other person?

6. What words would you use to describe what the other person *did*?

7. Have you ever encountered any behaviors in your life that matched those words?

8. When was the first time you experienced that kind of behavior? Who was it? What happened?

9. Do you see any connection between that earlier experience and the other person's behaviors in this conflict?

10. What words would you *like* to use to describe the other person's behavior?

11. What words would you use to describe yourself, your feelings and your responses to her/him?

12. What words would you *like* to be able to use to describe yourself and your responses to him/her?

13. What might you be able to do to help make those words become real? What could the other person do to support you?

20 Small Group Exercises for Dialogues on Culture and Conflict

In addition to these, a number of exercises and interventions have been invented, discovered, explored and improved by dialogue facilitators, diversity consultants, collaborative negotiators, mediators and other conflict resolvers to help people in small groups bridge the gaps that routinely arise as a result of stereotyping, prejudicial communications, encounters with bias or discrimination and cross-cultural conflicts. Here are twenty I find especially useful:

1. Ask people what they expect of the process, or who they think you are and what they would like you to say or do, or *not* say or do

2. Ask them to list the *positive* words that describe the other culture, and alongside them, the positive words that describe

their own, then exchange lists and compare them, pointing out similarities and differences in each side's perceptions

3. Consider conducting the same exercise, except more dangerously by eliciting the negative words and stereotypes that describe their *own* culture, then searching for neutral or positive words to reframe them

4. Elicit a hierarchy of conflicts by identifying which are most serious and which are least, compare similarities and differences, then do the same with conflict styles

5. Ask them to numerically rank the options for resolution available in their culture from war to surrender, elaborate those that lie in the middle and explore the reasons for choosing collaborative approaches

6. Ask them to state, pantomime, role-play, draw or script how conflicts are commonly handled in their cultures

7. Jointly design a consensus-based model for joint conflict prevention, resolution, transformation, learning and transcendence

8. Co-mediate in culturally diverse teams and invite each party or group to suggest someone from their culture who will act as a process observer and reflect or intervene if the process gets off track

9. Establish common backgrounds, points of reference and values for the process, for example, regarding the importance of cooperation, family, face, friendship and education, then connect these to conflict resolution

10. Ask questions like: "What does that mean to you?" Or, "What does the phrase 'good neighbor' (or some other word or phrase) mean in your culture?" Then list agreed-upon meanings for comparison or subsequent reference

11. Surface, acknowledge and model respect for cultural differences by asking people if they are proud of their culture. If so, ask why and of what; if not, also ask why and of what, then seek to reframe their concerns as expressions of caring and a desire for improvement

12. Or, more dangerously, ask if there is anything they dislike, are embarrassed about, or disapprove of in their own culture, why they feel that way, and again be prepared to reframe their responses

13. Ask them to describe the three most important lessons they have learned from their culture, who taught them and why they were important

14. Ask them to bring photographs or artifacts from their families, the homes they grew up in, or themselves as children, share these with each other and describe a crucible event that helped make them who they are today

15. Ask them to describe the most common stereotypes about their culture, say whether they think it applies to them (or to other people) and why, or, if not, why not. Discuss stereotyping and its emotional impact

16. Ask each person to list the main characteristics of heroes, victims, villains, mediators and others in their culture, then compare and contrast them, and apply them to the roles they are playing in their conflict

17. Ask them to write about their conflict in the form of a story or fable using neutral names and a third-person voice, for example, starting with "Once upon a time …" and ending with "… and they all lived happily ever after," then read their stories out loud to each other and discuss

18. As a mediator, facilitator or third party to their dispute, describe your own culture, list the stereotypes you and others have of it, or the stereotypes you were taught about other cultures and how you discovered they were inaccurate

19. Create a larger sense of culture by asking them what it contributes to their lives and those in their community, and what would be missed if it disappeared

20. Ask each person to bring a song, dance, poem, ritual, work of art, food, etc. from their culture to share at the next session, break bread together, then mediate and celebrate these cultural gifts together

While these techniques are useful in reducing stereotyping and prejudice in interpersonal cross-cultural disputes, they are sometimes less successful when the source of conflict is on a larger scale; or chronic and systemic; or when it flows from a prolonged history of socially sanctioned, economically reinforced, politically legitimized discriminatory practices; or where it is reinforced by on-going social inequality, economic inequity and political autocracy.

Systemic forms of discrimination such as "institutional racism," do not require or rely on personal prejudice, crude stereotyping or open expressions of bias. Instead, they imperceptibly and implicitly link values of unity, conformity and sameness with prejudice, bias and discrimination, often in order to maintain domination and control by privileged elites and reinforce social segregation based on status, wealth and power.

The *deepest* roots of prejudice and discrimination lie less in individual malice and personal spite than in social, economic and political systems and historical hatreds that are invigorated by inequality, inequity and autocracy. These lead to chronic conflicts that encourage a progression in aspirations from minority rights to nationalism, self-determination and collaborative partnerships, as stages of opposition to discriminatory treatment. (For more, see discussion in my book *Conflict Revolution: Designing Preventative Systems for Chronic Social, Economic and Political Conflicts* [Second Edition.])

40 QUESTIONS FOR DIALOGUES ABOUT PREJUDICE

Open and honest dialogues, especially when they are designed in ways that maximize the use of creative interventions, interest-based techniques and small group exercises, can assist people in becoming more aware of personal and systemic biases, and realize that differences are a source of creativity and celebration. These dialogues encourage pride in one's culture or background without denigrating anyone else's right to feel pride in theirs. They use storytelling to elicit empathy and person-to-person understanding, and group presentations to promote mutual learning. Specific conflicts can then be analyzed through simulations and role-plays, and alternative solutions generated through joint analysis of group experiences.

To facilitate these dialogues, I use the following 40 questions, which can be used either in large or small groups to design interactions and structure communications around prejudice, discrimination and cross-cultural conflict:

A. Questions About the Process:

1. What are your expectations regarding the conversation we are about to have about prejudice? What do you think is likely to happen? Why? Is that what you would like to happen? What kind of conversation about prejudice would you most like to have? Why? What do we need to do in order to have it?
2. What do the words "prejudice" and "discrimination" mean to you? What reactions do they trigger for you? What are your immediate, visceral, emotional and intellectual responses to them?
3. What do the words "race," "ethnicity," "gender," "sexual orientation," "religion," "social class" "disability" and "political beliefs" mean to you? What reactions do they trigger for you? What immediately comes up for you when you hear them? What do you feel like doing when you hear them?
4. What negative words, experiences, emotions and ideas do you associate with these words? What positive words, experiences, emotions and ideas do you associate with them?
5. How do stereotyping, prejudice and discrimination actually work? Could our ideas and feelings about prejudice, and our expectations about discussing them, *themselves* create a kind of prejudice? How? What could we do in our conversation to make sure that doesn't happen?
6. Do you believe there is value in talking together about these

words, experiences and idea? Why? What can we do to make our conversation useful?

B. Questions About Background:

1. When you were growing up, what was the nature of your family of origin, in terms of race/ethnicity/gender/sexual orientation/religion/social class/disability/political beliefs? How has your family changed?
2. What were the attitudes in your family toward people who were different in terms of race/ethnicity/gender/sexual orientation/religion/social class/disability/political beliefs?
3. How were race/ethnicity/gender/sexual orientation/religion/social class/disability/political beliefs spoken about in your family? How much room was there for diversity?
4. What did your family members say and do when confronted with stereotyping, prejudice or discrimination?
5. When did you first become aware of race/ethnicity/gender/sexual orientation/religion/social class/disability/political beliefs? How? What lessons did you learn from that experience?
6. What kind of neighborhood did you grow up in, in terms of race/ethnicity/gender/sexual orientation/religion/social class/ disability/political beliefs? What kind of mix or diversity was there in your neighborhood or community? What experiences did you personally have with prejudice or discrimination?
7. What kind of school did you attend, in terms of race/ethnicity/gender/sexual orientation/ religion/social class/ disability/political beliefs?
8. How many of your classmates, teachers or school administrators were from races/ethnicities/genders/sexual orientations/religions/social classes/disability/political beliefs different from yours?

9. What lessons did you learn in school about prejudice and discrimination, from classmates, teachers, administrators and others?

10. How were people who were different, in terms of race/ethnicity/gender/sexual orientation/ religion/social class/ disability/political beliefs, treated by police, courts, government, corporations, in your community?

C. Questions About Identity and Stereotyping:

1. How do you identify yourself, in terms of race/ethnicity/gender/sexual orientation/religion/social class/disability/political beliefs?

2. What, for you, creates that identity?

3. What do you think is the role of media in creating or distorting identity, and in stereotyping, discrimination and prejudice?

4. What are you most proud of about your race/ethnicity/gender/sexual orientation/ religion/social class/disability/political beliefs?

5. Is there anything you or member of your family do to declare, celebrate or acknowledge your identity? If so, what?

6. Is there anything you are ashamed of or embarrassed about regarding your race/ethnicity/gender/sexual orientation/religion/social class/ disability/political beliefs? Why? Where do you think that came from?

7. Have you ever felt like an outsider, a minority, stereotyped, discriminated against, or not seen for who you really are, for *any* reason? When? What happened? How did it feel?

8. Have you ever been an insider, part of a majority, dominating or discriminating against others, whether in school or a neighborhood or family or workplace? When? How did that feel?

9. What are the stereotypes you think others have of your race/ethnicity/gender/sexual orientation/ religion/social class/ disability/political beliefs? What is inaccurate about

those stereotypes? What would you most like them to know about you, and what it is like to be a part of your group?

10. What questions do you have to those in other groups, that you have always wanted to ask, but been afraid or embarrassed to ask?

D. Questions About Experiencing Prejudice:

1. What is the worst thing other people have said or done toward the race/ethnicity/gender/sexual orientation/religion/social class/ disability/political beliefs you identify with? What would you like to say to them about how it feels? What is one stereotype, prejudicial statement or discriminatory action you never ever want to hear or experience again?

2. Have you experienced prejudice or discrimination at work? Socially? What happened? How did it feel? How was it responded to or handled by others? By you? How could it have been handled better?

3. Have you observed or experienced prejudice or discrimination elsewhere in society, in corporations, governments, religions, law enforcement, media or other places? What is an example? How was it expressed?

4. Have you observed or experienced prejudice and discrimination as systemic, or reinforced and maintained by silence? Can you think of examples from current events reported in the media? How does politics influence prejudice and discrimination?

5. Have you ever had a prejudice or engage in discrimination against others? What led you to do that? How did it feel? Did you overcome it, and if so, how?

6. Do you feel you have any prejudices now? What are they? Are you doing anything to overcome them? Would you be willing to hear from others in the group about how you might do that?

7. If you met the person you have prejudices about and had some time to talk, what would you be curious about? What

questions would you want to ask them? What would you want him or her to know about you? What changes in their behavior would you want to request? What changes do you think they might want to request of you?

E. Questions About Responding to Prejudice:

1. What do you think keeps people from speaking up about discrimination? In being effective when they do speak up? What might be done to encourage them?

2. What do people generally do when they experience prejudicial or discriminatory statements or acts by others? What do you do? Is what you or they do effective in stopping the prejudice or discrimination? Why / why not? How do people respond when they are confronted? Is their response useful in

3. Have you done anything yourself to reduce prejudice or discrimination? Have you ever stood up for someone who was being treated prejudicially or spoken about stereotypically? What led you to do that? Have you ever confronted other people for their prejudicial or discriminatory acts or statements? How did it feel? How did the other person feel? What happened? What did you learn from that experience? In hindsight, what do you think you might have done better?

4. What is most difficult for you in responding to prejudicial acts and statements? What do you feel is most difficult for others? What do you think each of us might do better?

5. Imagine that I just made a stereotypical or prejudicial statement, or one that feels hurtful to you or others. How would you respond? Other ideas? What would you want to communicate to me? What do you think would be most effective in changing my attitude and behavior?

6. Is it possible to be prejudiced against people who are prejudiced? How? How might we respond to them in ways that don't make them avoidant, defensive or angry; and don't make us judgmental, self-righteous or uncaring?

7. What can each of us do to reduce prejudice and discrimination in our families, neighborhoods, schools, workplaces, organizations, media and institutions? What are some things we can do together? What support do you and all of us need in order to take those steps?

With these questions and techniques, along with others that have been practiced by mediators, dialogue facilitators, bias and prejudice professionals and conflict resolvers for several decades, we have enough to begin designing the difficult, often dangerous dialogues and courageous conversations that are needed to free us from suppressed resentments and defenses, unspoken angers and fears, and needlessly hostile and destructive conflicts, by teaching us how to speak to each other directly, openly, honestly and from the heart about sensitive personal and political issues; how to encourage empathy and caring; and how to help us work collaboratively to solve our common problems, develop the skills and capacities we need to reduce stereotyping, prejudice and discrimination, and create a better life for all.

IMAGINING INTEREST-BASED SOLUTIONS TO GLOBAL CONFLICTS

Man's capacity for justice makes democracy possible, but man's inclination to injustice makes democracy necessary. —Reinhold Niebuhr

People talk loud and long, in order to say as little as possible. The really true and interesting things are the intrigues in the background, about which not a word is mentioned. —Franz Kafka

Any real change implies the breakup of the world as one has always known it, the loss of all that gave one identity. —James Baldwin

Everything is theoretically impossible, until it is done. —Robert Heinlein

SEVEN

RETHINKING MIGRATION: DESIGNING DIALOGUES FOR IMMIGRANTS AND CITIZENS

The comfortable people in tight houses felt pity at first, and then distaste, and finally hatred for the migrant people. — John Steinbeck

In this world, shipmates, sin that pays its way can travel freely, and without passport, whereas Virtue, if a pauper, is stopped at all frontiers. —Herman Melville

We know that there is no help for us but from one another, that no hand will save us if we do not reach out our hand. And the hand that you reach out is empty, as mine is. You have nothing. You possess nothing. You own nothing. You are free. All you have is what you are, and what you give. —Ursula K. Le Guin

PEOPLE AROUND THE WORLD ARE ON THE MOVE, SEARCHING FOR BETTER lives, largely as a result of wars, natural disasters, climate change, economic crises, political repression and racial and religious intolerance. As a result, immigration related political conflicts have increased, along with hatred, prejudice and potentially genocidal forms of violence, fracturing once stable communities and alliances, escalating unrest and bringing misery and suffering to many.

As global problems extend their reach and increase in importance and severity, it is essential for us to discover better ways of responding to contentious social, economic and political issues, and come together across the political borders we created to keep others out, in order to listen, ask questions, discuss problems, understand each other, search for solutions and act together to implement them. It is essential that we build bridges rather than walls, and not allow ourselves to become silent or passive as difficult, dangerous and polarizing events drag us into their downward logic.

Perhaps the most divisive and important of these issues is immigration, which has become a wedge issue for ultra-right and neo-Nazi organizations. The unimaginable is now stirring, and we are moving toward a watershed in world events, a crossroads where values and ethics, democracy and human rights are put to a very real test, leading to increases either in hatred, violence and war; or dialogue, empathy and collaboration. The outcome depends largely on us.

Trends in Global Migration

A 2016 study by the U.N. High Commission on Refugees (UNHCR) found that migration has increased significantly in recent years, primarily as a result of wars, terrorism, poverty, political corruption, repressive governments and climate change. In 2017, UNHCR revealed that 65.6 million people worldwide had been forcibly displaced, a number roughly equivalent to the population of France, or enough to populate an entire nation. Of these, only 189,300 were resettled. In a single day in 2016, an average of 33,972 people fled their homes due to conflict or persecution.

The U.N. separates migrants into three legal categories, with a fourth reserved for those without nationality:

1. *Refugees*: According to the U.N., a refugee is defined as "an individual who has been forced to leave his/her country in order to escape war, persecution or natural disaster." About 22.5 million people were forced to flee their homes in 2016 to find safety, security or shelter, over half of whom were under the age of 18.

2. *Internally displaced persons*: In 2016, 40.8 million people were uprooted from their communities, fled their homes and sought refuge in another part of their own country. Some were displaced multiple times, nearly always because of wars, persecutions, natural disasters or famine.

3. *Asylum-seekers:* Also in 2016, 3.2 million people actively sought asylum in other nations, most often for political reasons and a desire to be protected by a foreign government.

4. *Stateless Individuals:* In addition, there were more than 10 million stateless people who were denied nationality and access to education, health care, employment and freedom of movement.

More than 55 percent of the world's refugees came from just three countries: Syria (5.5 million), Afghanistan (2.5 million), and Sudan (1.4 million) — all war regions. The top hosting countries for refugees were Turkey (2.9 million), Pakistan (1.4 million), Lebanon (1 million), Iran (979,000), and Uganda (940,000), which took in significantly more refugees than the U.S., Canada and Europe combined.

Eduardo Porter and Karl Russell, writing recently in The New York Times, cited an in-depth study based on surveys in the U.S. and a number of European countries, which found that people everywhere exaggerate their immigrant populations, with the largest overestimates made by the least educated, lowest skilled employees and those on the political right. The numbers of Muslim immigrants and their dependence on welfare were greatly overestimated, while their education and self-sufficiency were underestimated, generating fear and a sense of crisis, along with defensiveness and hostility.

While a relatively small number of migrants have sought refuge in the U.S. and Europe, far greater hostility has been expressed toward them in these countries, spilling over into physical violence, verbal aggression, widespread stereotyping and prejudice, fueled by fears of terrorism, poverty and disease. This hostility has been aggravated by conflicting cultural norms, including attitudes toward women, divergent religious practices, racial biases and general intolerance of outsiders.

These differences have divided communities and increased support for right-wing political parties that favor rejection and expulsion of migrants, triggering increased hostility also against native-born Blacks, Latinos, Jews, Arabs, Roma, and those who offer them hospitality or assistance. In the U.S., the predominant message has been, do *not* send us "your tired, your poor, your huddled masses yearning to breathe free," there is no welcome for you here.

Migration and International Law

There are a number of treaties and provisions in international law that safeguard the rights of migrants and spell out the obligations of nation-states. Article 13 of the *Universal Declaration of Human Rights*, for example, approved by all members of the United Nations, guarantees the freedom of travel:

> (1) Everyone has the right to freedom of movement and residence within the borders of each state.
>
> (2) Everyone has the right to leave any country, including his own, and to return to his country.

While these freedoms are important and deserve widespread protection, they do not expressly include the right to move *across* state borders; or the right to be accepted as an immigrant by other countries; or the right to be treated with kindness and consideration; or the right to hospitality, food and clothing; or the right to live wherever one wishes.

In 1990, the United Nations created the *International Convention on the Protection of the Rights of All Migrant Workers and Members of Their Families*, which offers migrant workers the same rights, benefits and guarantees, including health and safety, overtime pay, holidays, etc. as citizens of the country they are working in. Few countries, however, have signed this agreement, and many strongly oppose migration publicly, while privately welcoming it as a way of reducing wages and finding workers who are willing to perform the least popular, lowest paying tasks. Yet this extension of benefits could conceivably be applied to all migrants, reducing their poverty and altering their perception as impoverished and needing assistance.

There are a number of other rights in international law that are available to asylum seekers who have crossed an international border as refugees, but the 1951 Refugee Convention and international treaties generally do not protect "Internally Displaced Persons" (IDP's), even though they are by far the largest group of migrants. It is officially assumed that internal refugees will be protected by their own governments, yet these same governments are often the primary reason they are leaving.

According to the 1998 *Guiding Principles of Internal Displacement*, states are required to provide basic necessities, such as food, water, shelter, clothing, sanitation and medical services, and to "respect life and dignity," yet routinely deny them and claim sovereignty, both as a justification and a defense against international intervention, even for genocidal acts and the grossest human rights abuses. It is a principle of international law that every state has the discretion to deny entry to non-nationals, and while States are required in theory to recognize international human rights, in practice they have little interest in doing so. Indeed, in 2018 the U. S. withdrew from the U. N. Human Rights Council, which has sought to improve the rights of migrants. Other international laws and legal principles, including the *Universal*

Declaration of Human Rights, Geneva Conventions and the international law of war make it clear that civilians should not be targeted in warfare and that nations have a legal obligation to protect refugees from war, but without a strong and committed United Nations (See Chapter 9), and an interest-based approach to addressing both the reasons people migrate and the problems created by their departure, transit, arrival and assimilation, power- and rights-based solutions will inevitably be resorted to, and also fall short, generating chronic conflicts in their wake.

WHY WE MIGRATE

Conflicts over immigration are increasing in intensity within host countries, while immigrants, many of them children, are drowning, being raped, robbed, starved, killed and forced into slavery. Otherwise welcoming and hospitable citizens in wealthier nations are becoming frightened or angry, and refusing admission, fueling aggressive far-right political movements and sparking hostility even toward native-born citizens who look, speak or act differently.

If we regard these conflicts as concerning not just *immigration*, which suggests hordes of strangers from foreign cultures coming uninvited to live in our homes and neighborhoods, exhaust our resources and reduce our quality of life; but more broadly as *migration*, which suggests an impermanence that typifies most of our lives, we can see that every animate species on the planet, including our own, migrates continually in search of better conditions, and that a variety of conflicts naturally transpire as a result.

Hence, we are *all* migrants, moving about throughout our lives — not just physically or geographically, but mentally, emotionally, spiritually and relationally, gravitating from one set of ideas or beliefs to another, one job to another, one relationship to another, one stage of life to another, experiencing and stirring up conflicts throughout our transit from one domicile to the next.

What would you do if the place where you were born or chose to live turned into a death-camp, or a prison or a desert, or became disease-ridden and infectious? What would you do if staying put meant certain death, if the borders you designed to defend your freedoms turned inward to enslave you? How would you want others to respond if you were the one who was desperate to escape, and forced to beg for food and shelter?

And what if the problems you faced weren't as serious as war or genocide? What if it was grinding poverty, lack of potable water, inadequate medical care, intolerable weather, fires, earthquakes, tsunamis or other catastrophes? What if it was political dictatorship, religious intolerance, racial prejudice, caste restrictions or gender discrimination? What if it was just that you would rather live somewhere else?

Difficult questions arise also if we imagine ourselves as hosts: How many people do we let in? Who do we turn away? Where will they go if everyone rejects them? If we think of nations as analogous to families, how would we respond if they came to our house? Who would we invite to stay with us? For how long? Under what conditions? Who would we cast out? At what cost? And who or what would we become as a result?

The Somali poet Warsan Shire has written eloquently about the reasons we migrate and the experience of being a migrant, and I have included a brief selection from her poem *Home* because of its clarity, intensity and emotional power, and encourage you to read it unabridged (See, e.g., https://genius.com/Warsan-shire-home-annotated):

> *no one leaves home unless*
> *home is the mouth of a shark*
> *you only run for the border*
> *when you see the whole city running as well*
> *your neighbours running faster than you*
> *breath bloody in their throats*

the boy you went to school with
who kissed you dizzy behind the old tin factory
is holding a gun bigger than his body
you only leave home
when home won't let you stay.
... you have to understand,
that no one puts their children in a boat
unless the water is safer than the land
... no one would leave home
unless home chased you to the shore
unless home told you
to quicken your legs
leave your clothes behind
crawl through the desert
wade through the oceans
... i dont know what i've become
but i know that anywhere
is safer than here.

Centuries earlier, in a handwritten passage for an unpublished play, *The Book of Sir Thomas More*, William Shakespeare is reported to have written in similarly moving terms about the plight of migrants, and who we become when we exclude them:

Imagine that you see the wretched strangers,
Their babies at their backs and their poor luggage,
Plodding to th'ports and costs for transportation,
And that you sit as kings in your desires,
... What had you got? I'll tell you. You had taught
How insolence and strong hand should prevail,
How order should be quelled; and by this pattern
Not one of you should live an aged man,
For other ruffians, as their fancies wrought,
With self same hand, self reasons and self right,
Would shark on you, and men like ravenous fishes

Would feed on one another.
… whither would you go?
What country, by the nature of your error,
Should give you harbor? …
Why, you must needs be strangers. Would you be pleased
To find a nation of such barbarous temper,
That, breaking out in hideous violence,
Would not afford you an abode on earth,
Whet their detested knives against your throats,
Spurn you like dogs, and like as if that God
Owed not nor made not you, nor that the claimants
Were not all appropriate to your comforts,
But chartered unto them, what would you think
To be thus used? This is the strangers' case;
And this your mountainish inhumanity.

From these passages and others of equal eloquence, two important points emerge: first, few people leave their homes or countries of origin without some seriously pressing need or weighty reason; and second, any of us might someday find ourselves in a similar position and need to ask ourselves the obvious question: how would we want to be treated if it were us?

Two still deeper considerations emerge when we think about our collective responses to migration: first, by failing to act kindly, openheartedly and humanely toward others, we diminish what is kind, openhearted and humane in ourselves, turning into the opposite of what, at a deep level, we all value, cherish and believe in. Second, hidden beneath our hostile rejection of migrants lies a fear of strangers and a set of subconscious prejudices that also know no borders, but easily and swiftly expand to touch everyone who looks different, who does not belong, who dissents, or who extends a helping hand to others — i.e., to all those who have been discriminated against and picked on throughout history.

It is a simple step to extend hatred, exclusion, selfishness, bigotry and intolerance from immigrants to other races; to Jews, Catholics and Muslims; to Hutus and Tutsis; to women, gays and transgendered people; to Roma or "Gypsies;" to artists and bohemians; to communists and socialists; to those who are old or sick or disabled or poor or homeless; in short, to all "inferior," "sub-human" races, religions, genders, cultures, nationalities, ideas and beliefs; even to those whose physical appearances, social behaviors, personalities, values or ways of living do not fit the norm. To understand how and why this occurs, it is helpful to briefly consider the history of migration.

A Brief History of Migration

Of course, all species migrate and travel, and human beings are no exception. There is ample evidence over the course of many millennia that people have always migrated in search for food, safety and better places to live; that they have picked up stakes whenever they wanted, or were forced to, and searched for other lands where they could settle, beginning even before the first exodus from Africa hundreds of thousands of years ago.

In this sense, the history of the human race can be regarded as a history of migration, on the one hand mingling incredible acts of kindness toward strangers with a pervasive morality comprised of generosity, hospitality, peacemaking and cooperation; while on the other hand, combining countless acts of genocidal violence and implacable hatred of others with an equally pervasive amorality comprised of selfishness, xenophobia, war and greed.

In the beginning, human populations were mostly nomadic, following herds and searching for seasonal plants, much as the rest of animate life. With the rise of agriculture and domestication of animals, people began settling in one place and cities were formed, offering preferential rights and privileges to residents, amassing wealth, accumulating weapons, and building walls to defend themselves against foreigners, interlopers, bandits and outcasts, who increasingly used force to loot and plunder the accumulated riches and resources of others.

With war and conquest, these riches and resources began to assume the form of human property, or slavery, along with rape and tribute, and a need to manufacture weapons to defend fields and grazing lands, safeguard stockpiles of surplus wealth, and conquer other lands. Slavery and large-scale agriculture reinforced the need for permanent, professional armies and private militias, along with clearly defined territories and walls, borders and guards, and a consequent fear and suspicion of strangers who might wish to do the same to them.

First city-states, then regional alliances, then nation-states were formed; in part to create internal markets and maintain monopolies over the means of force and violence that allowed them to withstand sieges and foreign invasions, suppress internal revolts and riots, and successfully siege and invade others. The rise of stable states, together with legal institutions and professional political, military, merchant, religious and bureaucratic classes, reduced resort to civil wars and private vengeance by slaves, mercenary soldiers, migrants, workers and the poor, and to some extent deterred the lawless operations of corrupt merchants and bribe-seeking officials, as well as those of thieves, pirates, lesser tyrants, and those who operated freely outside the walls, in the spaces between settlements.

While Crete, Athens and other city-states were mercantile, sea-going powers and therefore more accustomed to migration, Sparta and other inland centers were agricultural and less open to strangers. A notable exception to the tendency to exclude foreigners began in early Rome with Romulus' promise of citizenship to the Sabines after the rape of the Sabine women; and later, in an effort to expand Roman influence and placate soldiers for their loyalty to the state. Historian Mary Beard wrote, in her book *SPQR*:

> To some communities over wide areas in central Italy, the Romans extended Roman citizenship. Sometimes this involved full citizen

rights and privileges, including the right to vote or stand in Roman elections while also continuing to be a citizen of a local town. In other cases they offered a more limited form of rights that came to be known ... as 'citizenship without the vote' ... [Others had] Latin rights. That was not citizenship as such but a package of rights believed to have been shared since time immemorial [including] intermarriage with Romans, mutual rights to make contracts, free movement and so on.

It has often been argued that the fall of the Roman Empire was a consequence, not only of barbarian invasions, but also of the acceptance and inclusion of foreigners and immigrants. The most famous historian of Rome, Edward Gibbon, in *The History of the Decline and Fall of the Roman Empire*, included immigration as a source of decline, but argued that Christianity was also responsible for the fall, as it led Roman leaders to favor religious pursuits and undermined their military spirit with a more generous turn-the-other-cheek, open, empathetic mentality.

More recently and provocatively, Oxford historian Peter Heather has argued that a crippling, unchecked wave of immigration and barbarian invasions led to the gradual dismantling of the Roman empire, with clear warnings for Europe and the U.S. Other scholars have disagreed vigorously, some arguing that the decline of Rome led to the rise of an even greater civilization centuries later. What many of these historians missed was the increasing impact of unresolved conflicts created by war, slavery, economic policies, political turmoil and environmental changes in forcing people to migrate in search of survival or better lives.

In Europe during the Dark Ages that followed, migration was regulated by feudal tenure, and permission from a local lord was required for serfs to travel or settle in a new area. Following the Black Death and resulting scarcity of skilled workers, the *Statute of Labourers* in England and similar legislation on the continent and in Russia made it a crime for serfs to leave the land to which they were entailed without their lord's written permission, or for skilled workers to migrate to new jobs or leave their places of employment. Similar rules governed migration in large areas of China and Japan over a period of centuries, restricting freedom of travel and work, and criminalizing migration.

Still, these restrictions were largely local and the modern nation-state, with fixed laws regulating migration did not really exist before the 18th century. There were no passports or clear, legally defined borders, and people for the most part identified ethnically, religiously, culturally or linguistically, rather than nationally. Until the invention of railroads, migration was mostly local, loosely regulated, subject to bribery and graft, and largely unrestricted.

Nonetheless, periodic mass migrations have always been triggered by wars, oppressive governments, climate changes, agricultural failures and communicable diseases, leading to violent anti-immigrant riots, such as those in London on "Evil May Day" in 1517; or the Alien and Sedition Acts passed by the U.S. Congress in 1798 requiring immigrants to live in the U.S. for 14 years instead of five in order to vote; or the rise of the "Know-Nothing" party in the U.S., which opposed immigration and newly arrived Irish, German and Catholic immigrants; or restrictions on Chinese immigrants who were brought to the U.S. in the late 19th century as miners and to help build the railroads.

Most of these anti-immigrant efforts were directed against those who sought to escape from oppressive conditions at home, or religious and political dissidents like those who fled England and Europe to the American colonies. With the rise of modern means of transportation in the 19th and 20th centuries, the scale and impact of these migrations increased enormously, accelerating the rise of protectionist and nationalist ideologies.

Much of the migration in recent history was sparked by the rise of colonialism and merchant capitalism, and fanned by competing nation-states in Europe, both to deport dissidents, criminals and the poor from overcrowded, impoverished cities; and to populate colonies, providing a source of cheap labor that could mine precious metals, extract raw materials, harvest cotton, sugar cane, coffee and other products, and produce handicrafts and commodities for export.

Perhaps the greatest migration in history took place as a result of the slave trade, in which millions of Africans were uprooted and forcibly migrated to other lands, especially to European colonies. Equally violent was the forced migration and removal of indigenous, Native American, Mexican and other communities, in order to take possession of their lands and natural resources.

The modern nation-state began to grow rapidly in the 18th and 19th centuries, triggered by a race for colonies; global competition for precious metals, raw materials and markets for mass-produced commodities; and intense battles for control of lesser developed countries. These, in turn, required fixed, clear boundaries, which forcibly united diverse tribes, cultures and communities that were otherwise distinct, driving them from ancestral lands into the factories, fields and cities that grew up around them, or forcing them to migrate elsewhere.

In the 20th century, migration increased even more rapidly, largely as a result of a sequence of revolutions in transportation, communication, warfare, politics and international commerce. These led to rapid increases in support for nationalism and isolationism; strengthening of sovereignty and military might; growing competition between colonial powers; and the swift establishment of legally enforceable borders and boundaries in order to defend local industries against foreign competition and keep rival products and peoples out.

Before 1890, immigration to the U.S. was regulated by individual states, but a rapid upsurge, rising to over a million immigrants a year, mostly fleeing poverty and persecution, intensified anti-immigrant sentiments directed primarily at "the new immigration" of Catholics from Italy and Jews from Russia, which led to restriction by the federal government and openly racist preferences for Northern and Central Europeans, who were viewed as more closely related to already assimilated immigrants, who had once been discriminated against themselves.

IMMIGRATION, CAPITALISM AND BARBARIANS AT THE GATE

With the rise of capitalism, migration was encouraged as a way of increasing the supply of cheap labor, leading to the Enclosures Acts that forced masses of peasants into factories, thereby increasing the supply of workers, reducing demand and cutting wages, while maximizing profits, dividing classes and pitting foreign against domestic workers. In 1870, for example, Karl Marx wrote about Irish immigration to England in a letter that sounds remarkably modern:

> The ordinary English worker hates the Irish worker as a competitor who lowers his standard of life. In relation to the Irish worker he regards himself as a member of the ruling nation and consequently he becomes a tool of the English aristocrats and capitalists against Ireland, thus strengthening their domination over himself. He cherishes religious, social, and national prejudices against the Irish worker. His attitude toward him is much the same as that of the "poor whites" to the Negroes in the former slave states of the U.S.A. The Irishman pays him back with interest in his own money.... This antagonism is the secret of the impotence of the English working class, despite its organization.

Except for their importance as a source of cheap labor, nearly all governments throughout history have seen immigrants as outsiders and threats to their stability and well-being, and with a few notable exceptions, consistently sought to keep them out. As Thomas Hobbes described it:

> [O]utside the Commonwealth is the empire of passions, war, fear, poverty, nastiness, solitude, barbarity, ignorance, savagery; within the

Commonwealth is the empire of reason, peace, security, wealth, splendor, society, good taste, the sciences and goodwill.

Many governments agreed, using the threat of "barbarians at the gate" to consolidate their power and wealth, justify economic inequalities and defeat internal and external rivals. As a result, those outside their borders have nearly always been regarded as nasty, evil and barbaric, stoking popular fears of domestic crime, loss of resources and foreign invasion, while justifying autocracy, domination and monopolization of power. As H. G. Wells wrote 75 years ago, in words that could easily be applied today:

Never have there been such crowds of migrating depressing people. They talk languages we do not understand ... they stimulate xenophobia without intention ... Their necessary discordance with the populations they invade releases and intensifies the natural distrust and hostility of man for man – which is the aim of all moral and social training to eliminate... For the restoration and modernisation of human civilisation, this exaggerated outlawing of the fellow citizen who we see fit to suspect as a traitor or revolutionary and also of the stranger within our gates, has to be restrained and brought back within the scheme of human rights.

The growing separation between wealthy, white, industrialized countries at the center in the North; and poorer, darker, agrarian ones at the periphery in the South, resulted in widespread hostility toward dark-skinned immigrants that was nearly always experienced by those at the center as an invasion by those at the periphery, and by those at the periphery as domination by those at the center.

The Role of Borders

The drive to erect and defend borders is grounded in three commonly cited win//lose, adversarial assumptions — that they are needed first, to defend against foreign invasions and wars; second, to safeguard homegrown wealth and resources and prevent them from being used or exploited by others; and third, to establish internal identity and cultural unity — all requiring the creation of a strong military to defend local sovereignty against foreign domination.

But these same assumptions also operate in reverse: borders are needed first, to justify invading other countries and declaring war on weaker states; second, to provide a platform for seizing and exploiting the wealth and resources of others; and third, to enflame a fear of others that unites people against other cultures, rationalizes autocracy and military control, and justifies dividing and conquering, controlling and dominating external, as well as internal opponents.

It has long been known, in pursuing these goals, that it is useful to inflame people's fears of alien, adversarial forces and bolster the idea that "they" are inhuman, inferior, morally evil, dangerous or out to get "us;" that they are naturally irrational, brutal, violent, murderous and untrustworthy. British novelist Hanif Kureishi writes:

> A necessary level of hatred is kept going with regard to the reviled figure of the immigrant. Integration can never continue; there has to be someone shoved off the map. Today it will be him, and tomorrow someone else; the circulation of bodies is determined by profit. The rich buy freedom: they can always go where they like while the poor are not welcome anywhere. But, all the time, by some perverse magical alchemy, those we need, exploit and persecute the most are turned into our persecutors ... Hate skews reality even more than love. If the limits of the world are made by language, we need better words for all this. The idea of the immigrant creates anxiety only because he is unknown and has to be kept that way.

The difficulty is that when it comes to our *own* survival and well-being, our desire for wealth or advancement, our wish to escape oppression and suffering, our need to support our families, we become profoundly vulnerable to fear and rationalization. We hope for, and often require the kindness of strangers ourselves, but are not nearly so quick or ready to offer it to others — especially when racial, sexual, religious, cultural, political and economic differences are used to incite panic and fear — that "they" will overpower us and destroy our freedoms; that they have nothing to lose and will respond only to military force; and that without it, they will try to take what is rightfully ours. Yet, paradoxically, as suggested above, these very same phobias can be used to justify our (defensively) doing the same to them.

These fears and rationalizations, along with the ways we state and respond to them, are of great consequence, ethically and morally, economically and politically, personally and relationally. In order to respond intelligently and effectively to the hatred of immigrants, it is necessary to concede that there are difficulties and downsides — not only with the wholesale exclusion and expulsion of migrants, but also with their unregulated admission and acceptance. These difficulties oblige us to think honestly and carefully about what I refer to as "the problem of sharing."

THE PROBLEM OF SHARING

Certainly, hospitality, kindness and sharing are highly desirable from the point of view of ethics, values morality, conflict resolution and social cohesion, but for immigration and mutual aid to operate *successfully* — especially with people from diverse cultures, religions, backgrounds and beliefs we require a number of higher order interest-based attitudes and behaviors, processes and relationships, skills and capacities, including, I believe, these:

- A strong capacity for empathy
- A deep desire and willingness to aid those in need
- A sense that burdens will be shared equally and equitably
- A recognition of the value and importance of reciprocity and mutual exchanges of generosity

- A rich assortment of opportunities to repay the kindness one has received
- A sense of shared understanding and relative well-being on all sides
- An ability to monitor and shape behaviors that clash with those of the host culture
- A set of processes for problem-solving, cross-cultural dialogue, collaborative negotiation, decision-making and conflict resolution
- A way of identifying, isolating and working to repair those who pose a danger to the people who host them

In a similar vein, Elinor Ostrom won the 2009 Nobel Prize in economics for showing, in contrast to orthodox economic principles and proscriptions, that groups of people are entirely capable of sharing and managing their common economic and natural resources when the following eight conditions are met:

1. The group and its purpose are clearly defined
2. The costs and benefits are shared equally
3. Decisions are made by consensus
4. Misconduct is monitored
5. Sanctions start out mild and escalate only as needed
6. Conflict resolution is fast and fair
7. The group has the authority to manage its own affairs
8. The relationship of the group with others is appropriately structured

By combining these conditions with the skills and capacities listed above, it becomes possible for us to imagine how we might create *practical*, collaborative solutions to most of the problems produced by immigration; to design courageous conversations and dangerous dialogues that reduce hostility and hatred directed at migrants; and to do so without diminishing our democracy or our capacity for caring. The ability to talk directly with each other, while at the same time jointly solving the problems that arise whenever people travel to new places, are equally essential in assuaging people's fears, as can be seen in the following sections, which are offered as a potential model or prototype for those who would like to organize dialogues over immigration in their communities.

Designing Dialogues on Immigration in Athens

No country is entirely walled off, permanently protected or immune from the problems and complications that accompany immigration; and no country has discovered a simple, surefire way to solve them. What we require is not war and violence, or prejudice and discrimination; not well-meaning pronouncements, self-righteous speeches or apathetic silence, but courageous conversation, authentic engagement, genuine listening and creative problem-solving. What we require is dialogue.

For years, Greece has been in a state of profound crisis as the issue of immigration has deeply polarized its population and strained its already inadequate resources. In this it is not alone, but a harbinger and bellwether of things to come elsewhere in the world. But where better to begin a dialogue on immigration than Athens, where Socrates first gave it power and meaning?

The last few years have been critical in Greece's history. The impact of the EU's fiscal crisis and imposed austerity reached a crescendo at the same time that scores of immigrants crossed into Greece to escape wars and violence in North Africa, the Middle East and Asia, and began living in large numbers in Athens, creating a strain on local communities and resources. For years, there were daily protests and riots in Athens, leading to the emergence of violent neo-Nazi political groups such as Golden Dawn, which frequently beat up immigrants and was reported to have considerable support in the military and police.

In response to a request for assistance from the Hellenic Arbitration and Mediation Centre, a small team from Mediators Beyond Borders International (MBBI), an organization I helped found, agreed to design, organize and conduct a series of dialogues that would assist Greeks and immigrants in building their skills in dialogue and peaceful engagement, reach agreement on potentially viable solutions to the difficult and contentious problems they were experiencing, and reveal better ways of responding to the growing strains placed on Greek society by a combination of economic crisis, austerity and immigration.

We thought that if we could collaborate in organizing successful dialogues between immigrants and Greek citizens, we might discover effective ways of increasing empathy and mutual understanding, brainstorming creative options and reaching consensus on recommendations for action concerning immigration, thereby helping reduce the growing threat of hatred and violence. And if we could achieve these goals in Athens where hatred and violence were at a high-pitch, perhaps we could do so in other places as well.

We began by forming an international team of mediators, conducting trainings for Greek mediators and organizing a series of dialogues between immigrants and Greek citizens that were facilitated by Greek mediators. Participants included representatives of the primary immigrant organizations, government officials, political and community leaders, religious organizations, police officials, officers in the Coast Guard, university professors and others, but *not* including Golden Dawn, since the immigrant organizations adamantly refused to attend if they were invited, and we were not certain that freshly trained dialogue facilitators would have the skills needed to respond to potentially violent encounters.

To clarify the reasons for this decision, I wrote the following explanation for members of the joint dialogue facilitation team, as proposed points of agreement for moving forward and conducting the dialogue without them:

1. We do not believe in excluding any person or group that wants to participate in dialogue.
2. We require a clear commitment to safety and ground rules from all participants that will allow people to actually talk to each other.
3. We come as capacity builders for Greek mediators, not as people who will run the dialogue ourselves.
4. Given the political philosophy and public statements of Golden Dawn, it is highly unlikely at this point that they would agree to the ground rules and safety concerns required of participants in dialogue.
5. Given the decision by the other political parties that they will not participate if Golden Dawn is invited, we respect their wishes and those of our Greek hosts and will not invite them to attend this dialogue.
6. We envision multiple dialogues of which this is the first, in hopes of laying the groundwork for future dialogues.
7. Given the political situation in Greece, with real attacks being made on immigrants and those who support them, we recognize that work needs to be done to create the conditions in which all parties will be willing to participate in dialogue with each other.
8. One element in creating those conditions is our contribution to the development of capacity and skill among Greek mediators who will gain some experience facilitating less difficult dialogues.
9. One topic we can encourage the Greek team to raise in the dialogues is how to expand it to reach all groups within Greek society.
10. In our trainings, we can present techniques and jointly search for ways of gaining agreement on the ground rules and safety concerns among groups that have publicly rejected them.

Strategically, we need to be able to facilitate and mediate skillfully with whoever shows up, and whatever arises; yet tactically, we need to build the skills and capacities needed for effective communication and collaborative engagement, often from scratch and gradually over time. Yet if dialogue is going to be successful as a method for responding to political conflicts, we cannot afford in the long run to leave anyone behind. This, however, raises the problem of limits, since it is possible to enter into dialogue solely for the purpose of crippling and destroying it, or to participate in democracy simply to extinguish it.

On a deeper level, all nations, political groups, minorities, cultures, classes, races and individuals seek to satisfy their self-interests, yet rarely recognize that doing so requires them to also satisfy the interests of others, *including* those of their opponents. Modern forms of warfare, ecological disasters, technological revolutions, economic globalization and similar issues no longer reward isolated, short-term, unilateral approaches to satisfying interests. The *long-term* interests of each of us are increasingly and immediately the interests of all, and *vice versa*.

GOALS OF THE ATHENS DIALOGUE INITIATIVE

The Athens Dialogue Initiative, as an international collaboration, was designed to educate, coordinate and build the skills and capacity of Greek mediators and Athenian civil society to facilitate dialogues and introduce community mediation over issues of immigration, among others. We imagined the Initiative progressing in five separate yet inter-connected programmatic stages that would be implemented over a three-year period, with the goal of later expanding to address other topics. These stages, as we saw them, were:

1. Develop an International Team of trainers, facilitators and mediators who would improve their skills in designing, organizing and conducting dialogues on immigration and other difficult and dangerous issues in a variety of countries and cultures
2. Create a cohesive network of mediators and other interested individuals and organizations in Greece who would continue

to facilitate dialogues, support community mediation and enhance communication over difficult issues in other areas, such as neighborhoods and schools

3. Improve techniques for facilitating civil society dialogues through international collaboration and hands-on experience

4. Design an on-going series of dialogue, communication and conflict resolution training programs that could assist Greek mediators, leaders and volunteers from core groups of immigrants and citizens in developing active listening, dialogue facilitation, mediation and other conflict resolution skills

5. Start an international public dialogue/consensus-building initiative that would stimulate constructive dialogues at a local level in other countries over a range of important social, economic and political issues

While the Athens dialogues proved highly successful, as described below, their elaboration and expansion to other countries and communities is still in progress.

Overview of the Athens Dialogue Process

We conducted the first dialogue in Athens in April 2013, led by a team of Greek and international mediators who had been trained for two days in dialogue facilitation techniques, in an effort to demonstrate that it was possible for people from diverse cultures, races, religions and backgrounds who disagreed with each other over these issues to learn from each other, deepen their understanding and work together to solve common problems.

The immigrant communities included members of the Kurds and Turkish Immigrants and Political Refugees Union, the African Women Union, the Syrian Immigrant Community, Asante NGO, Madagascar Committee and African Women Union, representing immigrants from Nigeria, Kenya, Somalia, Burkina Faso, Ghana, Ethiopia, Philippines,

Afghanistan, Pakistan, Egypt, Syria, Iraq, Kurdistan, Turkey, Guinea, Sierra Leone and Bangladesh. These immigrants and organizations were working together to form a unified organization that would represent all immigrants and refugees in Greece.

Feedback and evaluation took place after each event and a small group of professional researchers, process observers and small group reporters gathered qualitative and quantitative data regarding the experience and made proposals for improving the dialogue process and building skills in dialogue facilitation, mediation and dispute resolution among Greek mediators. The team met after the first dialogue to discuss and critique the experience and design a three- to five-year plan that would lay a practical foundation for future dialogues. Members of the International Team then returned to Athens to deliver a number of follow-up trainings and dialogues over the next three years.

The plan for the dialogues was as follows: as participants arrived, they were divided into diverse small groups and assigned to tables. Two lead mediators, one Greek and one International, were stationed at the front of the room throughout the process, with two additional mediators, also Greek and International, roaming and observing the small groups, ready to intervene if necessary.

Each small group was led by a Greek facilitator and co-facilitator, and assisted by a member of the International Team who acted indirectly as a coach and consultant. Each group selected from among its members a volunteer recorder, process observer, timekeeper and presenter, and agreed to report to the large group on their experiences after at the end of the dialogue. All dialogues were conducted in Greek, with volunteer translators assisting those who spoke other languages, including English, Arabic, Farsi, Swahili and others.

A GENERIC AGENDA FOR DIALOGUE

We created the following generic agenda for the dialogues, which was used to train facilitators and presented as a general guide to the conversation, while offering multiple options and alternative questions that allowed each facilitator to modify the agenda as they wished and select alternative paths in each small group as the conversation progressed. I offer it as a template for those who would like to design similar sessions, with notes to facilitators in brackets.

1. *Welcome!* Introduction of the team, overview of the agenda and context for the dialogue.

2. *Ground Rules:* The subject of ground rules is presented to the large group and the following questions are discussed in small groups and reported back to the group as a whole. Proposed ground rules are presented based on prior meetings with leaders and participant representatives. Topic: What ground rules are needed for us to have a successful dialogue?

- Small groups discuss the proposed ground rules. Additions or corrections are presented to the large group and agreed to by the group as a whole. Everyone is asked to commit to the ground rules.
- The large group is asked if it is ready to begin — if not, we stop, assess and correct.

3. *Introductions:* In small groups, each person introduces themselves by answering the following questions:

- What is your name? Does it have a meaning? If so, what is its meaning?
- Where is your family originally from?
- What is your personal experience with immigration? Your family's experience?
- What stories do you or your friends and family tell about their experience of getting here, or of living here and interacting with immigrants?

- What has it been like for you being an immigrant, or being a citizen of a country that others have immigrated to?
- Have you ever, in your life, in a family, neighborhood, school or workplace, been the new one, the one who just arrived? What was that like?
- Have you ever, in your life, in a family, neighborhood, school or workplace, been the one who has been there for a while, and experienced new people arriving? And what was that like?
- What is one thing you would most like others in the group to know about you before we begin?
- What is one wish or hope you have for our dialogue today? (Wishes and hopes are recorded on flip charts, a member of the small group presents to the large group, and they are posted around the room to remind participants of why they are here.)

4. *Framing the Discussion:* The following questions are addressed in each small group, at the discretion of the facilitator, allowing each person time to answer for themselves:

- Why did you decide to participate in this dialogue today?
- What life experiences have you had that have led you to feel strongly about this issue?
- What is one reason why you would like this issue to be discussed?
- What words or phrases would you use to describe the way immigration *should* be talked about in Greece, that you would most like to use to guide our dialogue today? (Words and phrases are recorded, a small group member presents to the large group and responses are posted around the room. The large group quickly reaches consensus on the words.)

5. *Identifying Problems and Difficulties:*

- What are the main problems or difficulties in connection with immigration that you believe need to be addressed?

- What is one successful method you have seen used to address these issues?
- What is one method that has not been successful, or that you believe has made the problem worse?
- (Answers to each question are recorded and the top 3–5 problems and successful and unsuccessful methods are listed.)
- (Discussion in the large group. A different volunteer reports to the large group listing the main problems, successful and unsuccessful methods.)
- (A volunteer process observer gives general (not personal) feedback at the request of the facilitator, or at the end of the session, on how the group did in their dialogue and what they might do better in future discussions.)

6. *Optional Questions:* (These questions can also be asked by facilitators if they feel it will be useful, or in response to conflicts within their small groups.)

- What is at the heart of this issue for you as an individual?
- Do you see any gray areas in the issue we are discussing, or ideas you find it difficult to define?
- Do you have any mixed feelings, uncertainties or discomforts regarding this issue that you would be willing to share?
- Is there any part of this issue that you are not 100 percent certain of, or would be willing to discuss and talk about?
- Even though you hold widely differing views, are there any concerns or ideas you think you may have in common?
- What underlying values or ethical beliefs have led you to your current political beliefs?
- What values or ethical beliefs do you think you might have in common?
- Do the differences between your positions reveal any riddles, paradoxes, contradictions or enigmas regarding this issue?
- Is it possible to view your differences as two sides of the same coin? If so, what unites them? What is the coin?

- What is beneath that idea for you? Why does it matter to you?
- Can you separate the issues from the people you disagree with? What will happen if you can't?
- Is there anything positive or acknowledging you would be willing to say about the people on the other side of this issue?
- What processes or ground rules would help you disagree more constructively?
- Instead of focusing on the past, what would you like to see happen in the future? Why?
- Are you disagreeing about fundamental values, or about how to achieve them?
- Is there a way that both of you might be right? How?
- What criteria could you use to decide what works best?
- Would it be possible to test your ideas in practice and see which work best? How might you do that?
- Would you be willing to jointly investigate your conflicting factual assertions? How would you do that?
- How is everyone in the group feeling right now about the tone of this discussion? What could we do to improve it?
- What could be done to make each side's ideas more appealing?
- Could any of the other side's ideas be incorporated into yours? How?
- Is there any aspect of this issue that either of you have left out? Are there any other perspectives you haven't described?
- Are there any other ways you can think of to say that?
- Do you think it would be useful to continue this conversation in order to learn more about each other and what you each believe to be true?
- How could we make this conversation more ongoing or effective?
- What could each of you do to improve the ways you disagreeing with each other in the future?
- Would you be willing to do that together?
- (The purpose of these questions is not to eliminate or discourage disagreements, but to place them in a context of

common humanity and allow genuine disagreements to surface and be discussed openly and in-depth. These questions reveal that political conversations need not be pointlessly adversarial, but can be transformed into authentic engagements by allowing opposing sides to come to grips with difficult, complex, divisive issues without being hostile or abusive.)

7. Responding to Prejudice, Bias, Discrimination and Stereotyping:

- What has your experience been with prejudice, bias, discrimination or stereotyping? Have you ever felt discriminated against for any reason?
- Have you had any stereotypes or beliefs about other people in the past that you later discovered to be false? How did you overcome them?
- Do you have any prejudices or biases now that you would like to overcome? What are you doing to overcome them?
- What do you believe are the main reasons for prejudice, or sources of hostility that need to be overcome?
- What are some ways of responding to prejudice, bias, discrimination or stereotyping that you think might be successful?
- (Ideas are recorded and a different member of the small group presents to the large group. Discussion of ideas in the large group.)

8. Responding to Bias Regarding Immigration: (with thanks to Ashok Pannikar)

- What has your personal experience been with immigrants who have come to your neighborhood or city?
- Are there any ways you think the experiences of a native Greek are different from the experience of an immigrant?
- Are there any ways you think the experiences of a native Greek

are similar to the experience of an immigrant?
- What worries you most about immigration?
- What do you think native Greeks are most afraid of regarding immigrants?
- What do you think most immigrants are afraid of?
- If you met an immigrant or a native Greek with strong views on immigration and had some time to talk, what questions would you most want to ask?
- What would you want him or her to know about you?
- What would you want him or her to think about you?
- What changes in behaviors would you want to request?
- What advice would you have?
- What kind of life would you wish for him or her?

9. Brainstorming Recommendations and Solutions:

- Is there anything you believe these problems have in common?
- What do you think might be done to help solve the problems the small groups earlier identified?
- If you were asked what the government could do to solve this problem, what would you recommend? The police? The church? The community?
- What do you think you might be able to do personally or in your families and communities to encourage future dialogue?
- (Ideas are recorded and a different member of the small group presents to the large group.)
- (Alternatively, facilitators reach consensus on problems to be discussed and ask everyone to join a team that will discuss the problem in-depth, ask each person to brainstorm possible solutions, then list and report to the large group on the top 5–8 solutions from their team. afterward, one volunteer from each team agrees to meet to consolidate and synthesize the recommendations and take them as a group to the organizations that could do something to implement them.)

10. Closure: What Will We Do Differently?

- What is one thing you learned in this session? What will you take away from this conversation?
- What is one thing you are committed to doing differently as a result of this dialogue?
- What recommendations do you have for future sessions?
- (Process observers give the small groups feedback on how they did in these discussions.)
- (Small group facilitators acknowledge participants, invite them to give feedback to the facilitator and encourage them to continue to dialogue in their families and communities.)
- (Each small group discusses their experience and brainstorms things that could be done to improve the next dialogue. A different small group member reports to the large group on their top 3–5 recommendations for future sessions.)
- (Participants are given an evaluation form to fill out.)
- (Large group facilitators thank participants, announce future meetings and thank the small group facilitators, recorders, process observers, presenters and members.)

11. Adjourn.

In each of the dialogues, there was active participation by people on all sides of the issue, with lots of energy and excitement, open and honest conversations, deep experiences of empathy, positive exchanges of experience and constructive suggestions for problem-solving. There was a great deal of positive feedback and requests for more dialogue, as well as ideas for improving the process.

SOME DEEPER QUESTIONS

What emerged from this experience, personally for me and many of the trainers, facilitators and participants, was a realization of the power and creative potential of dialogue in bringing diverse groups of people with apparently antagonistic political views and unresolved conflicts into positive, empathetic conversations with each other, leading to joint problem-solving, collaborative negotiation and consensus. These positive experiences raised a number of follow-up questions: Is it possible for people elsewhere in the world to do something similar? What would be required to create dialogues on immigration in other countries? Could we design dialogues for other political conflicts as well?

The dialogues successfully underscored the universality of migration as a *human* experience and the increasing artificiality of political borders in a world that is becoming far too interconnected and moving much too rapidly to get stuck in avoidable hostilities and needless animosities. They demonstrated on a small scale the need to rethink borders, boundaries, partitions and divisions. As a result, a second tier of questions regarding immigration arose:

- Based on our experiences with *internal* migration, for example, within the U.S. and member countries in the E.U., people are able to travel without restriction, so what prevents us from extending our idea of what is "internal" and opening our borders even wider?
- What safeguards would need to be in place to extend the freedom of travel between groups of countries in different regions, mirroring the freedom of travel within them?
- What would happen if all borders everywhere were reduced to a minimum, or eliminated entirely?
- Is this in fact the direction in which we are heading?
- How might we encourage frightened people to offer empathy and hospitality to those who are suffering and have lost their homes?
- Is it possible to do so without triggering large-scale nationalist, nativist and fascist reactions?
- What would be the social, economic and political costs and benefits of such a dramatic shift?

RETHINKING BORDERS

Many of those who seek to exclude foreign immigrants (as opposed to domestic ones) assume that the economic consequences of doing so would be catastrophic or deleterious. Yet the economic history of migration suggests otherwise. Michael A. Clemmons at the Center for Global Development in Washington DC estimated in 2011, in the *Journal of Economic Perspectives*, that the economic benefits from eliminating *all* barriers to emigration would

> ... amount to large fractions of world GDP — one or two orders of magnitude larger than the gains from dropping all remaining restrictions on international flows of goods and capital. When it comes to policies that restrict emigration, there appear to be trillion-dollar bills on the sidewalk.

Certainly, if we were to add up the amount spent by all nations establishing and maintaining borders, the economic impact of tariffs and national restrictions on trade, the incalculable cost of wars and conflicts over imposed boundaries and disputed territories, the gains that could be made from work by migrants, the increased tax revenues, the decreased political tensions and similar factors, an argument can be made that the benefits of an open border policy toward migration would far outweigh its costs.

While the economic outcome of immigration may be arguable, the ethical and moral consequences of refusing entry to those who are fleeing death and destruction, poverty and persecution, narco-trafficking and terrorism, rape and torture, gender and class discrimination, corrupt and tyrannical regimes, etc., are entirely clear, especially when we recognize that most of the migrants we are so frightened of are in fact children.

In *Fortress Europe: Inside the War Against Immigration*, Matthew Carr describes the history of migration and policies designed to discourage it:

> European governments ... created an extraordinarily elaborate and complex system of exclusion and control that is simultaneously ruthless, repressive, devious, chaotic and dysfunctional, and whose consequences are often strikingly at odds with its stated objectives.

Carr argues that the way forward for Europe is the Schengen agreement of 1985, which eliminates internal borders while allowing people to maintain independent identities and common borders for all. This, he writes, avoids the danger of "falling into something that may not be fascism but may not be far removed from it." A similar provision in the U.S. Constitution permits freedom of movement between states and territories inside the U.S.

The difficulty lies in deciding where the common boundary and freedom of travel ought to end. The traditional answer has been in our fear of others, our anxiety and desire for security, the strength of our military, and our conservative attitude toward political conflict and change. For these reasons, still deeper questions arise in connection with migration that concern the relationship between ourselves and others, the connection between freedom and security, and the emotions and attitudes we bring to diversity, conflict and change.

Before beginning to probe and search for answers to these questions, we need to imagine in detail what would happen if we were to approach migration in a completely different way, and ask even more imaginative, somewhat rhetorical questions, none of which we are now able to completely or finally answer:

- What do we imagine would happen if we allowed people to travel wherever they wanted? *Why* do we imagine it that way?
- Why *not* elevate the freedom to travel and migrate to a universal human right?
- What if everyone had a "Universal Passport," and we entirely eliminated or significantly reduced the innumerable bureaucratic, time-consuming, costly restrictions on the freedom to travel?

- What would it mean to become an *undivided* planet, a single species making space for each other and working collaboratively to solve our common problems?

Two Possible Futures

Clearly, a number of problems would arise if we completely abolished political borders, as they do whenever people travel without restriction inside a country. These include not just the obvious ones involving banned substances, crime and violence, but how we can support diverse individuals and conflicting cultures in communicating and co-existing with each other under stressful conditions, in jointly solving problems, in collaboratively negotiating and resolving conflicts, in satisfying their mutual interests and planning how they want to live together.

Indeed, it has been predicted by many scientists that substantial increases in population, together with climate change, species extinctions, rising sea levels, overfished oceans, drought and desertification, drug-resistant diseases, ballooning debt (estimated recently by Robert J. Samuelson as totaling over $247 trillion globally), aging populations, depleted natural resources and similar crises will trigger a *dramatic* upsurge in migration, and that hundreds of millions of people will be forced to move in the next 50 years, and condemned either to stay put and die, or migrate to more hospitable locations in numbers that will easily overwhelm local resources.

Indeed, it is arguable that the current crisis over immigration represents a subconscious awareness of this future possibility, especially in countries where migrants are most likely to seek a better life, and whose citizens are naturally drawn to defend their families, communities, cultures, possessions and livelihoods against what are likely to be increasingly desperate outsiders, conceivably by force if necessary. To avoid the devastation these migrations are likely to create, we will be compelled either to find new ways of solving these problems, or slip into increasingly barbaric and inhumane behaviors.

While the issues and difficulties are daunting, the potential advantages of instituting and enforcing an international human right to migrate and travel — not only in human lives, but in reduced costs, increased ethical and moral decency, added fairness, reduced fear and hatred, diminished chronic conflicts and less fractious political differences, make it worth seriously considering — reminding ourselves throughout, as Ludwig Wittgenstein wrote, that "What is thinkable is also possible."

Indeed, part of what makes our present condition seem so intolerable is the growing recognition that creative, constructive and collaborative solutions are in fact *possible*; that we do not *need* to act cruelly toward each other in order to overcome the difficulties we have created; and that our capacity for caring and compassion can remain alive throughout our differences.

The only ethical process and relational solutions to these conflicts, in my view, are interest-based, and include open and honest dialogue, creative problem-solving, collaborative negotiation, mediation and a rich array of other conflict resolution techniques that have proven successful in a wide range of disputes. The easiest of these, I believe, is simply to shift our *attitude* toward those we have endeavored so long and strenuously to keep out. As the poet Edwin Markham wrote in 1913:

> He drew a circle that shut me out —
> Heretic, rebel, a thing to flout.
> But Love and I had the wit to win,
> We drew a circle that took him in.
> That circle is ours to draw.

EIGHT

GLOBAL PANDEMICS, NATIONAL BORDERS AND POLITICAL PROBLEM-SOLVING

America's healthcare system is neither healthy, caring, nor a system. —
Walter Cronkite

*Doctors are men who prescribe medicines of which they know little to cure
diseases of which they know less in human beings of whom they know
nothing.* —Voltaire

*There are crimes against humanity the magnitude and cold brutality of which
cannot be understood, cannot be weighed or calculated on any scale or
spreadsheet — crimes, the motives for which are as commonplace, as banal, as
quarterly earnings and political careers.* —Hannah Arendt

SO FAR, WE'VE BEEN LUCKY. NONE OF THE HEALTH EMERGENCIES OR
potential pandemics we have been through in recent years has
achieved its deadliest potential. These health crises have included
outbreaks of bird flu, swine flu and Ebola; the spread of drug-resistant
bacteria and mosquito-born diseases, such the Zika virus; and the
gradually extending reach of other infectious and insect-borne diseases
that easily cut across political borders. At the same time, we have seen
how conflicted, bureaucratic, ineffective and "too-little-too-late" many

government departments and nonprofits have been in response to these emergencies. Before the next outbreak or pandemic, it would be wise for us to consider why this has been, and what we might do instead.

The first reason we have responded so poorly to health crises is quite simple: infectious diseases do not respect sovereignty or national borders, and potentially threaten everyone everywhere. From this simple fact we can only conclude that any serious effort to block their spread *has* to be organized internationally and collaboratively, even if it means a loss of sovereignty by nation states, whose resources and responses necessarily stop at their borders. The same facts and conclusions can be reached regarding environmental disasters, migration, crime, terrorism, climate change and other global problems.

The second reason is also quite simple: no government wants to admit that it is experiencing a pandemic or outbreak of infectious disease. No government is willing to slash potential income from tourism and trade, or promote panic among its citizens, or look ineffective by publicizing its health problems. No government is prepared, especially in the beginning when it is most important, to warn others about the true potential danger, or accept that the spread of disease is beyond its control. No government is prepared to admit that it is desperate and in need of international assistance. No government is ready to give international aid organizations full permission to do whatever they think is necessary to contain the disease without obtaining permission beforehand from local political authorities and overcoming innumerable bureaucratic roadblocks, which can take considerable time, when time means lives that are lost to disease. No government wants to surrender its sovereignty to political forces that may be hostile or indifferent to it. No government is willing to admit that by delaying the process of controlling disease in these ways, it is directly responsible for unnecessary deaths and the spread of infection.

So what will happen, inevitably and predictably, when serious infectious diseases begin to spread and fearful or corrupt government officials deny that there is a problem, suppress critical information about health issues that impact everyone, and block aid from reaching those who are most in need? What will happen when international aid organizations such as the World Health Organization are kept underfunded, inadequately staffed and ineffectual by these same governments, and starved of the resources and information that are vital to preventing global pandemics, all in the entirely legitimate name of national sovereignty? The answers are both obvious and preventable.

The Ebola Outbreak

Consider, for example, the Ebola virus that erupted in West Africa in December 2013, but was not diagnosed until March 2014, after it had already spread across several national borders. The World Health Organization (WHO) was contacted and its Global Outbreak Alert and Response Network (GOARN) tried to help, but WHO's already meager budget had been cut 20 percent in 2011, and emergency and epidemic funding was cut by 50 percent in 2012.

Guinea and Sierra Leone tried to reassure foreign investors that all was well by denying its extent and minimizing its importance. Guinea only allowed GOARN to report confirmed cases, but laboratory and public cooperation were initially restricted and only about half of all suspected cases were confirmed. As a result, only those who had personal contact with confirmed cases could be tracked down and quarantined, and there was inadequate funding even for these limited efforts, allowing a small outbreak to escalate into an epidemic.

Moreover, WHO's offices are located in Geneva, far removed from the most common places where diseases emerge, with country and regional offices that are staffed by people who are generally appointed by, and loyal to, local politicians. WHO staff members who were critical of their local governments' response to the epidemic and spoke out were reportedly silenced or sent back to Geneva. GOARN staff members also complained about obstructions, but were told there was no problem. In June 2014, aid groups declared the epidemic out of control and accused WHO of failing to respond. In August, WHO declared a global emergency and began to tackle the problem in earnest, eventually successfully controlling the disease. [See, e.g., report by Debora MacKenzie in *New Scientist*, 19-26 December 2015]

In *The End of Epidemics: The looming threat to humanity and how to stop it*, Jonathan D. Quick and Bronwyn Fryer identify seven steps that can be taken to reduce the threat of epidemics, among which are better communications and a stronger WHO, with reduced reliance on traditional "command and control" methods, all of which require more advanced skills. Peter Salama, who heads WHO's Health Emergencies Programme, is reportedly moving the agency rapidly in this direction, and for the first time attempting to track all potentially severe health risks around the world, leading to earlier responses and improved prevention.

CONFLICTS OVER BIRD FLU

It is important for us to recognize that what happened in connection with Ebola is not unique or surprising or exceptional. The same pattern has played out over and over again in every country where potential pandemics, environmental catastrophes and similar problems have emerged. For example, consider what happened in connection with the H5N1 virus, otherwise known as avian influenza or bird flu.

It is predictable that the convergence of extreme poverty and reliance on poultry for survival anywhere in the world will create favorable conditions for avian diseases such as bird flu, to mutate into a form that can be transmitted by air between human beings, which will lead to a catastrophic crisis for which we are woefully unprepared. Scientists estimate that only two or three, or at most a mere handful of mutations or instances of viral gene swapping are needed to transform bird flu into a virulent, deadly human form similar to Spanish

Influenza. The difficulties mentioned in connection with Ebola, combined with the ease of international travel, panic and a desire to escape infection will then allow the virus to spread rapidly to other countries, creating a global pandemic.

The process of preparing vaccines for bird flu happens, in a simplified version, like this. Blood samples are taken from infected individuals by local health officials wherever there are outbreaks. These samples are sent to the WHO for analysis and tracking. The samples are then sent to large pharmaceutical companies to prepare vaccines, which are then sold for a profit on the world market. WHO rules allow commercial firms to make vaccines and patent them without sharing the profits with the viruses' countries of origin, and national governments are not permitted to make cheap generic versions of these vaccines.

The difficulty with this process is that the countries where bird flu outbreaks occur most often cannot afford to vaccinate their poorest citizens. So, in 2007, Indonesia, which is a hot spot for bird flu outbreaks, stopped exporting blood samples to WHO labs, on the ground that they would be used to make vaccines that Indonesia and other poor countries could not afford and could not duplicate. In an article in *New Scientist*, Indonesian health minister Siti Fadillah Supari explained her refusal to provide further blood samples to WHO:

> In 2005, when bird flu arrived, we needed Tamiflu [the antiviral drug that can cure H5N1]. We contacted Roche, [the Swiss company that holds the drug's patent and its only source at the time]. They said we couldn't have any, we would have to wait two years, because industrialised countries had already made advance purchase orders.

At the time, countries such as the U.S. and the UK, fearing an H5N1 pandemic, had placed orders for millions of doses of Tamiflu to be stockpiled in case of global spread, which would take Roche years to manufacture. Other buyers had to get in line, yet the rich countries had no H5N1 cases and the poor countries couldn't get the vaccine. "We already had 20 cases," said Supari. "That's unfair distribution." She argued that fair distribution of flu drugs and vaccines should be based on need, and on which country had actual outbreaks of the disease, rather than on profits, political power or wealth. The drug companies refused. Meanwhile, WHO officials feared that by the time this problem was worked out it could be too late to develop a vaccine for any pandemic that would emerge from Indonesia or elsewhere.

In April 2011, after years of impasse and unresolved conflicts between the parties, an agreement was finally reached in which poorer countries would receive help accessing vaccines and antiviral drugs in return for providing viral samples. The International Federation of Pharmaceutical Manufacturers and Associations, which represented 26 research-based drug manufacturers, pledged to donate drugs and technology covering half of the $58 million annual cost of boosting defenses in the poorest nations, and pledged to "reserve at least 10 percent of pandemic vaccine manufacturing capacity on a real-time basis, for donation to the WHO and/or supply at tiered prices, to developing countries."

While clearly a step forward, it is obvious that these measures are still inadequate and unable to prevent a global pandemic. Since they stopped sending virus samples, more than 15 Indonesians died of the virus and many more fell ill, fortunately without it mutating into a pandemic form, yet *every* human infection represents an opportunity for the virus to adapt further, become airborne and spread to people, thereby becoming pandemic.

Similarly, during the H1N1 swine flu pandemic in 2009–2010, many developing countries complained that they had no life-saving antivirals or vaccines to combat the new virus. WHO helped distribute 78 million vaccines, donated by rich nations and drug companies to 77 developing countries, but regulatory and other hurdles slowed the process, and again, we were lucky that the pandemic turned out not to be as destructive as it might have been.

No one contends that the drug company agreement will prevent pandemics from spreading, or that these bird flu or swine flu response patterns will be enough to prevent a new pandemic from occurring, or that the present drug distribution system is going to work if it does. The drug companies, under the agreement, are able to choose between donations and sharing their intellectual property in vaccines, so that even if low-cost generics were available, it is likely that the poorest people in the poorest countries will not be adequately vaccinated beforehand or in time, allowing the virus to spread to pandemic proportions.

Without a coordinated international response, scientists are nearly unanimous in noting that significant outbreaks of infectious diseases *will* occur before the end of the century, causing global pandemics that will inundate our capacity to respond, triggering panic, mass migrations, heightened competition for scarce vaccines, militaristic responses and political polarizations that will result in widespread illness, massive deaths and enormous economic losses, making future health problems even more difficult to solve.

As we grow more connected and interdependent globally, a health disaster anywhere on the planet can easily turn into a catastrophe elsewhere, making it clear that global problems require global solutions. As outbreaks of disease are naturally chaotic and unpredictable, even small, seemingly insignificant changes anywhere can produce vastly larger ones later.

What Is the Solution?

Violence, bitter conflicts and divisive attitudes are widespread over whether some of these problems even *exist*, who is responsible for them, and how to fix them. Our conflicting cultures, political and religious beliefs, attitudes, national processes and competitive economies, together with efforts to maintain power and control by means of hierarchy, autocracy, bureaucracy and national sovereignty are restraining us from reaching agreements, finding solutions and preventatively addressing these issues before they spiral out of control. How, then, do we solve these problems?

If military force, litigation and similar power- and rights-based processes will not work, and take too long even when they do, the only alternatives remaining are inclusive, international, *interest-based* solutions, including designing conflict resolution systems that encourage open and honest communications, informal problem-solving, public dialogues, collaborative negotiations, consensus building, prejudice reduction, conflict coaching, ombuds services and mediation. In the specific context of potential pandemics such as Ebola, bird flu, swine flu and similar outbreaks, a minimally effective start seems to me to include at least the following steps:

1. Develop international treaty language that grants authority and strengthens the ability of WHO and GOARN to coordinate global efforts to eradicate and control the spread of infectious diseases
2. Increase funding for the treatment of infectious diseases, including a "superfund" for pandemics
3. Establish a special international fund based partly on profits made by pharmaceutical companies from sales to wealthy countries, for the rapid development of pandemic vaccines
4. Require pharmaceutical companies to make vaccines for the treatment of diseases labeled "pandemic" by WHO available to countries in order of the number of infections in each country
5. Require pharmaceutical companies to make all biomedical intellectual property acquired through international agencies open and available to the United Nations and its member states
6. Fund and encourage the production of less costly generic vaccines
7. Create regional medical "rapid response teams" in areas where pandemics are occurring, or can be predicted
8. Attach a U.N. mediator, dialogue facilitator and/or ombuds

staff member to every international medical response team to assist in resolving conflicts in the field, coordinate multinational efforts and facilitate community dialogues aimed at increasing understanding of what is being done to control the outbreak, coordinating community health efforts and reducing prejudice against those who have been infected

9. Protect WHO and GOARN personnel who are critical of local efforts from being punished or transferred for their views

10. Hire additional full-time professional mediators, facilitators and ombuds personnel at the U.N., WHO and GOARN to resolve conflicts between nation states and international authorities over differences regarding prevention and treatment protocols and facilitate local community dialogues, provide feedback and recommend improved responses

OTHER GLOBAL PROBLEMS WE ARE NOW REQUIRED TO SOLVE

More broadly, the difficulty is not just that individual nation states are prone to resist international coordination in responding to pandemics or health care emergencies, it is that the problems we face as a *species* are increasingly global in scope, requiring us to move beyond nationally organized response mechanisms and autocratically, hierarchically and bureaucratically imposed solutions that have evolved over the course of centuries, in order to solve them. The most critical and important of these problems, in my view, are:

- CO_2 and methane emissions
- Exhaustion of the oceans
- Species extinction
- Decreasing bio-diversity
- Air and water pollution
- Deforestation
- Terrorism

- Nuclear proliferation
- Drug-resistant diseases
- Global pandemics
- Overuse of fertilizers
- Loss of arable land
- Religious intolerance
- Biological weapons
- Torture
- Sexual trafficking and abuse
- Genocide
- "Ethnic cleansing"
- Prejudice and intolerance
- Cyclical economic crises
- Narcotics smuggling
- Organized crime
- Vaccinations for diseases
- Over population
- Unregulated currency trading
- Destructive technologies

None of these problems can be solved locally, or nationally, or even by a consortium of nation-states. Neither can they be solved using military force, litigation, rule making, hierarchical command structures, autocratic decision-making processes or bureaucratic rules and regulations. In other words, neither power- nor rights-based processes, neither nation-states nor international organizations as presently constituted, are capable of creating sustainable solutions or avoiding destructive outcomes.

Thus, our most powerful problem-solving institutions, including the nation-state, have been outpaced and eclipsed by the problems they are required to solve and the information needed to solve them. And what is worse, the borders we have created to keep these problems out have made collective action and interest-based processes more difficult to carry out or implement in time.

As Albert Einstein famously declared after atom bombs were detonated over Hiroshima and Nagasaki, "Everything has changed, except the way we think." The potential for disaster, created by a combination of national borders and international problems, ease of travel and ease of transmission, vaccines for the wealthy and pandemics for the poor, increases every day, and it does not take great foresight to recognize that we are inadequately prepared for what is likely, at some point, to occur.

In the end, there are only two approaches we can take to solving these problems, and others like them: first, those in the wealthiest countries can hope and imagine that they will be able to isolate and selfishly defend themselves against these problems, and that those in the poorest countries will be the only ones to suffer and die; or second, we can agree to address these issues together in an intelligent way by increasing our skills and capacities to communicate across borders, collaboratively solve common problems, engage in dialogue over difficult issues and mediate our more imperative disputes.

To achieve these goals, we require not only advanced methods in science and technology, but *equally* advanced methods in effective communication, joint problem-solving, collaborative negotiation, dialogue and conflict resolution. These techniques and skills are currently available and skilled practitioners are ready to use them.

As Abraham Lincoln reminded us, "A house divided against itself cannot stand." Nor can a nation, a species or any important relationship. There are thousands of ways we can listen and learn from each other, work together to solve our common problems and prepare for environmental crises and potential pandemics. It is essential for our survival that we fund them and make them a priority.

NINE

STRENGTHENING THE UNITED NATIONS: TOWARD A "CONFLICT REVOLUTION"

---

there is only one blood,
the same life that animates us all!
Since one unique mother begat us all,
Where did we learn to divide ourselves?
— Kabir

The chief reason warfare is still with us is neither a secret death wish of the human species, nor an irrepressible instinct of aggression, nor, finally and more plausibly, the serious economic and social dangers inherent in disarmament, but the simple fact that no substitute for this final arbiter in international affairs has yet appeared on the political scene.
—Hannah Arendt

And now let us believe in a long year that is given to us, new, untouched, full of things that have never been, full of work that has never been done.
—Rainer Maria Rilke

AS THE REACH AND DESTRUCTIVE CAPACITY OF HUMAN CONFLICTS continue to escalate; as migrants stream across borders fleeing terrorism and civil war; and as ethnic and religious differences, environmental pressures and economic dislocations uproot families and communities around the world, it is increasingly clear that the conflict resolution capacity we presently possess is entirely inadequate.

It is equally clear, as described in earlier chapters, that the problems we face can no longer be solved by individual nation-states, and that regional and international cooperation will be more and more necessary, forcing us to cross the borders we created over centuries to keep others out, favor local economies and defend national sovereignty against presumptively hostile neighbors.

It would be natural to look to the United Nations to encourage, guide and facilitate this international cooperation. The U.N. already has some skill and capacity to mediate and facilitate the peaceful resolution of conflicts, but it needs orders of magnitude more. Its limited mandate, lack of significant enforcement capacity, restricted funding and politically constrained operations imposed by adversarial, sovereignty-conscious nations, both in the Security Council and the General Assembly, have narrowed the range of its interventions and kept it from responding to a broad array of religious, ethnic, gender, political, social, economic and intrastate disputes that are becoming increasingly destructive and consequential.

Fortunately, the U.N. could, with a small number of relatively inexpensive and easily implemented improvements, become a vastly more powerful preventive force in resolving not just international disputes, but a growing number of subnational, intra-state and internecine conflicts.

What the U.N. Is Doing

From its inception, and with international agreement on the *Universal Declaration of Human Rights*, the U.N. has been the hope of war-weary, impoverished and oppressed people everywhere. Among its fundamental purposes are the prevention of war and protection of human rights, and mediation is recognized as an important tool for carrying out these missions. Article 2 of the *Universal Declaration of Human Rights,* for example, provides:

> Everyone is entitled to all the rights and freedoms set forth in this Declaration, without distinction of any kind, such as race, colour, sex, language, religion, political or other opinion, national or social origin, property, birth or other status. Furthermore, no distinction shall be made on the basis of the political, jurisdictional or international status of the country or territory to which a person belongs, whether it be independent, trust, non-self-governing or under any other limitation of sovereignty.

While gender and similar categories are not explicitly mentioned, they are arguably included in the term "other status." More problematically, however, Article 2 states:

> Nothing contained in the present Charter shall authorize the United Nations to intervene in matters which are essentially within the domestic jurisdiction of any state.

It was originally proposed that international law would determine what is "solely within the domestic jurisdiction" of a state, but when the U.S. Congress demanded that the reference to "international law" be removed, it was deleted. Nonetheless, Article 8, asserts:

> Everyone has the right to an effective remedy by the competent national tribunals for acts violating the fundamental rights granted him by the constitution or by law.

For decades, groups and nations have violated these and other Articles, and little has been done, partly because military intervention, political censure and economic sanctions have been considered the only options; and partly because of liberal use of the veto power by permanent members of the Security Council. Originally, the Soviet Union proposed that permanent members of the Security Council have a veto over all decisions, but a compromise permitted vetoes only on "substantive" matters, while the peaceful settlement of disputes was categorized as a "procedural" matter.

Mediation is expressly called for in Article 33 of the U.N. Charter:

> 1. The parties to any dispute, the continuance of which is likely to endanger the maintenance of international peace and security, shall, first of all, seek a solution by negotiation, enquiry, mediation, conciliation, arbitration, judicial settlement, resort to regional agencies or arrangements, or other peaceful means of their own choice.
>
> 2. The Security Council shall, when it deems necessary, call upon the parties to settle their dispute by such means.

This broad provision would seem to allow the U.N. to act in support of mediation even when member states disagree, especially where global issues or human rights are involved, and military intervention or litigation at the World Court cannot rectify the problem. Yet vesting the right to call on the parties to mediate in the Security Council means that little or nothing can be done in most intrastate conflicts. Former U.N. Secretary-General Ban Ki Moon, however, has called for an expanded role for mediation in intrastate disputes:

> As a result of the economic downturn, climate change and the growing depletion of resources, from arable land to water to oil, disputes within and between States may become more common in the future. Our organization and our partners will need all of the knowledge, skill, wisdom and resources we can muster to meet this daunting challenge. Since one of the most promising approaches to the peaceful settlement of disputes is skillful third-party mediation, we, the United Nations, have a responsibility to "we the peoples" to professionalize our efforts to resolve conflicts constructively rather than destructively and to "save succeeding generations from the scourge of war.

In 2006, the U.N. established the Mediation Support Unit (MSU) in the

Department of Political Affairs to provide administrative and logistical support and advice to envoys, mediators and negotiators. The MSU is charged with strengthening the mediation capacity of regional and sub-regional organizations and being a resource on mediation knowledge, policy and best practices. Yet in visiting the MSU's headquarters with a team from Mediators Beyond Borders in 2009, we quickly realized that their tiny staff and limited offices, however dedicated, could not conceivably be adequate to meet the multiple, growing challenges of global conflict.

To encourage mediation efforts beyond its limited capacity, the MSU established a rapid-response Standby Team of Mediation Experts in 2008, consisting of seven (now nine) highly regarded individuals who can be deployed individually or as a group as experts at no cost, to advise and assist in resolving disputes. Yet they are extremely busy, with more than 100 missions in 2014, and unable to provide consistent support for long-term, integrated, multitier capacity building.

Other efforts have been made to supplement the U.N.'s limited capacity, including the formation of a Group of Friends of Mediation by Finland and Turkey, which includes 48 Member States and seven regional organizations, whose goals are to:

- Raise awareness of the need for and utility of mediation at all stages of the conflict continuum especially with a view to preventing conflict
- Encourage relevant actors, including regional and sub-regional organizations, to undertake mediation activities and to engage more women in mediation
- Highlight the importance of the full and effective participation of women at all stages and at all levels of peace processes as well as the crucial role of gender expertise in mediation
- Provide a forum to bring together expertise and to share lessons learned between different actors
- Create, foster and expand the network of mediators
- Improve cooperation and coordination amongst different

actors, in order to increase complementarity and coherence of efforts
- Increase the capabilities for mediation, especially within the U.N. framework
- Promote mediation-related capacity building, including through regional arrangements and networks
- Promote the development of guidelines and/or a code of conduct for mediation, taking into account the specific nature of each conflict
- Mobilize more resources in order to secure sustained funding for mediation activities
- Support the development of early warning response capabilities
- Provide political support to U.N. appointed mediators

The Group has developed a "Guidance for Effective Mediation" and encouraged "contacts and links between mediation communities and networks as essential in order to improve the coordination and cooperation, and to address the challenges of a diverse and crowded field of mediation." However, the Group does not have a mechanism for directly providing a full range of conflict resolution services to local communities, including capacity building, which is where mediation organizations like the International Section of ACR, Mediators Beyond Borders, Partners Global and similar organizations might be helpful.

REFLECTIONS ON NORTH AND SOUTH KOREA

When I wrote this section, a meeting was being organized in Singapore between the U.S. and North Korea, and it seemed worthwhile to reflect on how it happened that the world suddenly changed and we shifted from mutual animosity, personal insults and threats of impending nuclear annihilation to a series of agreements between North and South Korea, pledges of a nuclear-free zone, release of prisoners and genuine face-to-face dialogue, promising a real "conflict revolution."

If there is a Nobel Prize in this, it is unlikely to be given to Kim or Trump, but might be given to South Korean President Moon for breaking the ice and taking the first small steps toward the other side, but perhaps also to Kim's sister, to the athletes on both sides at the Winter Olympics, and to the North Korean cheerleaders, whose positive presence and willingness to participate together in a global sporting competition demonstrated something essential that is often overlooked in nearly every conflict.

While the United Nations had little or nothing to do with initiating these talks, it might easily have done so, as one of the few organizations to which both parties belong, and with an agreed-upon mandate to prevent war. What would need to shift for the U.N. to begin taking these preventative steps when member countries start acting with open hostility and aggression toward one another?

To begin answering this question, let's consider the problem from a different perspective. If we ask the question: how far apart are people in conflict, I believe there are three correct answers:

1. They are an infinite distance from one another, because the gap between them seems unbridgeable and there appears to be no clear way of overcoming the hostility, intractability and impasse that divides them.
2. They are no distance apart at all, because they are inseparable in their conflict, and bound together by it.
3. They are exactly *one* step apart, because either side can move unilaterally to end the hostility, intractability and impasse on *their* side, and invite the other side to do the same.

We need to remember now, with humility and hindsight, all the U.S. government, TV pundit and press descriptions of Kim Jung Un as "crazy," "insane," "aggressive," "threatening," etc., and may then be prompted to ask:

1. Are these not also descriptions the other side might reasonably make of us?
2. How do we distinguish responsive conflict behaviors from innate evil?
3. Are they not descriptions that each side commonly makes of the other side in nearly every conflict? Why? How do we discern their real purpose?
4. What happened to those descriptions? What *precisely* was done that eliminated or changed them? What can we learn as mediators from these shifts? And,
5. How might we change *all* the descriptions we use to portray our opponents in every conflict in a more positive and affirming direction, without losing sight of the differences between us, but allowing us to invite them into honest dialogue, creative problem-solving, collaborative negotiation, mediation and other conflict resolution processes?

While the rhetoric of war has shifted for the moment regarding North Korea (as of the writing of this book), it has increased with respect to Iran, and can easily escalate in all our conflicts — in part because our choice of language creates a self-fulfilling prophecy by encouraging others to respond in kind. Thus, perceiving the other side as aggressive and unreasonable leads us to act in ways that cause them to respond aggressively and unreasonably, thereby "backward engineering" our response, creating an excuse for causing them harm in the first place and justifying our further efforts to seek their destruction through violence. Notice that there are three quick consequences that apply to all our conflicts:

1. Resorting to hostility, violence and war appears reasonable and acceptable *only* if the other side can be shown to deserve it, by reason of their innate evil or insanity or hostility or ill will toward us

2. It is far easier to convince ourselves and others to fear people who are different from us and disagree with our actions than it is to trust them, or be willing to talk openly, equally and honestly with them about our differences and how we might work together to resolve them

3. As a result, it is often necessary for third parties to intervene and act as mediators, facilitators of dialogue, searchers for common ground, promoters of empathy, designers of conversations, reframers of language and initiators of collaborative solutions

If the world can shift in the space of a few weeks from impending nuclear war and willingness to slaughter millions of innocent civilians to conversations that invite collaborative negotiation, dialogue and problem-solving, so can everyone in every conflict. All it takes is a little openness, a little courage and a little cheerleading.

It is within the unique prerogative of the United Nations to convene representatives of nation states, such as the U.S. and North and South Korea, and assist them in discussing, negotiating, problem-solving and mediating their conflicts — not just accidentally or occasionally, but routinely and continuously. To do so, the U.N.'s interest-based skills and capacities will need to be strengthened exponentially.

40 Ways We Might Strengthen the United Nations

It is clear that the United Nations can be strengthened in small ways that significantly increase its mediative skills and capacities, for example, in at least the following 40 ways, 10 in each category, to which many others may be added. Some of these have already begun, but each can be expanded, and provided with higher levels of support.

Structural Changes:

1. Transfer the Mediation Support Unit out of the Political Department and place it directly under the Secretary-General, quadruple its budget and staff, and expand its express authority to include intra-state, ethnic, religious and environmental conflicts.
2. Integrate the Mediation Support Unit with the office of the Assistant Secretary General for Ombuds and Mediation Services, which supports U.N. employees in resolving internal disputes.
3. Conduct periodic "conflict audits," linked to a collaborative conflict resolution systems design process, in order to: identify high conflict areas, predictors of conflict and potential preventative measures; encourage informal problem-solving; open outlets for constructive expression of differences; support interest-based options; and create "loopbacks" to negotiation.
4. Cease relying exclusively on a handful of international mediators, but work with the Group of Friends of Mediation to develop a comprehensive list of *thousands* of mediators and dialogue facilitators who can intervene in all levels and varieties of conflict in diverse communities around the world.
5. Encourage all delegations to future U.N. meetings to include among their members one or more skilled mediators, collaborative negotiators and facilitators who can assist in bridging differences as they occur.
6. Assign one or more U.N.-employed mediators, facilitators or ombuds employees as liaisons to every delegation, work group and problem-solving meeting.
7. Reduce reliance on Security Council and member state approval for mediation efforts, especially where violations of human rights are concerned, and allow the Secretary General and MSU to initiate mediation wherever conflicts arise.
8. Focus on *integrated* capacity building in conflict resolution,

problem-solving, dialogue facilitation, collaborative
negotiation and similar methodologies.

9. Form *multiple*, regionally based international rapid responses
teams that can travel quickly to emerging trouble spots before
they become violent.

10. Establish a permanent election oversight team to establish
international standards for electoral fairness, supervise
elections and mediate electoral contests.

Process Changes:

1. Don't wait for conflicts to reach impasse, but intervene early
and throughout the life of every conflict, organizing dialogues,
facilitating problem-solving and negotiations, and conducting
mediations.

2. Hire many more professional mediators from all countries,
with contributions from member states based on their history
of conflict.

3. Arrange for, facilitate and mediate regular *direct* meetings
between heads of hostile, opposing nation states, without
waiting for talks to break down.

4. Conduct in-depth, inclusive, collaborative evaluations of the
process used in Copenhagen and similar negotiations to
identify what works and what needs to be improved.

5. Develop a comprehensive set of process recommendations for
future negotiations, secure agreement to implement them
before meetings and conferences, brief delegates on them
before they arrive and agree on next steps to be taken
whenever consensus is not reached.

6. Appoint fast-forming, diverse problem-solving teams with
experts representing adversarial nations, regions, groups and
ranges of opinion, with professional mediators and facilitators
to aid them in their work.

7. Conduct open dialogue sessions on critical topics without
attempting to reach agreement, providing opportunities for

free-ranging small group discussions and recommendations on ways of reaching consensus.

8. Allow mediators and facilitators to redesign meetings if they aren't working, discuss what isn't working openly, invite suggestions and propose ways of fixing them.

9. Routinely debrief joint sessions and ask participants to recommend ways of improving future sessions.

10. Periodically conduct process checks to make sure everything is on track and make improvements as needed,

Protocol Changes:

1. Create rich, comprehensive algorithms, international conflict resolution protocols, model mediation language, and annexes to all existing agreements that encourage a broad range of collaborative, interest-based dispute resolution processes including mediation, negotiation, dialogue and similar methods, especially where violations of human rights are concerned.

2. Consult widely with diverse public and private sector mediation organizations and private mediators who have experience designing dispute resolution systems, and invite them to teach and propose ways of improving conflict resolution protocols.

3. Send experienced negotiators, facilitators and mediators to meet with parties in advance of international meetings, conferences and negotiating sessions to help set targets and timetables, and suggest protocols that could lead to better and quicker agreements.

4. Simplify and reduce the rigidity and formality of U.N. protocols, rules and processes, especially regarding mediation, problem-solving, negotiation and agreement drafting processes.

5. Shorten large meetings and break participants up into small, diverse, informal teams to brainstorm alternatives, agree on

protocols, common goals or shared values, and reach consensus recommendations on problems, led by U.N. mediators and facilitators.

6. Appoint facilitators and mediators to propose ground rules and protocols in advance of every international conference or meeting.

7. Focus not only on reaching large, comprehensive, global agreements, but smaller, specialized, limited, tentative, provisional and local agreements, then work to introduce them to a larger constituency.

8. Draft international treaty language mandating mediation for all nations, even in intra-state and human rights disputes.

9. Establish a World Arbitration Service and protocols for arbitration.

10. Agree on minimal standards for mediation and arbitration of international territorial, commercial and human rights disputes.

Culture and Training Changes:

1. Build a culture that seeks to solve problems at the lowest level through dialogue, collaborative negotiation and problem-solving, and empowers people to select from a range of options for resolving conflict.

2. Prioritize conflict prevention over conflict management and interest-based solutions over power- and rights-based ones.

3. Promote a respectful, inclusive, "elicitive" approach to cultural differences regarding conflict that encourages learning and diverse approaches to conflict.

4. Significantly expand lists of global mediators, facilitators and conflict resolution trainers, and the MSU library of conflict resolution books and training manuals, and translate them into local languages.

5. Offer an expanded array of free trainings for individual delegations and political leaders in human rights, as well as in

communication, problem-solving, dialogue, collaborative negotiation and conflict resolution skills.

6. Create an online conflict resolution forum and "TED Talk" series with talks by peacemakers around the world.
7. Videotape mediation practices around the world and offer an expanded array of online distance learning in dispute resolution.
8. Facilitate "virtual dialogues" on "dangerous" topics, especially those connected with human rights.
9. Offer a diverse range of incentives, skills and resources to motivate parties to use these processes.
10. Use "action research" and integrated fact-finding teams to research and resolve factual disputes, conduct post-conflict interviews and recommend preventative measures.

Out of this list of possible changes, I believe the highest priorities are to *exponentially* expand the use of mediation, dialogue and collaborative negotiation techniques; to dramatically increase funding and authority to intervene in intrastate disputes where violence and human rights are involved; and to initiate a comprehensive "conflict resolution systems design" process for the U.N. as a whole that would initiate an internal improvement process that could consider multiple possibilities for strengthening its conflict resolution capacity.

CONFLICTS AND BORDERS

All conflicts can be seen as taking place at the boundaries and borders that separate us, whether as individuals, families, cultures, organizations or nations. Every conflict can therefore be regarded as a line of demarcation, splitting us into opposing sides, competitive positions, unfamiliar cultures, foreign experiences and hostile camps that isolate and alienate us from one another.

Yet these same boundaries and borders are also places of *connection*, of unifying possibilities, of spaces where we can come together. Conflict resolution can then be regarded as a *consensual* crossing of borders, whether interpersonal or international. *Non*-consensual border crossings are experienced as boundary violations and vigorously resisted, but consensual crossings are experienced as acts of empathy and friendship, indicators of kindness and affection, and precursors to collaboration, problem-solving, forgiveness and reconciliation, even when the parties are nation states.

To significantly expand our global mediation capacity and move beyond "us versus them" conflicts, we need to recognize, as suggested earlier, that it is no longer useful to divide ourselves into "Us" and "Them." The "Them" we hate is simply the flip side of our own fear, accompanied by poor communications, primitive conflict resolution skills, failures of collaboration, accumulated pain and disappointment, and a history of reliance on militaristic power- and legalistic right-based interventions, leading to widespread loss of capacity for empathy and compassion, and a lack of commitment to strengthening interest-based conflict resolution skills and capacities.

I believe the next great leap in human history will be to develop these collaborative, interest-based skills and use them to search together for solutions to our most chronic social, economic and political conflicts; to find ways of crossing the man-made, insecure, anachronistic boundaries and borders that foster fear, prejudice, hatred and war; and to support international collaboration, democracy, human rights and conflict resolution.

Strengthening conflict resolution capacity in the U.N. can teach people globally how to disagree without killing each other; how to initiate open, honest dialogues and collaborative negotiations over difficult and dangerous issues; how to discuss gender, religion, culture and politics with an eye to empathy and learning; and how to build the skills and integrated conflict resolution capacity our human family requires.

Applying them will require even *higher* levels of skills and capacities in conflict resolution, much more catalytic conversations, far deeper transformations, leading, I believe, to a global "conflict revolution" in which we *systemically* shift from power- and rights- to interest-based methods of living together and solving problems on our one fair, finite and fragile planet. In doing so, we need to recognize, with Pablo Casals, that "The love of one's country is a splendid thing. But why should love stop at the border?"

INTEREST-BASED DEMOCRACIES AND ALTERNATIVES TO CONFLICT

The ideal subject of totalitarian rule is not the convinced Nazi or the convinced communist, but people for whom the distinction between fact and fiction (i.e., the reality of experience) and the distinction between true and false (i.e., the standards of thought) no longer exist. —Hannah Arendt

It is not the strongest of the species that survive, nor the most intelligent, but the one most responsive to change. —Charles Darwin

Direct government as at present generally understood is a mere phantom of democracy. Democracy is not a sum in addition. Democracy is not brute numbers; it is a genuine union of true individuals. —Mary Parker Follett

TEN

THE FORMS, LIMITS AND EVOLUTION OF DEMOCRACY

The average man votes below himself; he votes with half a mind or a hundredth part of one. A man ought to vote with the whole of himself, as he worships or gets married. A man ought to vote with his head and heart, his soul and stomach, his eye for faces and his ear for music; also (when sufficiently provoked) with his hands and feet. If he has ever seen a fine sunset, the crimson color of it should creep into his vote... The question is not so much whether only a minority of the electorate votes. The point is that only a minority of the voter votes. —G. K. Chesterton

Conformity need not be monitored, dissent has *to be. In any hegemony, dissent defines the limits and the final shape or legitimacy of a system, not conformity.... You are taught to fight established authorities according to the conventions authorized by the authorities themselves, so that rebellion gradually becomes a matter of apprenticeship and learning correct radical praxis according to texts produced in the global citadels of knowledge.* — Ashis Nandy

Life is always a tightrope or a feather bed. Give me the tightrope. —Edith Wharton

DEMOCRACY IS NOT ONLY POLITICAL; IT IS ALSO SOCIAL AND ECONOMIC, organizational and familial, substantive and procedural. Politically, it calls on us to transcend autocratic, win/lose, power- and rights-based forms of decision-making; socially, it summons us to eliminate inequalities in status, dignity and respect; economically, it invites us to reduce inequities in income and wealth; organizationally, it encourages us to flatten hierarchies and work in self-managing teams; familiall, it asks us to accept gender equality and eliminate patriarchy; substantively, it empowers us to participate in making decisions and own the task of directly governing ourselves; and procedurally, it enables us to collaborate and move from unilaterally imposing our will or voting to consensus-based forms of decision-making and problem-solving.

These are all interconnected and interdependent, making it far more difficult to nourish or sustain a political democracy when people are raised in authoritarian, patriarchal families and spend most of their lives studying or working in hierarchical, autocratic organizations. Yet if higher order skills are required for democracy to succeed, these need to be learned while we are young and practiced repeatedly in families, schools and workplaces, in order to produce an interest-based "default setting" that support a *culture* of dialogue and mediation.

FORMS AND VARIETIES OF DEMOCRACY

Most countries today consider themselves democratic in some broad, undefined sense, but every nation and culture, group and faction, politician and citizen has widely varying ideas about what that means and involves. Democracies thus take many different forms, based largely on history and culture, but also and perhaps more significantly, on the strength and intensity of our political conflicts and the level or order of our skills and capacities in resolving them.

If this is true, it follows that there are three fundamental varieties of democracy, each based on one of three primary approaches to resolving conflicts. If we regard democracy as *itself* a conflict resolution process, it can take either a power-, rights-, or interest-based form. In its power-based form, democracy is largely authoritarian, hierarchical, autocratic, dominating, bullying, violent and patriarchal. In its rights-based form, it is predominantly legalistic, electoral, representative, argumentative, controlling, coercive and bureaucratic. In its interest-based form, it is principally collaborative, participatory, consensus-driven, diverse, egalitarian, respectful and human.

The difference between these forms is partly a function of our skills and capacities, with power-based forms requiring the lowest level of skill or capacity and taking the least amount of time and effort; and interest-based forms requiring the highest skills and capacities, and entailing the longest time and most effort. The skills and capacities required for power-based forms of democracy are simply those of exercising authoritarian will and responding violently or aggressively toward one's opponents, demanding merely obedience. Alternatively, rights-based forms and processes, required higher levels of skill and capacity in order to promulgate laws, establish rules and regulations, define roles and responsibilities, set standards, make legal adjudications, competitively negotiate agreements, settle or compromise on solutions, and permit or prohibit a variety of acts and behaviors, necessitating compliance.

In interest-based forms of democracy, *exponentially* higher orders of skill and capacity are required that are rarely found in power- or rights-based forms. These include skills in active and responsive listening, empathy and compassion, non-violent communication, appreciative inquiry, creative and paradoxical problem-solving, collaborative negotiation, open and honest dialogue, emotional intelligence, cultural sensitivity, consensus building, teamwork, appreciation of diversity, prejudice reduction and bias awareness, reframing, group and circle facilitation, restorative justice, systems design, mediation, forgiveness and reconciliation, and others, inviting participation and ownership.

What is often missed is that chronic conflicts are created, intensified, exacerbated and made interminable and intractable *precisely* by the use of power-based processes, which backward justify their use. Similarly, conflicts are settled, compromised, adversarially negotiated and adjudicated using coercive rights-based processes, which also backward justify their use. And we can easily see that when conflicts are listened to empathetically, openly discussed, collaboratively resolved, emotionally transformed, systemically transcended and genuinely forgiven using interest-based processes that do not rely on force or coercion, the success of these processes similarly backward justifies their use.

Hence, each approach regards itself as necessary and successful, and fails to recognize or appreciate that its evolution to a higher form of democracy requires the development of significantly higher-order skills and capacities, but also that these *free* us, not only from lower forms of conflict that rely on force or coercion and are more likely to generate chronic conflicts, but from entire *categories* of conflict that no longer require our active attention and prevent us from evolving equally advanced levels of caring, connection and relationship.

For these reasons, it is helpful to recognize that we have been evolving over centuries from primitive power-based political forms to higher level rights-based approaches, to still higher level interest-based methods for resolving social, economic and political conflicts, and that we will be able to move much more rapidly and directly toward interest-based political democracies by practicing and perfecting the skills and capacities we need to make it successful.

How Democracies Die

While interest-based forms of democracy are essential if we want to design processes that are equitable and inclusive, and foster relationships that are egalitarian and collaborative, they are vulnerable to violent and aggressive approaches to conflict, and have sometimes failed, triggering retreats to power-based methods that deform democratic processes and defend win/lose outcomes, encouraging prejudice and discrimination, reinforcing hierarchical relationships and supporting continued domination.

In recent months, democracy has been pushed significantly backward in the U.S., Europe and elsewhere, and replaced by authoritarian, power-based approaches to conflict, which primarily consist of suppressing it through violent, hostile and aggressive acts. Centuries earlier, Socrates asserted that "[T]yranny is probably established out of no other regime than democracy," but what we have largely overlooked is that it is *specifically* the failure of rights-based democracies to resolve chronic political conflicts that feeds fascist and neo-Nazi movements.

For the most part, as mediators, facilitators and conflict resolvers, we have little control over the power to dominate in any society, economy or polity, or over the success of autocratic power- or bureaucratic rights-based institutions in resolving chronic political conflicts. But we *do* have some control over the level of interest-based skills and capacities that are available to resolve them, and it is here that democracy and conflict resolution meet in potentially catalytic, synergistic and transformative ways.

Because rights-based democracies rely on elections, they can be manipulated, corrupted and hacked by power-oriented authoritarian cliques. And because great advantages in status, wealth and power can be obtained by doing so, the ability to resolve internal conflicts between citizens and build interest-based skills and capacities becomes highly politicized and increasingly essential.

In rights-based forms of democracy, elections are the primary, nearly exclusive manifestation of democratic processes and relationships, and as a result, the manipulation of electoral processes to *appear* fair and inclusive while allowing widespread denials of fairness and inclusion, limits their ability to resolve chronic conflicts. The ineffectiveness and failure of lower order rights-based processes that rely on representative elections and legal coercion to resolve deep-seated social, economic and political conflicts, *invites* the use of still lower order power-based processes that rely on autocracy and authoritarian violence, all in unspoken defense of continuing domination. As Hannah Arendt wrote:

> [Political] parties, because of their monopoly of nomination, cannot be regarded as popular organs, but ... are, on the contrary, the very efficient instruments through which the power of the people is curtailed and controlled. That representative government has in fact become oligarchic government is true enough, though not in the classical sense of rule by the few in the interest of the few; what we today call democracy is a form of government where the few rule, at least supposedly, in the interest of the many. This government is democratic in that popular welfare and private happiness are its chief goals; but it can be called oligarchic in the sense that public happiness and public freedom have again become the privilege of the few.

The corruption of the U.S. electoral process not only by bribery, but control over the finances and operations of political parties was noticed and commented on over a century ago by the journalist Karl Marx:

Nowhere do "politicians" form a more separate and powerful section of the nation than precisely in North America. There, each of the two major parties which alternately succeed each other in power is itself in turn controlled by people who make a business of politics, who speculate on seats in the legislative assemblies of the Union as well as of the separate states, or who make a living by carrying on agitation for their party and on its victory are rewarded with positions.... It is precisely in America that we see best how there takes place this process of the state power making itself independent in relation to society, whose mere instrument it was originally intended to be. Here there exists no dynasty, no nobility, no standing army, beyond the few men keeping watch on the Indians, no bureaucracy with permanent posts or the right to pensions. And nevertheless we find here two great gangs of political speculators, who alternately take possession of the state power, and exploit it by the most corrupt means and for the most corrupt ends — and the nation is powerless against these two great cartels of politicians, who are ostensibly its servants, but in reality dominate and plunder it.

By making elections expensive and politicians dependent on media and money, the illegal bribery of politicians, which became widespread and commonplace in the 19th century, took a new form in the 20th, with the rise of entirely legal political advertising, lobbying and corporate campaign contributions made possible by the U. S. Supreme Court's decision in *Citizens United*. While the form and style changed, the content and outcome have remained the same.

As rights-based political processes and the skills and capacities they required expanded, the right to vote also expanded to include, at least on paper, men who were not property owners, formerly enslaved people, women and 18 year-olds, making it doubly important for a minority of those at the top to find ways of guaranteeing the continuation of political domination by a minority at the top over a much larger majority at the bottom, by inventing electoral processes that were needed to secure the support of those in the middle.

Yet these entirely *procedural* battles for electoral fairness, extension of the franchise and inclusion in political decision-making concealed a transformational potential, in part because the dominated nearly always outnumber the dominators, but also because the availability of fair and inclusive rights-based political processes make it possible for democracy to evolve even further, leading to the development of higher order interest-based skills and capacities, and giving rise to more diverse, egalitarian and collaborative forms and relationships.

In the U.S., following the Civil War, Blacks were systematically prevented from voting in order to undo the 13th, 14th and 15th Amendments to the Constitution and maintain the dominant wealth, status and power of Whites. Similarly, non-property owning men and women were denied the right to vote in order to maintain the dominance of property owners and men. It was not until the civil rights and women's revolutions of the 1960s and 70s that voting rights for Blacks began to be enforced, or much later that large numbers of Blacks, Latinos and women began running as political candidates, making it possible for more diverse, egalitarian and collaborative relationships to emerge, marking a new stage in the transition from power- to rights- to interest-based democracies.

As a result, the battle — even for rights-based democratic processes — continues today, in opposition to partisan restrictions on Constitutionally protected voting rights, including onerous registration requirements, gerrymandering, obscure forms of voter identification, exclusion of felons from voting lists, unlimited personal financial contributions, attack advertising, voting machine fraud, election hacking and countless other schemes designed to skew the electoral process in favor of a social, economic and political hierarchy that accepts the continued domination of wealthy contributors, men, Whites, Anglos and others.

These measures result from the perception that democracy will eventually result in a loss of unequal status, inequitable wealth and autocratic power for some, and must therefore be undermined, manipulated, biased and gamed in order to win, even at the cost of fundamental political principles, or indeed, of basic morality, elementary ethics and widely accepted, deep-seated values.

While these efforts have been vigorously opposed by groups like Vote Riders and others, it is important to consider carefully the limitations of power- and rights-based forms of representative democracy and to think in greater detail about what an interest-based, collaborative, participatory form of democracy might look like, along with the skills and capacities it is likely to require.

FROM REPRESENTATIVE TO PARTICIPATORY FORMS OF DEMOCRACY

While nearly all definitions of democracy recite the rights of citizens to make substantive decisions and vote on issues, the *actual* activity of representative democracy nearly everywhere boils down to the simple act of voting once every few years, individually and alone in a silent, isolated booth, for candidates we suppose will represent us in government. Very little of this is substantively democratic, or even political, as there is not much opportunity to discuss, debate or engage in dialogue over the issues, and while electoral campaigns go on and on seemingly forever, the act of voting is over in an instant. And it is then not the citizens, but their duly elected representatives who vote on legislation, appoint officials and decide how the government will spend monies raised in taxes, all allegedly in accordance with our wishes.

Jean-Jacques Rousseau observed as early as the 18th century that "The people of England deceive themselves when they fancy they are free; they are so, in fact, only during the election of members of parliament: for, as soon as a new one is elected, they are again in chains, and are nothing." While Joseph Stalin more cynically commented, "It is enough that the people know there was an election. The people who cast the votes decide nothing. The people who count the votes decide everything." And novelist Douglas Adams has Galactic President Zaphod Beeblebrox announce that the job of politicians was "not to wield power," but to attract attention from it, and from those that do.

In reality, especially in the U.S., candidates are most often wealthy individuals who have been endorsed by a small coterie of leaders in one of just two main political parties, funded primarily by wealthy donors and required to speak hypocritically out of both sides of their mouths in order to win votes from deeply divided and vastly diverse constituencies. They are then required to launch negative attack ads against each other, disregard unpopular, dissenting and minority voices, no matter how correct they may be, and make promises they cannot possibly keep. Once elected, they are hated by nearly half the voters, subjected to intense lobbying by corporations and special interests, bribed with favors and pressured into voting along pure party lines, or they are sidelined and their legislative ideas eviscerated.

The result is a dishonest, truncated, power- or rights-based process in which popular participation in direct decision-making is virtually abolished, diversity and dissent are discouraged, and integrity is all but eliminated in favor of conformity, hierarchy and control. More subtly, as Ashis Nandy wrote in *The Intimate Enemy* regarding the experience of dissent under colonialism in India,

> Conformity need not be monitored, dissent *has* to be. In any hegemony, dissent defines the limits and the final shape or legitimacy of a system, *not* conformity. ... You are taught to fight established authorities according to the conventions authorized by the authorities themselves, so that rebellion gradually becomes a matter of apprenticeship and learning correct radical praxis according to texts produced in the global citadels of knowledge.

At a deep level, democracy requires participation by citizens, and successful participation requires more advanced skills in critical thinking and political dialogue, both of which include an ability to imagine alternative futures, invent fresh approaches, appreciate diversity and dissent, solve complex social problems, and respond to conflicts constructively and collaboratively. Yet these are the primary political tools of the dominated, and hence have to be defined, molded, marginalized and channeled into safe waters by power- and rights-based political processes if domination is to continue unabated.

Therefore, while large numbers of people may vote or participate in minor ways in electoral campaigns, the core ideas, systems, processes and relationships are structured, sieved and slanted so they will have little or no impact on core policies and programs, and those without power will only rarely be allowed to participate in highly restricted, behind-closed-doors decision-making meetings.

As a result, the primary stimulus for many people's participation in politics is anger or fear, directed personally against politicians they naturally distrust and pre-determined policies they naturally abhor, in part because they had little or no say in selecting them. But these negative attitudes and emotions are often themselves apolitical and undemocratic, as they ignore the underlying political systems and structures that gave rise to their distrust and rarely convince others to protest or dissent or act in organized, extra-electoral ways, and sometimes even get in the way of active participation, dialogue and real political change.

Popular anger and fear, along with the "populist" political movements they periodically inspire, are nearly always emotional responses to unresolved political conflicts, rejections of corrupt right-based forms of democracy, and predictable outcomes of exclusionary political processes and hierarchical relationships that dismiss and divide people, rather than pay attention to and connect them. Interest-based approaches like dialogue and mediation, on the other hand, encourage people not only to express intense, heartfelt "pre-political" emotions, but offer a rich set of methods and techniques for responding both personally and systemically, and using emotional intelligence to turn anger and fear in the direction of problem-solving and transformational change.

While people often initially become politically active as individuals out of anger, fear, or negative responses to what they dislike, lasting participation is maximized only when they are able to transcend these responses and turn their displeasure in a positive, problem-solving direction by thinking, discussing, planning and working collaboratively with others, and imagining how they might use their anger and fear to bring what they care most deeply and passionately about into reality — not against others, but *with* them.

As long as democracy, public policy and political conflicts are experienced as belonging exclusively to elites, politicians, officials and experts; as long as the forms of democracy are primarily power- or rights-based, popular participation will be easily divided, dismissed and discouraged, allowing decisions to be made by small groups of elected representatives and their wealthy lobbyists and contributors, rather than by the people whose interests and capacity for dialogue lie at the heart of every substantively democratic system.

At the beginning of democracy in Athens, a process called "sortation" required every freeborn male citizen to serve every few years as a legislator, magistrate and juror, chosen by lot rather than by election. Indeed, elections were widely viewed as undemocratic and leading to oligarchy. Aristotle wrote, for example, in *Politics*:

> Democracy arose from the idea that those who are equal in any respect are equal absolutely. All are alike free, therefore they claim that all are free absolutely... [and as they] are all equal, claim equal participation in everything ... It is accepted as democratic when public offices are allocated by lot; and as oligarchic when they are filled by election.

While sortation has a number of advantages and disadvantages and is being experimented with in a number of countries and communities today, it is simply one of many ways that democracy might be redesigned to become less oligarchical, hierarchical and corruptible. In *Conflict Revolution*, I listed 30 additional ways of improving elections, which are revised and may be worth repeating here:

1. Approach elections as consensus-building efforts that identify potential solutions to important public problems, organizing discussions and dialogues over shared values, vision, strategies and problem-solving ideas
2. Facilitate public dialogue sessions in neighborhoods and communities in advance of elections to discuss key issues, explore disagreements, and agree on common goals and recommendations for action
3. Restructure and democratize the electoral system to increase diversity, direct participation and undiluted representation of minority interests
4. Provide free public campaign financing for all candidates,

remove soft money bribery from politics and reduce incentives
for graft, corruption and politically motivated appointments

5. Prohibit campaign contributions and expenditures in excess of
minimal agreed-upon amounts and impose fines or disqualify
candidates, contributors, lobbyists and those they represent
who exceed them

6. Equalize access to media and require limited free advertising
to all candidates, with fines or disqualification for those who
run personal attack ads or information that is intentionally
dishonest

7. Create a Voter Bill of Rights and a Constitutionally protected
right to vote

8. Ask the United Nations to establish expanded international
standards for elections to include in its Charter and
Declaration of Human Rights

9. Shorten the number of days for state primaries to reduce costs,
media hype, hypocrisy and opportunistic appeals to narrow
sectional interests

10. Institute joint nonpartisan election management teams to
oversee the process as a whole

11. Provide for automatic, universal, secure, lifetime registration,
with opportunities for Election Day registration

12. Establish a national Election Day work holiday and allow early
voting by mail and email

13. Extend the right to vote to everyone whose income or property
is taxed, including recent immigrants and former felons

14. Prevent removal from voting lists without ample advance
notice to those removed, with opportunities to appeal and
penalties for partisan removals

15. Use online voting, with machines that are reliable, publicly
owned and tamperproof, and an easily accessible paper trail to
confirm results

16. Require candidates to mediate ground rules for debates,
dialogues and campaigns in advance, agreeing on the kind of
campaign they will run

17. Mediate and arbitrate disputes between candidates or parties that violate ground rules, and censure, fine or disqualify those responsible

18. Formulate party platforms as vision statements drafted with input from facilitated dialogues and local citizen assemblies, adopted by consensus

19. Focus on issues rather than personalities by encouraging meaningful dialogues over important social, economic and political issues

20. Arrange for multiple, facilitated, in-depth local dialogues that include independent candidates, write-ins and "fringe" political parties, eliminate "stacking" of audiences and encourage public questioning and discussion

21. Schedule in-depth discussions of especially divisive issues in mediated public policy forums and televised town hall meetings, facilitated by professional mediators with ample time for audience participation

22. Eliminate gerrymandering of electoral boundaries by using algorithms (see, e.g., research by Jonathan Mattingly and other mathematicians), elected officials and balanced, community-based citizens commissions to draw nonpartisan voting lines that give minority constituencies a voice

23. End winner-take-all elections by using percentage or proportional representation, or instant runoff voting (i.e., allowing second choice votes to count) or fusion voting (i.e., allowing two or more parties to nominate the same candidate), or similar alternatives

24. Decentralize political decision-making by having voters vote directly and securely on important issues from their homes, workplaces and publicly accessible computers

25. Require multilingual ballots and poll workers who are fluent in languages likely to be used by voters online and at each polling place

26. Require polling places to be wheelchair accessible and ballots to be printed in Braille and large print, or available in audio

27. Eliminate the Election College and make the popular vote conclusive

28. In the event of close outcomes, recount or repeat the process from scratch

29. Continue to conduct dialogues following elections regardless of who won, and require losing candidates to be included as advisers to newly elected governments

30. Publicly evaluate the process afterward and agree on improved procedures for the next election

Whichever of the many suggestions and proposals for reforming democracy we choose to adopt, it is especially important today that we consider the ways advanced computer and internet technologies impact democratic processes, and how they might be used to corrupt, or make it more direct and participatory.

COMPUTER TECHNOLOGY, ELECTIONS AND PARTICIPATORY DEMOCRACY

Extraordinary advances in computing and technology have completely altered the stage, setting and backdrop in which elections and democracy take place. On the negative side, electoral results are now being tabulated by machines that are vulnerable to hacking; emails and documents of political parties and candidates are being broken into and faked; social media platforms are being manipulated by people in other countries to influence domestic election results, and the entire electoral system is increasingly vulnerable to being fixed or gamed.

On the positive side, with the development and ubiquity of computers, smartphones, tablets and similar devices, and especially with the anticipated advent of quantum computing, it is (or soon will be) *technically* feasible for everyone to vote in a secure way on any number of important issues rapidly, regularly and directly. Moreover, using interest-based skills and capacities, it will be possible for nearly all social, economic and political decision-making processes to be designed in ways that invite mass discussion, debate and dialogue, and produce better outcomes than would be possible using power- and rights-based systems.

Among the principal arguments and justifications cited over centuries for requiring democratic decisions to be made indirectly by elected representatives and professional politicians, has been the difficulty in researching and understanding complex political issues, the supposedly superior intelligence and experience of elites, the length of time required to present these issues to the public and allow them to deliberate and make wise choices, and the idea that masses of people are more susceptible to bias and emotion and will therefore make poorer, more prejudiced and less fair decisions.

Yet we know that the best decisions are those that are publicly discussed and debated by many people, where diverse ideas and perspectives are elicited and synthesized, where there is permission to dissent and opportunity to critique, and where efforts are made to reach consensus, or to collaboratively negotiate and search for options that satisfy interests, rather than simply voting pro or con.

Yet modern technology and social media make it easy to network people in ways that are fundamentally non-hierarchical and difficult for private interests or wealthy elites to dominate or control. For this reason, Paul Mason, along with others, argues that "the main faultline in the modern world is between networks and hierarchies …," in other words, between collaboration and control, or democracy and domination.

If computers and connectivity represent a new sort of status; if information and data reflect a new kind of wealth; and if technical "know-how," scientific capacity and theoretical understanding epitomize a new form of power, not only does the nature of politics and political conflict, but the entire *landscape* of what is possible in democracy have to shift from autocratic power-based hierarchies and representative rights-based bureaucracies to interest-based, collaborative, socially networked, direct, *participatory* forms of decision-making.

It will then become *possible* for us, using internet technology (which is expanding more rapidly than our ability to understand or avert its long-term consequences), to jointly design processes and relationships that invite people to participate in dialogues, make decisions and respond to conflicts in collaborative ways, based on positive attitudes and emotions that flow from higher order interest-based skills and capacities; on caring, community and social networking. These lie beneath anger and can stimulate the learning, openness, honesty, trust and empathy that are essential for collaborative problem-solving, democratic dialogue and conflict resolution.

Not only is it technically feasible for everyone on the planet to participate actively in raising, discussing, critiquing, refining, voting and reaching consensus on important social, economic and political issues, it is also possible to connect people globally in conversations and dialogues that reinforce diversity, dissent and minority rights while supporting individuality and creativity in problem-solving. What is more, it is possible to do these in stages, phases or branching processes that move from issue identification and clarification to research and analysis, to dialogue and option generating, to consensus and implementation seamlessly, accurately and rapidly enough to outperform both autocratic and representative forms of government.

Computer programs known as "deep neural networks," for example, have learned in the last few years to converse intelligently with humans, drive cars, win at video games, beat chess and Go champions, find cancer cells and planets in distant galaxies, analyze particle collisions, design new drugs, make scientific discoveries, prove mathematical theorems and perform many other high level functions. Recently, Google's DeepMind AI program AlphaGo, created by Dennis Hassabis and team, learned to defeat the best human Go player through supervised learning, in which researchers fed the program 100,000 top amateur games and taught it to imitate what it saw, then put it through reinforcement learning in which the program played itself and learned from the results.

A newer version, AlphaGo Zero, began as a blank slate, knowing only the rules of Go, and playing games against itself. After three days of training and 4.9 million training games, AlphaGo Zero defeated AlphaGo 100 games to zero. In chess, it took four hours to defeat the best chess programs. Subsequently, the DeepMind team released AlphaZero, which used AlphaGo Zero's approach and achieved superhuman levels of play within 24 hours in chess, shogi and Go, discovering new techniques that *vastly* exceeded human knowledge accumulated over 3,000 years of play. We can only imagine the impact this technology will have on other human "games" and forms of problem-solving.

Equally significantly, rapid progress is now being made in two key areas: first, evolutionary computing, which has defeated human players in a variety of computer games by evolving on its own to become more successful; and second, quantum computers, which are expected shortly to achieve "quantum supremacy," permitting calculations that are orders of magnitude beyond the capacity of the most advanced digital computer it is possible to create.

These innovations suggest that, for the first time in history, it will become possible, using advanced computer technology, to detect, analyze and propose solutions to complex social, economic and political problems, and design programs similar to those used in mathematics and physics, or to play computer games, or to identify dogs and cancer. This, of course, in no way guarantees that human-selected criteria or computer-identified solutions will be beneficial, or not be used to promote ruinous militaristic or power-based outcomes.

We therefore need to carefully consider how it might be possible to avoid these outcomes and at the same time direct our full scientific and technological capacity at radically re-invigorating and re-inventing democracy — not just in its ability to compute and calculate data, but in enhancing our understanding of dialogue and mediation, deepening our empathy and emotional intelligence; improving our processes and relationships; expanding popular participation in problem-solving and decision-making; and preventing chronic conflicts at their source — not just politically, but socially and economically, familially and organizationally, substantively and procedurally.

What, then, in broad, general terms, might an interest-based, technologically advanced, socially collaborative, participatory form of democracy look like? The answer, of course, depends on the unique characteristics of each circumstance and is beyond the scope of this book, and possibly even our present ability to answer. A *generic* answer, however, I believe, is that it will look a lot like the interest-based skills and capacities, collaborative arts and sciences, conflict resolution processes and methods described in earlier chapters and practiced today in diverse ways in cultures and settings around the world. (For more on this topic, see my book, *Conflict Revolution: Designing Preventative Solutions for Chronic Social, Economic and Political Conflicts* [Second Edition].)

It would be mistaken, of course, to imagine that a simple technological fix will cure all the ills of democracy, and it is important to acknowledge that every new technology poses fresh risks and problems that could not have imagined beforehand. It is also important not to rely exclusively on technology, computers and social media, but continue to maximize direct, person-to-person, face-to-face dialogue and communication, as virtual forms of participation sometimes slip into flaming and cyberbullying, and are less engaging, offering fewer opportunities for emotionally satisfying communications, and failing to spark the creativity and quality of energy that flows from personal presence, or the empathy and attentiveness stirred by personal encounters.

We know from history that revolutions and paradigm shifts in math, science and technology inevitably trigger corresponding revolutions and shifts in society, economics and politics, driving them to adapt and evolve, and by developing more advanced skills and capacities. Yet while math, science and technology are constantly changing, often without regard to what people think of them, social, economic and political changes are often actively resisted, even violently opposed, creating limits on our ability to adapt and evolve, and exacerbating chronic conflicts.

Chronic conflicts are a natural and inevitable outcome of diversity in any complex adaptive system. They appear most frequently, powerfully and intractably in systems that have started to evolve and entered a "phase transition," or period of "criticality," in which they become increasingly unstable, allowing small changes in one area to impact what happens in other areas, triggering cascading consequences, chaos and "emergent" phenomena that are vastly different from anything that might have been predicted or imagined beforehand, yet are linked to the fundamental limits that characterize the system. It is the same, I believe, with political conflicts and the evolution of democracy.

The Limits of Democracy

Because each new evolution in the level or form of democracy requires higher order skills and capacities that have not yet fully emerged, in order to become successful and sustainable; and because these skills and capacities are still being invented, discovered, learned and practiced; and because they are often doubted, dismissed, discouraged and undermined by those who accept the status quo or seek to dominate and control others; and because chronic conflicts often become more intense as new skill sets emerge, but before they are accepted and make improved outcomes possible; new forms of democracy are perceived as getting in the way of traditional methods for resolving conflicts, and may be blamed or viewed as leading to increased anarchy and chaos.

When this occurs, people may become frightened of change and seek an end to political conflicts through the deceptive security of power-based dictatorships that suppress dissent, diversity and democracy; or through the tranquilizing regulation and comparative calm of rights-based bureaucracies and representative forms of government. Yet, as these higher order skills and capacities multiply, consolidate and become successful, fears of change begin to lessen, opening paths to systemic transition.

When Plato wrote in *The Republic* that democracies inevitably succumb to tyranny, he did not consider the possibility that significant advances in conflict resolution skills and capacities could make them *more* stable and successful, or that widespread application of those skills to political conflicts might improve the ability to resolve chronic social, economic and political conflicts at their source without triggering the fears of anarchy and chaos that lead people into the vicious, violent arms of dictators and tyrants.

Clearly, using lower order, adversarial, win/lose power- and rights-based methods will predictably generate a large number of intractable chronic conflicts that will, in turn, place limits on the expression, expansion and evolution of more advanced collaborative, interest-based forms of democracy. At the same time, conflicts that appear intractable at a lower level of skill can easily be resolved at a higher one. Indeed, *all* approaches to politics find their limits in some set of conflicts that cannot be resolved within their lower order confines, in exactly the way that certain three dimensional problems cannot be solved using two dimensional skills.

I use the word "limit" here in its mathematical sense, as a value, bound, border, or fractal dimension that can be approached asymptotically, and by degrees; a region of criticality and transition; a place where something ends — in this case, a more primitive form of democracy — and something entirely new begins. Consider, for example, the following forms and varieties of democracy, and what I regard as their likely evolutionary limits:

1. Social Democracies and the Limits of Prejudice, Discrimination and Inequality:

Societies are arenas of shared communication and interaction, in which status and prestige are conferred either innately or individually, by character or category, generically or behaviorally, equally or hierarchically. The *social* form of democracy is one in which people are regarded as *innately* equal in their entitlement to dignity and respect; their right to be judged by their behaviors rather than their genetics; their diversity and individuality; their freedom to socialize, associate and form fresh relationships, connections, networks and communities, and create environments in which it is more acceptable to be caring, creative and collaborative than hostile, constrained and competitive.

Inequalities in status lead to social stereotyping, chauvinism, bigotry, prejudice and discrimination, which reinforce hierarchy and domination, most often based on race, gender, nationality, religion, sexual orientation, physical disability, appearance and similar reasons, each of which reduces the effectiveness of social democracy by disconnecting us as human beings and weakening our ability to collaborate in solving social problems.

Without equal entitlement to dignity and respect in social communications and interactions, chronic conflicts will inevitably arise, relationships will become oppressive, empathy and creativity will be stifled, and love and caring will begin to die. Power- and rights-based approaches to social communication and interaction *cannot* succeed in preventing these outcomes or solving complex social problems, whether in couples, families, schools, workplaces, neighborhoods or societies as a whole, because they foster stereotypes, prejudices and discriminations that divide people into hostile, competitive and conflicted social camps, and by doing so, reject diversity, block consensus, undermine dialogue, suppress empathy and caring, and impede collaboration.

2. Economic Democracies and the Limits of Capitalism, Poverty and Inequity:

Capitalism first became dominant using a potent combination of financial prowess, cheap factory-produced commodities and representative, rights-based democracies to undermine feudal aristocracies, secure favorable commercial legislation, manipulate markets and break down barriers to trade erected by protectionist foreign and local governments.

Capitalism gave birth to democracy and enthusiastically supported it, yet at the same time, has *systematically* limited and undermined it; for example, by keeping the social welfare state weak; encouraging bias and prejudice against minorities; creating hierarchical workplaces and authoritarian corporations; inequitably distributing wealth and repressing employee organizations; controlling elected representatives through campaign contributions and lobbying, and opposing direct popular participation in decision-making, among others.

Capitalism is a limit on the evolution of interest-based forms of democracy because it produces, promotes and profits from inequalities in social status, inequities in wealth and autocracies in political decision-making. It favors power- and rights-based processes because they are friendly to hierarchies and bureaucracies, monetize virtually everything, promote commercial exchange, protect private property and prioritize *financial* bottom lines over moral and ethical, or societal and relational ones. Adam Smith wrote, for example, that "The necessity of civil government grows up with the acquisition of valuable property ... till there be property there can be no government, the very end of which is to secure wealth, and to defend the rich from the poor."

More ominously, capitalism permits the wealthy to purchase, own and profit from natural resources, not only exhausting the land on which our food is produced, but poisoning the water we drink and polluting the air we breathe. Merely through the sale of fossil fuels, it is irrevocably heating our planet, altering our weather, raising sea levels, extinguishing countless species and threatening the survival of millions, if not all.

In recent years, we have seen a shift in the evolution, organization and operations of capitalism, as production and distribution have become more globalized and integrated across national borders; financial markets have become more computerized and integrated internationally; and robotics, artificial intelligence, the internet and neural net programming have dramatically reduced or eliminated dependence on human labor.

These have led the *form* and nature of wealth to shift from the extraction of raw materials and manufacture of commodities to the invention of apps, search engines and financial algorithms; the analysis of "big data," delivery of information, and provision of services; and the creation of networks and platforms that connect people electronically around the world, all of which lie outside the nation-state.

Most recently, these shifts have revealed a new level of vulnerability in corporations to popular opinion and permitted the use of social media to pressure businesses and governments to act more democratically and humanely on a wide range of social, economic and political issues. More profoundly, they have led to the development of new skills and capacities, and a consequent reimagining of the possibilities for political democracy. As Peter Drucker wrote:

> That knowledge has become *the* resource, rather than *a* resource, is what makes our society 'post-capitalist.' It changes, ... fundamentally, the structure of society. It creates new social dynamics. It creates new economic dynamics. It creates new politics.

Yet the "new politics" these post-capitalist dynamics create require a *corresponding* evolution in the forms of political democracy, which depend on the elimination of limits placed by capitalism on the political process in order to dominate, manipulate and control it using campaign contributions, lobbying and other methods that corrupt political integrity, increase poverty and economic inequity, and stifle creative, collaborative approaches to political problem-solving. These can only be reversed by democratic methods that implicitly permit the redistribution of socially created wealth and allow for democratic participation in decisions regarding the uses of socially important information. Rana Dasgupta, for example, has commented recently in the London Guardian:

> If we wish to rediscover a sense of political purpose in our era of global finance, big data, mass migration and ecological upheaval, we have to imagine political forms capable of operating at that same scale. The current political system must be supplemented with global financial regulations, certainly and probably transnational political mechanisms, too. That is how we will complete this globalisation of ours, which today stands dangerously unfinished. Its economic and technological systems are dazzling indeed, but in order for it to serve the human community, it must be subordinated to an equally spectacular political infrastructure, which we have not even begun to conceive.

Dasgupta goes on to describe how the decline of the nation state has given rise to a widespread "apocalyptic nationalism" as antiquated political systems and structures are increasingly overwhelmed by issues that are simply beyond their capacity to handle, necessitating the development of new global economic and political institutions, and consequently a new global definition of citizenship.

3. Power-Based Political Democracies and the Limits of Fascism, Dictatorship and Control:

Political democracies will always remain incomplete, conflicted and repressed where families and societies are authoritarian, patriarchal and unequal; and where corporations and workplaces are dictatorial, discriminatory and inequitable. While there are many different forms and varieties of democracy, they are all holistically connected and interdependent, interacting like waves that cancel and amplify each other in the spaces where they intersect.

Somewhat less obviously, the strengthening of higher order skills and capacities in one arena, form or variety of democracy inevitably trickles over and impacts others, supporting their mutual success and sustainability as newly-emergent systems. The *daily practice* of extending dignity and respect to others in couples, relationships, families, schools and workplaces, especially to those who have been subjected to stereotyping, prejudice and unequal treatment, will produce widespread political ramifications, as will the extension of participatory democratic forms of problem-solving and decision-making.

More ominously, the opposite is also true. The *destruction* of political democracy by fascists, dictators and tyrants inevitably leads to the annihilation of social and economic democracies, and of family and workplace democracies as well — indeed, it is often their very purpose. For this reason, the daily practice of individuals in treating women and minorities, foreigners and employees with dignity and respect, becomes contested territory in an undeclared war over hegemony and control, even in small, seemingly insignificant conflicts where it seems not to matter — yet each is an essential, integrated part of the underlying project of maintaining domination and control.

For domination and control to replicate and succeed, those who are dominated must, at least tactically and temporarily, accept their subordinate status, wealth and power, or if not, they must be violently and decisively pushed down whenever they assert their right to dignity and respect, or seek to participate equally in solving problems and making decisions, along with those who are courageous enough to support them.

For this reason, patriarchy is required in couples and families so that men can dominate and control relationships; prejudice is required in societies so that one race, gender or religion can dominate and control "inferior" ones; hierarchy is required in workplaces, schools and corporations so that employers, administrators and executives can dominate and control employees, students and consumers; and autocracy is required in politics so that leaders can dominate and control citizens and competing nation-states. Yet if just *one* of these arenas ceases to support hierarchical domination and control, the ability of the others to do so is diminished and compromised as well.

Hence, fascist movements always begin by playing off widespread fear, envy and hatred of others, but inevitably expand to rigidly define and enforce gender roles; to glorify patriarchal families and subordinate women; to reinforce hierarchy and obedience in workplaces, schools and corporations; to undermine education, science and mathematics; to oppose artistic freedom and cultural innovation; to brutalize language, burn books, murder journalists and extinguish independent media.

Recently, Benjamin Carter Hett has written, in *The Death of Democracy: Hitler's Rise to Power and the Downfall of the Weimar Republic,* that the Nazi's should be viewed as "a nationalist protest movement against globalization," together with a "victim mentality" directed not only at Jews, Communists and others, but at democracy itself as a political system. Conflicts and crises under fascism were therefore "manufactured by a political right wing that wanted to exclude more than half the population from political representation and refused even the mildest compromise." In my view, this was done not only to undermine democracy and justify the use of violence and genocide, but to resolve conflicts by exterminating everyone the Nazi's feared, hated and found responsible for them; in part by fomenting conflicts with the left that drove frightened people to seek security in a combative, ruthlessly anti-democratic government.

A number of recent books have explored the ways democracies end or die, but ultimately, the story everywhere is nearly always the same: fascists are backed financially by wealthy supporters, and popularly by displaced, marginalized workers, who feel their continued racial, religious and gender dominance, or place in the social, economic and political hierarchy, are being lost and threatened by the leveling, egalitarian aims of democracy and its evolution beyond power- or right-based methods and values.

In 1935, Sinclair Lewis wrote *It Can't Happen Here,* to show that it can, followed by Phillip Roth's *The Plot Against America,* which reached a similar conclusion. Formally, all that would be required for fascism to succeed in the U.S., or by analogy in any rights-based democracy, is a supportive electorate, a willing President, a majority in Congress and a five to four vote of the Supreme Court. The question poses itself: what might be done to prevent such an outcome?

Mediation and dialogue by themselves are insufficient, since even though they are capable of moderating and settling social, economic and political conflicts, without an interest-based orientation toward resolving conflicts at their chronic, systemic source, they can easily be twisted and distorted by fears of conflict, and end up being willing to trade justice for a *pretense* of harmony, peace and civility.

To illustrate, several attempts at mediation took place immediately before the outbreak of World War II between Germany and England, mediated initially by Walter Runciman, with later mediations taking place directly between Adolf Hitler and Neville Chamberlain regarding the fate of the Sudetenland in Czechoslovakia. The infamous Munich Agreement that allowed Germany to annex Sudetenland was in fact *mediated* by Benito Mussolini, but without the participation of the Czechs or any other concerned parties. At first wildly celebrated, the agreement was soon reviled and denounced as "appeasement."

The ultimate aim of fascist movements is not to resolve conflicts, or engage in dialogue, or negotiate with their opponents, or seek to evolve and transcend the reasons that gave rise to their disputes, but to violently and forcibly suppress them at their persistent evolutionary source — in their very *desire* for freedom and equality, for diversity and individuality, for creativity and caring, for dignity and independence. As a result, they are driven to oppose life itself — and therefore *eventually* fail, but not without immeasurable loss and destruction. (For more on fascism and mediation, see *Conflict Revolution: Designing Preventative Solutions for Chronic Social, Economic and Political Conflicts* [Second Edition].)

4. Rights-Based Political Democracies and the Limit of Bureaucracy, Autocracy and Coercion:

Perhaps the paramount limit of rights-based forms of democracy is bureaucracy, which is often seen as a method for reducing the chaos and anarchy of conflicts, and tying dictatorial, power-based approaches to decision-making in a knot by obfuscating, delaying and sidetracking *all* efforts to bring about systemic change. Hence, it is important to consider how interest-based forms of democracy and responses to political conflicts might be designed in ways that minimize or prevent the manipulation of political decision-making and immobilization of change by rights-based bureaucracies. As Simone Weil warned decades ago,

> Whether the mask is labeled Fascism, Democracy or Dictatorship of the Proletariat, our great adversary remains the Apparatus – the bureaucracy, the police, the military. Not the one facing us across the frontier or the battle lines ... but the one that calls itself our protector and makes us its slaves. No matter what the circumstances, the worst betrayal will always be to subordinate ourselves to this Apparatus, and to trample underfoot, in its service, all human values in ourselves and in others.

Bureaucracies also promise a kind of safety from the dangers created by political conflicts, which are remedied by impersonal rules and regulations, unemotional policies and procedures, exhaustive repetition, boring trivia, inhuman facelessness and apathetic uncaring. Hannah Arendt described it precisely:

> [T]he latest and most formidable form of ... domination [is] bureaucracy ... which could be properly called rule by Nobody. If, in accord with traditional political thought, we identify tyranny as government that is not held to give account of itself, rule by Nobody is clearly the most tyrannical of all, since there is no one left who would even be asked to answer for what is being done.

255

Interest-based approaches to conflict resolution like dialogue and mediation respond to bureaucracy by attempting to reduce reliance on "one size fits all" methodologies, individualizing rules and regulations, humanizing choices, shifting the locus of problem-solving and decision-making from officials to those who are closest to the problem, acknowledging emotions, eliciting expressions of caring, satisfying interests, encouraging people to learn collaboratively, trying out solutions before institutionalizing them, allowing issues to remain open for revision and improvement, and similar techniques.

Max Weber defined bureaucracy as a "search for domination through knowledge," arguing that bureaucracy converts the state itself into a new form of private property for public bureaucrats and generates a "blind trust in authority through a combination of passive obedience, of trust in authority, ... of an ossified and formalistic behavior, of fixed principles, conceptions and traditions."

In *Conflict Revolution: Designing Preventative Systems for Chronic Social, Economic and Political Conflicts*, I wrote about rights-based bureaucracies as follows:

> The veiled, yet deeply embedded values of bureaucracy are those of control, conformity, formality, diffused responsibility, discouragement of initiative and impersonal compliance, each of which generates chronic conflicts. For these reasons, German sociologist Robert Michels argued that bureaucracy is inextricably linked with what he called "the iron law of oligarchy," because increasing complexity and bureaucratization cause power to be concentrated in the hands of an elite that is then able to rule dictatorially, even within political parties that claim to value democracy. Michels believed that superior skills in administration themselves lead to oligarchical rule, domination, bureaucracy and the loss of political power and principles through electoral moderation and a desire for efficiency and success ... Bureaucracy concentrates access to communication at the top, reinforcing isolation and apathy below. This ... allows those in the middle to manipulate information, control communication networks

and consolidate their power. It also allows them to use their positions to acquire unique, secret knowledge and skills that make them difficult to replace, ossifying leadership and alienating the public ... while distancing themselves personally from responsibility.

In contrast to rights-based reliance on abstract legal formulas, interest-based democracies require not only popular participation in governing, but an openness to creating customized solutions by practicing higher order skills in collaborative negotiation, consensus building, dialogue and mediation that are essential for it to expand and become sustainable.

5. Interest-Based Political Democracies and the Limits of Consensus, Collaboration and Ownership:

Interest-based democracies only evolve, expand and become sustainable as they propagate and grow more successful in resolving internal and external conflicts, and solving problems that lie beyond the skills and capacities of power- or rights-based methodologies. As indicated above, it is the *inability* to resolve these conflicts that not only drives people to embrace less satisfying power- or right-based methods, but always defines, uniquely for each historical period, the limits of social, economic and political democracy.

For interest-based democracies, as well as for all others, there are really two kinds of limits: first, those that drag existing processes and relationships backward into less evolved, yet more familiar forms; and second, those that propel them forward into newer, more advanced forms and practices. While the backward limits are clear and consist of a return to power- and rights-based methods, the forward limits are less so, in part because we have yet to understand or implement interest-based democracies fully, or to discover and develop the advanced skills and capacities that are needed to support them on a sufficiently broad or global scale.

We can, however, be clear: first, that the ability to evolve socially, economically and politically is both predictable and increasingly essential; second, that it is interactive, cumulative and chaotic, relying sensitively on what has gone before; and third, that it is exponential, as each new advance requires a higher order of skills and capacities in order to tackle higher orders of complexity in the problems that need to be solved.

For the present, it is clear that at the heart of interest-based forms of political democracy lie the catalytic, transformational arts and sciences of collaboration, consensus, empathy, emotional intelligence, direct participation and ownership — not just of the problems, but of the processes, the relationships and the solutions as well, each of which is required if urgent global problems are to be addressed and solved as rapidly and competently as power- and right-based processes.

Interest-based processes therefore require even more advanced skills and capacities — in learning how to live together in diverse communities and act according to shared values, ethics and morality; in shifting our attitudes and intentions toward "foreigners" and opponents; in cultivating individuality, empathy and connectedness; in deepening our capacity for caring and intimacy; in behaving humanely, with dignity and respect toward the least among us; in facilitating dialogues and mediating disputes with our opponents. Often, and at present, it is political conflicts that limit our ability to act in these ways, and dialogue, mediation and other collaborative arts and sciences that point the way forward.

Ultimately, democracy requires *ownership* of the entire social, economic and political system, including the decisions, processes and relationships that shape it. Ownership, in turn, requires still more advanced skills, since, as owners, there is no one left to blame, other than ourselves, for whatever is not working, and blaming ourselves is pointless, time-consuming, exhausting and depressing, as it is much easier and far more enjoyable to just fix it. But fixing it, when we disagree about whether and how to do so, demands dialogue and conflict resolution skills.

A Return to Reality: Battles Are Raging

Lest we lull ourselves into wishfully thinking that all democracy consists of are a few interesting ideas and interest-based techniques, it is important to remind ourselves that very real battles are now taking place here and around the world between those who favor interest-based forms of democracy and those who are actively seeking to replace it with prejudice and discrimination; or who favor dictatorship and fascism; or who advocate autocracy, theocracy and plutocracy; or who are simply frightened of conflict and chaos and prefer legalistic, rights-based solutions.

The battles that are now taking place between these alternative political futures will have consequences that significantly impact our lives and those of generations to come, just as they did following World War II. Conflicts are taking place in nearly every community over most, if not all of the issues discussed in this book and more, and the outcome is far from certain.

What is essential for us to understand is that these battles are *simultaneously* being waged over the *way* they are waged — that is, over whether it is better to attack each other aggressively, violently and personally, even in the name of dignity, peace and respect; or to engage in collaborative, non-violent, empathetic dialogue and mediation in an effort to reconcile our differences.

These hidden, unacknowledged, yet immensely consequential battles are being waged in *every* conflict, every mediation, negotiation and dialogue, every conversation about race and gender and a long list of social, economic and political issues that divide us. In every one of these conversations, we are asked to choose between whether we will wage peace or war; whether we will respect each other and listen to those who disagree with us, or disrespect and dismiss them; whether we will act democratically or dictatorially, caringly or hatefully, collaboratively or violently. We are consequently at a moral and ethical crossroads that is *disguised* as a political conflict. But we are also at a political conflict that is disguised as a moral and ethical crossroads —

in other words, we are increasingly living in a time when morality has political consequences and politics has moral import. As a result, it is not only our opposition to hatred that matters, but our skill and capacity in working respectfully and democratically, ethically and morally, caringly and collaboratively to oppose it.

We know from personal experience, if not from Mohandas K. Gandhi and Dr. Martin Luther King, Jr., Cesar Chavez and Mary Parker Follett, Gene Sharp and Desmond Tutu, along with countless others, that when we respond to hatred with hatred, even when we win, hatred also wins and in this way, plants its seed in future generations, sometimes in the form of petty personal animosities, but also politically in the form of large-scale fears and hatreds, and routinely as adversarial, inhumane attitudes and immoralities in ordinary, everyday conflicts. As Albert Einstein expressed it, in words that still ring true,

> I believe that America will prove that democracy is not merely a form
> of government based on a sound Constitution, but is, in fact, a way of
> life tied to a great tradition, the tradition of moral strength. Today more
> than ever, the fate of the human race depends upon the moral strength
> of human beings.

WHAT IF IT'S TOO LITTLE AND TOO LATE?

It may come to pass that the methods and techniques, skills and capacities advocated here are insufficient to prevent the downfall of democracy, as they proved to be in Germany, Italy and Spain before World War II, in which case we will have lost something precious and irreplaceable, and will be forced to respond with whatever tools remain. But sooner or later, it will be necessary for us to learn how to talk to our opponents about our disagreements and learn to live together, rather than slaughter each other, as we have done for centuries.

Our history as a species has, for several millennia at least, been one of unremitting willingness to use violence for social, economic and political gain; and while, as Steven Pinker has shown, the long-term trend appears to be away from violence, it is possible that this pattern and way of thinking will nonetheless stall us at a strategic moment in our development of the higher order skills we need to support political dialogue and sustain interest-based approaches to democracy, problem-solving and conflict resolution. A character in Pakistani novelist Camilla Shamsie's *Broken Verses* offers the following advice:

> It's true, that in concrete battles the tyrants may have the upper hand in terms of tactics, weapons, ruthlessness. What our means of protest attempt to do is to move the battles toward abstract space. Force tyranny to defend itself in language. Weaken it with public opinion, with supreme court judgments, with debates and subversive curriculum. Take hold of the media, take hold of the printing presses and the newspapers, broadcast your views from pirate radio channels, spread the word. Don't do anything less than all you are capable of, and remember that history outlives you. It may not be until your grandchildren's days that they'll point back and say, there were sown the seeds of what we've now achieved.

Nonetheless, it may be "too little and too late" in various parts of the world to prevent a combination of fascist violence, authoritarian control, private greed, fear of foreigners and prejudice from gaining political power and using governmental power and military force to dominate and suppress efforts at expanding social equality, increasing economic equity and supporting political democracy, as has happened on numerous occasions before.

Yet, in each of these cases, violent, dominating, authoritarian, power-based, adversarial approaches have finally failed — in my view, because they are simply too hostile to be human, too simplistic to solve complex problems, too egotistical to avoid hubris, too repressed to permit open and honest conversations about things that matter.

As Margaret Mead wrote, "For the human species to evolve, the conversation must deepen." And it must do so not just in the shape of ideas or content, but attitudes and behaviors, methods and techniques, processes and relationships — in other words, it must allow us to learn new skills and capacities that we can use to match, step-by-step, our scientific and technological evolution, our growing artistic and emotional acumen, and whatever else we may need to solve our problems and support our continued life together.

In my experience over 38 years practicing mediation and facilitating dialogues, except for a few rare instances, the effort to resolve conflicts has *always* been too little and too late, because nearly no one agrees to talk until their conversations have already ceased being civil. Yet *every* effort we make to communicate and resolve our differences helps us avoid future ones and learn how to handle them better, and therefore, it is *never* too little or too late.

More importantly, the idea that what we do will be too little or too late merely encourages us to surrender, helping to bring about the very problems we trying to solve. We can never know in advance whether our efforts will make a difference, but we must make them anyway, because it is the only way we can keep hope alive and preserve our humanity. Failing that, we will be forced to take sides against the forces that divide us, knowing that by doing so, we may be destroying something precious that gives us hope and makes us human.

The choice is ours, both individually and collectively, yet as our skills and capacity continue to increase, so do the possibilities for more evolved personal, familial and organizational, as well as social, economic and political forms of democracy. We have opportunities every day to demonstrate that conflicts *can* be successfully understood, respectfully discussed and collaboratively resolved without slipping into the antagonistic emotions and adversarial behaviors that keep us divided.

By doing so, we become privileged: first, by being able to witness the transformation and transcendence of conflicts on a small scale; second, by being able to experience the deep, heartfelt connections and caring that lie beneath all our conflicts; and third, by being able to catch a small glimpse of what our future as a species might be. The last word, as always, belongs to poets. Here, then, is Adrienne Rich:

> *What would it mean to live*
> *in a city whose people were changing*
> *each other's despair into hope? –*
> *You yourself must change it. –*
> *what would it feel like to know*
> *your country was changing? —*
> *You yourself must change it. —*
> *Though your life felt arduous*
> *new and unmapped and strange*
> *what would it mean to stand on the first*
> *page of the end of despair?*

ABOUT THE AUTHOR

Kenneth Cloke is the Director of the Center of Dispute Resolution in Santa Monica, California. He is a mediator, arbitrator, consultant and trainer who specializes in resolving multiparty conflicts and designing dispute resolution systems for organizations. He holds BA and JD degrees from UC Berkeley, and PhD and LL.M. degrees from UCLA. He did post-doctoral work at Yale, is a graduate of the National Judicial College, and teaches at Pepperdine University, Southern Methodist University, USC and Saybrook University. He is the founder and first president of Mediators Beyond Borders. Learn more at www.kencloke.

INDEX

groucho, 19
guidance, 214
guidelines, 126, 214
guilt, 84, 128, 132
guin, 159
guru, 99
guys, 38
gypsies, 168
gyrus, 39

H

hacked, 231
handicap, 19
hanif, 175
hannah, 197, 209, 225, 232, 255
harassed, 138
harassment, 70–71
harbinger, 178
harmony, 6, 254
harsh, 42, 64
haruki, 131
harvard, 4, 39
hassabis, 243
hateful, 88, 133
hatefully, 259
hatred, 15, 88, 110, 159–160, 167–168, 175–177, 179, 195, 223, 253, 260
hatreds, 15, 32, 149, 260
havel, 1, 3, 81
healthcare, 197
heather, 170
heating, 249
hegemony, 20, 227, 236, 252
heinlein, 157

hellenic, 178
herds, 168
heredity, 8
heretic, 195
herman, 159
heroes, 141, 148
herzliya, 45
heterarchical, 124
hett, 253
hierarchically, 8, 205, 248
hierarchies, 39, 228, 242, 249
hierarchy, 9, 28, 53, 147, 203, 234, 236, 248, 252–253
highcontext, 142
hiroshima, 207
histocompatibility, 42
historian, 169–170
historians, 170
hitler, 22, 253–254
hobbes, 173
hobgoblins, 35
homeless, 168
homogenizing, 139
homophobic, 5
homosexuals, 38
hooligan, 45
hormone, 37
hormones, 36
hostile, 17–18, 23, 26, 34, 41, 44, 65, 89–90, 93, 117, 132, 134, 145, 155, 167, 188, 198, 210, 219, 222, 231, 248, 261
hostilely, 84
hostilities, 32, 191

hostility, 15, 20, 62, 95, 107, 109, 112, 115, 141, 161–162, 164, 174, 177, 188, 215, 217
hubris, 261
humane, 167
humanely, 167, 250, 258
humanity, 4, 117, 188, 197, 200, 262
humanizing, 256
humans, 39, 41, 243
humanselected, 244
humiliation, 18, 94
humility, 79, 215
humorous, 18
hutus, 168
hypocrisies, 92
hypocrisy, 54, 239
hypocritical, 54
hypocritically, 235
hypothesize, 51

I

idealistic, 95
ideals, 29–30, 70
ideas, 4–6, 18, 23, 26, 30, 32–33, 47–53, 57, 60, 66–67, 72–73, 75, 81, 83–84, 89, 94–95, 102, 104–106, 109–111, 115–118, 120–121, 125, 127, 133, 137, 140, 150, 154,

CPSIA information can be obtained
at www.ICGtesting.com
Printed in the USA
FFHW020402151118
49391223-53738FF